FACT, FICTION, *and* FOLKLORE
in HARRY POTTER'S WORLD

Books by George Beahm

The Vaughn Bode Index (Heresy Press, 1975)

Kirk's Works: The Art of Tim Kirk (Heresy Press, 1977)

How to Sell Woodstoves (George Beahm Publisher, 1980)

How to Buy a Woodstove—and Not Get Burned! (George Beahm Publisher, 1980)

Notes from Elam (as editor and publisher, GB Publishing, 1983)

Write to the Top: How to Complain & Get Results—Fast! (The Donning Company, 1988)

The Stephen King Companion (Andrews McMeel Publishing, 1989)

The Stephen King Story (Andrews McMeel Publishing, 1990)

War of Words: The Censorship Debate (Andrews McMeel Publishing, 1993)

Michael Jordan: Shooting Star (Andrews McMeel Publishng, 1994)

The Stephen King Companion (revised edition, Andrews McMeel Publishing, 1995)

The Unauthorized Anne Rice Companion (Andrews McMeel Publishing, 1995)

Stephen King: America's Best-Loved Boogeyman (Andrews McMeel Publishing, 1998)

Stephen King from A to Z (Andrews McMeel Publishing, 1998)

Stephen King Country (Running Press, 1999)

Stephen King Collectibles (a packaged book for Betts Bookstore, 2000)

The Patricia Cornwell Companion (St. Martin's Press, 2002)

The Essential J. R. R. Tolkien Sourcebook (New Page Books, 2003)

How to Protect Yourself & Your Family Against Terrorism (Brassey's, 2003)

Muggles and Magic: An Unofficial Guide to J. K. Rowling and the Harry Potter Phenomenon (Hampton Roads Publishing, 2004)

The Harry Potter Encyclopedia of Fact, Fiction, and Folklore (Hampton Roads Publishing, 2005)

Stephen King Collectibles: Updated & Revised on CD-ROM (a packaged book for Betts Bookstore, 2005)

The Bittersweet Impermanence of Things, with Noriko Beahm (2006)

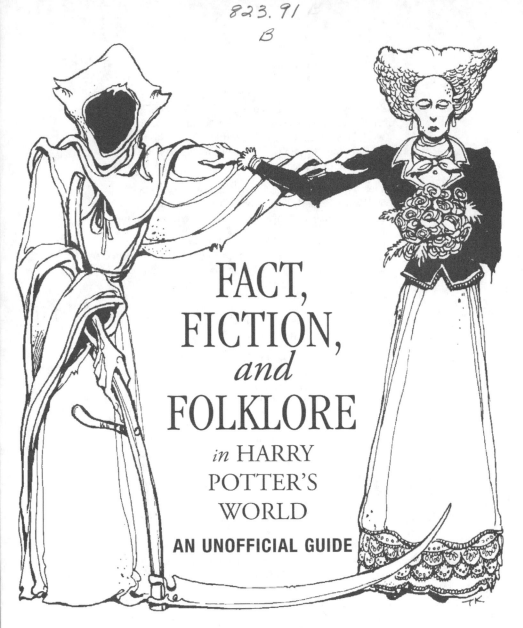

FACT, FICTION, *and* FOLKLORE

in HARRY POTTER'S WORLD

AN UNOFFICIAL GUIDE

GEORGE BEAHM

With illustrations by
Tim Kirk and Birtton McDaniel

HAMPTON ROADS
PUBLISHING COMPANY, INC.

Cover design by Steve Amarillo
Cover art: wizard hat © Thinkstock; all other images © Jupitermedia Corp.
Interior illustrations by Tim Kirk and Britton McDaniel;
small eyeglasses © Anne Dunn Louque

Hampton Roads Publishing Company, Inc.
1125 Stoney Ridge Road
Charlottesville, VA 22902

434-296-2772
fax: 434-296-5096
e-mail: hrpc@hrpub.com
www.hrpub.com

If you are unable to order this book from your local
bookseller, you may order directly from the publisher.
Call 1-800-766-8009, toll-free.

Library of Congress Cataloging-in-Publication Data

Beahm, George W.
  Fact, fiction, and folklore in Harry Potter's world : an unofficial guide / George Beahm.
      p. cm.
  Summary: "Fact, fiction, and folklore in Harry Potter's world : covering the first five
Harry Potter novels, this book presents more than one hundred entries that thoroughly
examine the myths, legends, literature, and historical references of J. K. Rowling's fictional
universe"--Provided by publisher.
  ISBN 1-57174-440-1 (pbk. : acid-free paper)
  1. Rowling, J. K.--Characters--Harry Potter--Handbooks, manuals, etc. 2. Potter, Harry
(Fictitious character)--Handbooks, manuals, etc. 3. Children's stories, English--Handbooks,
manuals, etc. 4. Fantasy fiction, English--Handbooks, manuals, etc. 5. Wizards in litera-
ture--Handbooks, manuals, etc. 6. Magic in literature--Handbooks, manuals, etc. I. Title.
  PR6068.O93Z527 2005
  823'.914--dc22
                                    2005010369

                            ISBN 1-57174-440-1
                           10 9 8 7 6 5 4 3 2 1
                  Printed on acid-free paper in Canada

for Linda and Tim Kirk

Aa' lasser en lle coia orn n' omenta
    gurtha,
Aa' i'sul nora lanne'lle,
Aa' menle nauva calen ar' ta hwesta e'
ale'quenle,
        Aa' menealle nauva calen ar' malta,
        Tenna' ento lye omenta.

The fame thing is interesting because I never wanted to be famous, and I never dreamt I would be famous. . . . I imagined being a famous writer would be like being like Jane Austen. Being able to sit at home in the parsonage and your books would be very famous and occasionally you would correspond with the Prince of Wales's secretary. You know, I didn't think they'd rake through my bins, I didn't expect to be photographed on the beach through long lenses. I never dreamt it would impact my daughter's life negatively, which at times it has. It would be churlish to say there is nothing good about being famous; to have a total stranger walk up to you as you're walking around Safeway, and say a number of nice things that they might say about your work. I mean, of course you walk on with a bit more spring in your step. That is a very, very nice thing to happen. I just wish they wouldn't approach me when I'm buying items of a questionable nature. Always, always. Never when you're in the fresh fruit and veg section. Never.

—*J. K. Rowling, interviewed for the BBC2,*
produced by the Newsnight team (2003)

Contents

· Honeydukes Sweetshop · Knockturn Alley · Madam Malkin's Robes for All Occasions · Madam Puddifoot's · Magical Menagerie · Obscurus Books · Ollivander's: Makers of Fine Wands since 382 B.C. · *Sidebar: "Alivan's: Makers of Fine, Handcrafted Wands"* · Post Office · Scribbulus Everchanging Inks · Shrieking Shack · Three Broomsticks · Whizz Hard Books · Zonko's Joke Shop

Rowling has imagined this universe in such minute and clever detail that we feel we've been admitted to a looking-glass world as palpable as Tolkien's Middle-earth or L. Frank Baum's Oz—a Grimm place where the fantastic and the fabulous are routine, but also a place subject to all the limitations and losses of our own mortal world.

—*Michiko Kakutani,* New York Times

The Enchanting World of Harry Potter

When Joanne Rowling first saw a copy of *Harry Potter and the Philosopher's Stone* at a Scottish bookstore, she later told an interviewer that it "was better than receiving any literary award! I wanted to sneak it off the shelf and sign it, but I was worried I'd be told off for ruining the books, so I didn't."

Rowling needn't have worried. Even as an unknown author, she would likely have been welcomed in the bookstore and asked by the store manager to sign the few copies on hand.

That was in 1997 and since then, how times have changed!

When those few hundred copies of her first book were published and found their way into libraries and independent booksellers, Harry Potter ("the boy who lived," as he's known in the wizarding world) became the heart of a phenomenon that has enchanted millions of Muggles worldwide. Harry Potter, who has unruly black hair, round eyeglasses, and, most distinctive of all, a lightning-shaped scar on his forehead, is a student at the magical wizarding school, Hogwarts; he has followed in the footsteps of his late parents, James and Lily Potter.

The unprecedented popularity of the Harry Potter novels is such that Pottermania—a pop culture phenomenon on the order of the Beatles—has gone far beyond the boundaries of his homeland, England, where Rowling's roots are firmly planted. Since 1997, 260 million copies have sold worldwide, and in 62 languages. Clearly, the magic of Harry Potter has cut across international boundaries to reach the broadest possible spectrum of readers: gender, age, and religious affiliations are not obstacles.

At a time when the pace of life is increasingly frantic and people closet themselves in their own worlds, an astonishing thing will happen on July 16, 2005, when the sixth Harry Potter novel is published. A collective hush will descend on millions of readers worldwide as they share a common yet private experience: televisions, computers, video games, radios, and cell phones will be turned off as the readers turn on to the magic of storytelling, each transported from the Muggle world to Harry Potter's magical world.

In the United States, Scholastic is publishing a record-breaking 10.8 million copies in hardback. Weighing in at 672 pages, with a color cover by Mary GrandPré, *Harry Potter and the Half-Blood Prince* will prompt Muggles everywhere to rush to bookstores to pick up their reserved copies; many bookstores, in fact, have scheduled Harry Potter events, complete with giveaways, readings, costumed performers, and other entertainment. These will draw record crowds. In my small corner of the world, at a Barnes and Noble bookstore in Newport News, Virginia, its event drew over a thousand people who showed up for a midnight Harry Potter party when the previous book was published.

Barbara Marcus (then president of Scholastic Children's Books) told *USA Today* (March 30, 2005) that "We know, based on past experience, that readers will want a copy the minute it goes on sale. We wanted to be ready so that every single child, every single person who started out with *Harry Potter* when it began and every family that wants multiple copies will be able to get them."

The wise Muggle will reserve a copy, for if publishing history repeats itself, *Harry Potter and the Half-Blood Prince* will sell out and bookstores will be beseeching Scholastic to ship more copies immediately.

In 2003, when *Harry Potter and the Order of the Phoenix* was published, Scholastic—concerned about overeager booksellers buying more copies than they could sell—cautiously tailored the book shipments as close as possible, to minimize massive book returns.

But the demand for the book was more than the publisher had imagined. For instance, on publication day in southeast Virginia, the big chain bookstores and independent booksellers were forced to hastily scribble door signs that read: "We are sold out of the new Harry Potter novel." It was a common sight to see frustrated parents with disappointed kids in tow enter a bookstore only to leave empty-handed. All copies, so to speak, had flown the coop.

With an additional four million copies to be printed for *Harry Potter and the Half-Blood Prince,* Scholastic may well have enough stock on hand to satisfy the demand; but if not, history will surely repeat itself.

Total secrecy on the order of the Manhattan Project surrounds the book's contents to protect it from inadvertent disclosure from any source: No review copies will go out prior to publication, embargoes are placed on all copies to ensure none are sold before the publication date (a warning is prominently printed on each book carton), and woe to the journalist or bookseller who breaks the rules!

Typically, in the book industry, a publisher will print hundreds, sometimes thousands, of copies to be given to the media, with the hope of garnering as many early reviews as possible to boost sales, but review copies aren't necessary to sell a new Harry Potter novel. No matter what the critics say, Potter fans will buy it sight unseen. Clearly, review copies would be superfluous.

> The five years I spent on *Harry Potter and the Philosopher's Stone* were spent constructing The Rules. I had to lay down all my parameters. The most important thing to decide when you're creating a fantasy world is what the characters *can't* do.
> —J. K. Rowling, *interviewed by South West News Service (2000)*

Ernest Hemingway, who was fond of holding court to expound on his theories of writing, spoke the plain truth when he talked about his "iceberg" theory of writing. In *Death in the Afternoon,* Hemingway wrote:

> If a writer of prose knows enough about what he is writing about he may omit things that he knows and the reader, if the writer is writing truly enough, will have a feeling of those things as strongly as though the writer had stated them. The dignity of movement of an iceberg is due to only one-eighth of it being above water.

Rowling would, I think, be in complete agreement. The Harry Potter universe is so richly imagined and detailed that what Rowling omitted—entire notebooks of back story that will never see print—would fill a very large book, which raises the question: Would she ever publish such a book? Perhaps. Though she is adamant that she's only going to publish seven Harry Potter books, an eighth book with detailed information about Hogwarts *may* be published to benefit a charity, she said in a recent interview. If so, great! Harry Potter fans will buy it, just as they did her two other charity books, *Fantastic Beasts & Where to Find Them* and *Quidditch Through the Ages*, which have raised millions of dollars to benefit a British-based nonprofit organization, Comic Relief.

Until that tantalizing possibility materializes, however, we are left with the sobering realization that we are closer to the end of the Harry Potter novels than we would wish: After *Harry Potter and the Half-Blood Prince,* only one more Harry Potter novel remains to be published, its title and contents shrouded in secrecy.

As to its eventual publication date, no one knows, but given the two-year interval between the current novel and the previous one it's possible that book seven will be published sometime in 2007.

In any event, book seven's publication will be met with mixed emotions: joy on one hand because we will finally know the end story of Harry Potter and his inevitable showdown with Lord Voldemort; sadness on the other because the final chapter about the boy wizard will have been written. Then Rowling is putting down her pen, turning off the computer, and taking a long-postponed but well-deserved break from writing.

There will be no more Harry Potter stories—a point Rowling emphatically reinforces in virtually every interview—because the seven-book series was designed from the beginning to be a self-contained story arc with closure. Despite rampant rumors and news stories "reporting" that there will be an eighth book comprised of "outtakes" and deleted scenes, the Christopher Little Literary Agency has adamantly denied it: spokesman Neil Blair, quoted in a BBC news story (October 21, 2002), said, "There is no truth in the story that . . . there is going to be an eighth book in the series. . . ."

Looking back at this juncture, it's worth celebrating what Joanne Rowling has accomplished. If you want to get a clear picture, you'd have to talk to booksellers, publishers, media figures, and the movie stars who have appeared in the film adaptations; perhaps most telling, talk to a young child whose impatience to read the next Harry Potter novel will rival that of his anticipation on Christmas Eve.

Writing novels is all about the magic of words.

As writer Ray Bradbury once observed, the popular notion that a picture is worth a thousand words is false—one *word* is worth a thousand pictures.

Think of what these words conjure up in your mind's eye: Hogwarts. The Forbidden Forest. He-Who-Must-Not-Be-Named. The Mirror of Erised. Honeydukes. The Patronus. Quidditch. The Ministry of Magic. O.W.L.s. Hagrid. Dumbledore. The Pensieve. The Grim. Wands.

Ray Bradbury knows whereof he speaks.

Part of the magic in reading the Harry Potter novels is that they are written on several levels and for different audiences. A child will enjoy the story-telling itself, the characters, and the imagery, but a well-read young adult will likely understand some of the allusions, the clever wordplay, and the many historical, mythical, and literary references that are embedded throughout the books. And a grown adult will, if he's reasonably well read, enjoy it on multiple levels.

It should come as no surprise that Rowling was a teacher. With a degree in French and the classics from the University of Exeter in Scotland, she is well versed in myth and legends, especially Greco-Roman. She supplemented this education, as most writers do, with extensive reading outside the class-room. From Jane Austen to J. R. R. Tolkien, books have always been an inte-gral part of Joanne Rowling's life.

As a writer, Rowling is unquestionably a gifted storyteller with a positive genius at plotting. There's a good reason why everything in the Harry Potter universe interlocks so neatly. Did you know, for instance, that she spent five long years writing, and rewriting, the first Harry Potter novel and plotting the next four?

The happy result is that Rowling knows the Harry Potter universe inside and out, as she should, being its creator. Hers is a fully realized secondary universe with a wealth of detail, which is why there's virtually no interview question—no matter how specific—that she cannot answer; in many instances, keen-eyed readers spot revealing clues and query her, but she nec-essarily deflects these questions, since answering them will give away too much in terms of what is to come.

Also seasoned Harry Potter readers know that even the most seemingly innocent fact could be significant. For instance, the fact that Harry Potter has his mother's eyes is, on the face of it, merely a matter of genetics. But this fact, repeated throughout the novels, could prove to be of paramount importance.

As a result of these kinds of seemingly innocent but suggestive details, Harry Potter websites delight in speculation, and numerous books about Harry Potter range from educated guesses to fanciful imaginings that border on the laughable. But it's all in good fun as any Potter fan will tell you.

This book was written with the realization that the Harry Potter universe is an artful blend of imagination and inspiration from the real world, incorporating its myths and legends. Given the dual constraints of time and selectivity, I've chosen to focus on discussing people, places, and things from the Harry Potter universe that, in many instances, overlap with the Muggle world. This linkage allows for reasonable speculation, since a great deal of the conflict in the novels derives from the intersection of the two worlds. Harry, after all, lives in both, as (obviously) does J. K. Rowling.

In this book, I discuss fabulous beasts, witches and wizards, magical artifacts, and some of the places frequented by the wizarding world: more than 300 separate entries, some short, some long, but all (I hope) fun and fanciful, factual and informative.

Obviously, given the complexity of the Harry Potter universe, it's impossible to discuss the stories without revealing a few spoilers. I have tried to minimize them, so new readers can enjoy discovering the Harry Potter universe for themselves—a key component of reading the novels in the first place.

Like you, I eagerly await the final two volumes that chronicle Harry Potter's sixth and seventh years at Hogwarts. When Harry graduates at the end of his seventh year, he will come of age and be free to practice magic. He will probably leave the Muggle world behind to become a permanent resident of the wizarding world.

And then, sadly, the Harry Potter stories come to an end.

Will time treat Harry Potter kindly? We have certainly seen books that have enjoyed great popularity and high sales, only to be forgotten years later. Personally, I think Harry Potter will live . . . forever. So does master storyteller Stephen King, who wrote this dead-on assessment in a review of the fifth Harry Potter novel in *Entertainment Weekly:*

> Will kids (and adults as well) still be wild about Harry 100 years from now, or 200? My best guess is that he will indeed stand time's test and wind up on a shelf where only the best are kept; I think Harry will take his place with Alice, Huck, Frodo, and Dorothy, and this is one series not just for the decade, but for the ages.

Writers like J. K. Rowling are so rare that you can count them on one hand, which is all the more reason to celebrate her and her work; in less than a decade her print runs have gone from 500 to nearly 11 million in the U.S. alone. At that level of success, the media coverage predictably focuses on both J. K. Rowling as a personality and the millions of dollars produced by merchandise and the movies. Those things matter but not to the reader, who simply wants to read a well-told story from a writer who wants to spin a fantastic tale.

In doing just that, Rowling has sparked the imaginations of millions of people. What writer could ask for anything more?

George Beahm
Williamsburg, Virginia
April 5, 2005

Tanya: Where do you come up with the words that you use, the names of the classes and spells and games, etc. For example, the Patronus Expectumous, was it?

J. K. Rowling: That's Latin. Go and look it up. A little investigation is good for a person! Mostly, I invent spells, but some of them have particular meanings.

—*Yahoo chat sponsored by Barnes & Noble*
(October 20, 2000)

Section 1

Fabulous Beasts and Ferocious Critters, Ghoulies and Ghosties, and Long-Leggety Beasties, and Things That Go Bump in the Night

Both the Muggle world and the wizarding world are filled with a magical (in every sense of the word) menagerie of animals that amaze and delight and instill in us a sense of wonder.

Drawing on the natural and the supernaturnal, the normal and the paranormal, creatures of the day (and night) that are part of the Harry Potter universe, or alluded to, are penned in this section.

From the Abominable Snowman to the zombie, this section's entries tell us a little about each one, and their connections to the Muggle world.

Some of the references herein can be found at greater length and detail in the excellent book *Fantastic Beasts & Where to Find Them* by Newt Scamander, who we are told, "was awarded the Order of Merlin, Second Class, in 1979 in recognition of his services to the study of magical beasts, Magizoology."

The quoted definitions throughout this and the other sections are from the *American Heritage Dictionary of the English Language* and *Merriam-Webster's* online dictionary.

Abominable Snowman

In Scamander's *Fantastic Beasts & Where to Find Them,* there is an entry for "Yeti," with a notation that it is also known as the Abominable Snowman, a creature with white fur, standing 15 feet tall.

Clearly, a close encounter with a Yeti would be a memorable experience,

so it comes as no surprise that the bombastic Gilderoy Lockhart published a book claiming an extended association with this fabled creature, *Year with the Yeti.*

Scamander is correct in pointing out that the Yeti is also known as the Abominable Snowman, but incorrect in stating that it's known as Bigfoot, which is clearly its North American cousin, also known by the name Sasquatch.

Those who hunt the Yeti (or, at least, hunt for information about this creature) have yet to find it, for the same reason that those who hunt the Loch Ness monster have yet to find it: Sightings are inconclusive. The scientific conclusion is that those who have purportedly seen the Yeti have in fact seen a creature, but have misidentified it as a Yeti.

Typically cited as being spotted above the snow line in the Himalayan mountain range—depending on its region, the snow line is 14,700 to 17,000 feet

above sea level—the Yeti remains elusive, and is most likely a creature of imagination, not a rarely seen creature who haunts remote and high mountain regions.

Abraxan

In the Harry Potter novels, Abraxans are elephant-sized Palomino horses with wings that make their appearance when a dozen of them are drawing a carriage carrying students to Hogwarts from Beauxbatons, one of two other schools of witchcraft and wizardry in Europe (the other school is Durmstrang).

The inspiration for the name likely came from the word *abraxas,* which has a place as a god in Egyptian culture and also in demonology. It is frequently used as an amulet, and the magical word *abracadabra* is derived from it. In numerology, its seven Greek letters translate to 365, which corresponds to the number of days in a year.

It is obviously connected to Greek mythology, to Pegasus, from the word *pegasos* (the Greek word for "spring"), a winged horse who sprang to life from drops of blood from Medusa, one of the Gorgon sisters, when beheaded by Perseus.

Tamed by Bellerophon with a golden bridle given to him by Athena, Pegasus later bore him in battle against the Chimaera.

Not only a symbol of poetic inspiration, Pegasus also symbolizes flights of imagination.

Pegasus, a northern constellation, can best be seen in October.

Abraxan: Aethonan

Aethonan is cited in *Fantastic Beasts & Where to Find Them* under the listing for "Winged Horse" as a breed found mainly in Britain, and the likely inspiration is Aethon. In Greek mythology, Aethon (the son of Hyperion) is the sun god and Pegasus carries his chariot daily from east to west. In Roman mythology, Aethon is one of the names of Helios's horses (the others are Phlegon, Eos, and Pyrois) that carries Helios's sun chariot across the heavens.

Acromantula

> *Do some of the beasts appear in your dreams sometimes and give you nightmares?*
>
> J. K. Rowling: No. They haven't yet and I don't think they will but I, myself, am like Ron because I too am afraid of spiders, so the Chamber of Secrets would be the one I fear most.
>
> —*Interviewed on* Blue Peter *on cBBC (March 12, 2001)*

In *Harry Potter and the Chamber of Secrets,* in Hagrid's hut, the Minister of Magic (Cornelius Fudge) and Lucius Malfoy—the chief instigator to remove Albus Dumbledore from his position as Hogwarts headmaster and incarcerate Hagrid in Azkaban—don't know they have visitors: Using his father's invisibility cloak, Harry Potter overhears the dastardly plan, as does Ron Weasley. Knowing the two boys are in earshot, Hagrid drops the none-too-subtle clue that anyone who wanted to know what was really going on should follow the spiders.

Harry and Ron take Hagrid's advice, which leads them deep into the Forbidden Forest, where they encounter a giant spider, an Acromantula named Aragog, whom Hagrid has befriended and raised. (The well-meaning Hagrid also found Aragog a wife, an Acromantula named Mosag.)

In *Fantastic Beasts & Where to Find Them,* Scamander notes that these creatures, which originated in Borneo, were specially bred by wizards to be used as guards for dwellings or treasures. With its eight 15-foot-long legs and near-human intelligence, and armed with a poisonous secretion, the Acromantula is indeed a formidable beast, which is why Harry and Ron are justifiably horrified when Aragog tells them about his personal history, but decides in the end that although he would not bring his old friend Hagrid to harm, his friends enjoy no such privilege: They are suitable prey, at which point Harry and Ron beat a well-timed retreat.

In truth, real-world spiders do have eight legs and do have poisonous secretions, but the estimated 34,000 species of spiders, from the class Arachnida, are typically small; in fact, the largest is the tarantula, which usually grows only to three inches; however, some can grow up to ten inches and may eat small birds, toads, mice, and frogs.

Scamander cites Borneo, located northwest of the South China Sea in the Malay Archipelago, as the birthplace of the Acromantula, a name that may be a combination of "acro" (meaning height) and tarantula (the biggest known spiders in the world), which makes sense: An Acromantula, then, would be a large spider.

It's possible, given Rowling's intimate knowledge of Tolkien's *The Lord of the Rings*, that a partial inspiration for Aragog and Mosag is Tolkien's own Shelob, which he said was a philological joke, since it translates to "female spider." A giant spider with a poisonous sac to paralyze or kill her prey, Shelob, who lives deep in the bowels of Cirith Ungol, is, like Aragog and Mosag, a formidable enemy and nearly bests Frodo and his manservant, Sam.

Armadillo

Harry Potter deliberately spills a bottle of armadillo bile, used as an ingredient in potions in Professor Snape's class, in order to stay behind after class to listen in on a conversation between Snape and Professor Karkaroff.

There is no conclusive reason why armadillo bile would be useful as an ingredient for potions, since standard texts do not make any special note of it.

Ashwinder

A gray serpent with fiery eyes, the Ashwinder emerges from a magical fire and lays its flammable eggs under a sheltering rock or log.

Its name may be a combination of its color (ash) and its method of locomotion (sidewinding), which is unusual for snakes, producing a J-shaped pattern in the sand.

This species of snake recalls the sidewinder, a gray snake found in the southwest United States, which lays its eggs under rocks to protect them from the heat of the desert sun.

B

Banshee

In his Defense Against the Dark Arts class, Professor Lupin teaches his students how to defend themselves against a boggart, a shape-shifting creature, which assumes the shape of each person's worst fear. For Seamus Finnigan, his worst fear is a banshee, a nonmalevolent female spirit specifically associated with Irish mythology, which sometimes makes a distinction between the banshee's physical presence and aural presence: Its physical presence presages one's own death, whereas its aural presence presages the death of someone in the family.

Therefore it's obvious why Seamus Finnigan fears and doesn't want to see a banshee: It would signal his impending death.

Derived from Irish Gaelic ("bean woman" or "spirit woman"), the banshee typically makes her appearance at night and is instantly recognizable for her sustained and unmistakable keening sound.

Professor Gilderoy Lockhart's book *Break with a Banshee* is one of the required texts for his class, but as most of his students discovered, his books tend to be more fiction than fact; in actuality, he simply mines other people's experiences and passes them off as his own. So when he claims to have banished the Bandon Banshee, the claim can be discounted, since proper credit should have been given to an unnamed witch about whom we know little except that she is harelipped.

Basilisk

Deep in the bowels of Hogwarts, an ancient beast lies in wait, to be summoned once again by one who speaks Parseltongue, a language that few witches or wizards can speak—a language most often associated with Dark Wizards and the house of Slytherin, from which most dark wizards have come.

From the basilisk's presence spiders flee, even giant ones like Aragog and Mosag. A fearsome creature—whose real-world origins may be found in the Indian cobra—"basilisk" comes from the Greek word *basileus*, which means "king." Thus it is known as the King of Serpents, blessed with long life, able

to kill with a single glance, and virtually invulnerable, except to attack by weasels, which can secrete a deadly venom, or the sound of a crowing cock. It can also die of fright if it sees its own reflected image.

A creature from Greek and Roman mythologies, the basilisk was known in the Middle Ages as a cockatrice, and had the body of a snake and the head, wings, and feet of a rooster.

Beetle

First-year Hogwarts students are given a shopping list of required items, which include a set of brass scales, needed for weighing ingredients for potions. (One of the most taxing and procedural classes students can expect to take is Potions under Professor Severus Snape.)

It's not surprising that one of the ingredients used in potion-making is the beetle, for ancient Egyptians considered it sacred; in fact, it was most frequently fashioned as a talisman.

Derived from the Latin word *scarabaeus*, the scarab was an important Egyptian symbol of rebirth, which is why it was frequently used as an amulet positioned over the heart of a mummy, since the human heart was removed during the mummification process and the amulet served in the afterlife as that person's new heart.

In the wizarding world, any good apothecary store would carry scarab beetles and beetle eyes; in fact, most witches and wizards buy theirs at Diagon Alley at the Apothecary, though there'd almost certainly be an apothecary store in the magical village Hogsmeade near Hogwarts as well.

Bicorn

In *Harry Potter and the Chamber of Secrets,* when Hermione brews a batch of Polyjuice Potion, the horn of this creature is used as one of its ingredients.

In French myth, the bicorn is a beast that feeds on good husbands, and thus is always well fed and fat.

In sharp contrast to the bicorn, the chechevache feeds on good women (presumably wives), and it's a bag of bones because there are so few of them (according to the man who wrote this legend).

Though no description exists of the bicorn (or the chechevache), we may infer that it has two horns because of its root word, *bi* for "two."

Black Dog

In *Harry Potter and the Prisoner of Azkaban,* just before Harry boards the Knight Bus, he spots a large creature. Stan Shunpike, the conductor of the Knight Bus, asks an alarmed Harry what he was looking at. Harry replies he thinks he saw a massive dog, but he isn't sure because he didn't get a clear look.

In northern England, folklore holds that seeing a Barghest, a large goblin dog that makes its appearance only at night, is ominous: A glimpse means the victim will die in the short term, perhaps in a few months, but a good look means death is imminent.

Some of the more famous spectral dogs included the Black Dog of Winchester and the Padfoot of Wakefield. In East Anglia, the black dog, identified by its one eye, was known as Black Shock.

No doubt about it: Seeing one

The Black Dog

Though clearly not the spectral beast known in English folklore, the unofficial mascot of Martha's Vineyard in Massachusetts is a black dog, but of a benign variety. Its logo can be found on a wide range of products, available from

www.theblackdog.com.

of these large black dogs would indeed be a shock, especially since its appearance always signals death.

See also: Sirius Black.

Blast-Ended Skrewt

It's not surprising that the Ministry of Magic's Department for the Regulation and Control of Magical Creatures, responsible for cataloging fantastic beasts, would not have known about this creature, since it was created during a breeding experiment when Hagrid crossed a manticore with a fire-crab.

Hagrid, who is well known for his unusual affinity for dangerous pets, is obviously not going to inform the Ministry, either, which is likely why no listing of this one-of-a-kind creature appears in *Fantastic Beasts & Where to Find Them.*

Since a fire-crab can emit fire from its rear end, and a manticore has the tail of a scorpion, one wonders what natural emissions are produced by the Skrewt, whose discharge is likely somewhat explosive. (Blast-end is a term associated with the use of explosive devices and mining.)

Bloodhound

The Ministry of Magic's Department for the Regulation and Control of Magical Creatures keeps albino bloodhounds on hand to rid them of a creature called a nogtail.

Though a bloodhound would be a good choice, since it's unsurpassed for its scenting ability, one wonders why these would be albino, since that would make them unusually susceptible to sunburn—which means that their ability to track would ideally be limited to overcast, cloudy, or rainy days, or at night.

Boarhound

When Hagrid takes some of the students into the Forbidden Forest, he is accompanied by his large dog, Fang, a boarhound.

The ferocious name of Hagrid's dog belies its gentle nature, though it can be fiercely protective when threatened or when its owner is threatened. Hence the boarhound makes an ideal guardian.

In Germany, in the sixteenth century, these dogs were used to hunt boars. Today, however, they are principally valued as pets and for show purposes.

The wild boar makes an especially formidable creature to hunt because of its speed and sustained strength, which is why it was favored for hunts.

It's worth noting that a boar's head was once considered a delicacy, so it's not surprising that in the magical community of Hogsmeade, near Hogwarts, there's a Hog's Head tavern, a favorite place for fellowship, food, and drink, though its patrons are usually a little on the shady side.

Boggart

The boggart is a shape-shifting creature that feeds on its victim's emotions and assumes the shape of the victim's worst fear. Few can claim to have seen it in its natural state, though Alastor "Mad-Eye" Moody can spot them, as he does at Sirius Black's ancestral home at Grimmauld Place.

First encountered by Hogwarts students in Professor Lupin's class, Defense Against the Dark Arts, the boggart, which favors confined, dark quarters, emerges to confront each student in turn, assuming various shapes—Neville Longbottom fears Professor Snape, Ron Weasley fears spiders, Parvati Patil fears mummies, and Seamus Finnigan fears banshees.

Defending oneself against the boggart requires using a wand and stating the word "riddikulus," which will force the boggart to assume a ridiculous shape, invoking laughter.

It proved especially useful as a teaching tool to Professor Lupin outside his classroom, when he used it to help build confidence in Harry Potter by having the boggart assume the shape of a dementor so Harry could practice his Patronus charm.

Understandably, it

can appear to be a formidable opponent and, as such, was employed in the Triwizard Tournament as a guard in the maze that the student champions had to negotiate.

In English and Scottish legend, a boggart is a fairy that, by turns, could be either helpful or hostile. When helpful, it would help clean the house, but when hostile—particularly the boggart of Yorkshire, said to be a brownie—it could be destructive.

As with Rowling's house elves that accept gifts of food, the historical boggart accepts milk and bread, but little else, since boggarts are easily offended.

To get rid of a boggart, offer a suit of clothes. It will then don the clothes and simply vanish. You are sure never to see it again.

Boomslang

When Hermione Granger scoured Hogwarts for the ingredients for the Polyjuice Potion she wanted to concoct, some of the more esoteric ingredients proved difficult to find, notably boomslang, prized for its shredded skin, a stock of which is kept by Professor Snape, which was her illicit source for this snakeskin.

This snake *(Dispholidus typus)* can be found mostly in the savannas of sub-Saharan Africa. Its venom is poisonous, homotoxic, causing hemorrhaging by perforating the victim's blood vessels.

Bowtruckle

In Professor Grubbly-Plank's class, Care of Magical Creatures, the students study the bowtruckle, a tree-dwelling insect that uses camouflage to blend in with its arboreal surroundings. Fiercely protective of itself and the tree it inhabits, the bowtruckle can be placated with an offering of wood lice.

The bowtruckle's Muggle counterpart is the Phasmid, leaf-eaters that physically resemble sticks (other Phasmids resemble leaves). Found predominantly in Australia, the largest is the Titan Stick Insect *(Acrophylla titan)*, which measures almost ten inches in length. (In comparison, a bowtruckle is eight inches in length.)

Bugbear (Blood-Sucking)

When Hagrid discovers roosters killed on Hogwarts grounds, in *Harry Potter and the Chamber of Secrets,* he suspects either foxes or Blood-Sucking Bugbears.

A mythical beast whose name is derived from Middle English or Welsh (*bugge* or *bwg*) plus the *bear* suffix, it's usually cited to frighten small children.

Its closest cousins include the boogeyman and hobgoblin.

There is likely no direct relationship between the Bugbear and the bedbug, but it's interesting to note that the bedbug will feed on poultry when it can't feed on people, the latter being the source of the expression "Don't let the bedbugs bite."

Bundimun

This small creature's secretions can destroy house foundations.

Though there are no such Muggle creatures, house fungus *(Merulis lacrymans)* is a real, and costly, concern. If the wood used to construct the floor of the house itself has not been properly seasoned, or if the humidity is high or ventilation is poor, especially in cool, dark areas where moisture is present, house fungus (dry rot) can set in, destroying floors and causing houses to collapse.

Cat

> When I was working in London in the late 1980s, I used to eat my lunch in a nearby square on sunny days; and a large, fluffy ginger cat [that] looked as though it had run face-first into a wall used to prowl around the sunbathers there. I assume it lived in a nearby house. I didn't ever get close enough to give myself an asthma attack, but I became distantly fond of this cat, which prowled among the humans, looking disdainful and refusing to be stroked. When I decided to give Hermione an unusually intelligent cat, I gave him the appearance of this haughty animal, with the slightly unfair addition of bandy legs.
>
> —*J. K. Rowling, in an interview cited on hp-lexicon.org*

Harry Potter and the Sorcerer's Stone begins with an unusual event: Harry's uncle, Vernon Dursley, is taken aback when he thinks he sees a cat reading a map, and then reading a road sign.

It is a sign of the times, for strange doings are in the works on that auspicious day. On an otherwise ordinary "dull, gray Tuesday," Dursley has had a close encounter with the wizarding world. On that day, the streets teem with strangely dressed people, and the skies are filled with an unusually large number of owls, along with a downpour of shooting stars at night.

Magic is in the air.

Vernon Dursley—a man bereft of imagination—merely assumes he's seeing things and leaves it at that, but in fact his eyes did not deceive him. He *did* see a cat reading a map; he *did* see the same tabby reading a street sign; and he *did* get hugged by someone from the wizarding world who wore a violet cloak and exclaimed that this was a day of celebration, even for Muggles.

Muggles?

It's a word that Vernon Dursley had never heard before, but one that would have tremendous significance for him and his family. They would soon receive an addition—albeit unwelcome—to their family, which would be left on their doorstep at Privet Drive: Harry Potter, the only child of James and Lily Potter, both recently deceased.

The tabby cat in question was no ordinary cat: It was, in fact, Professor Minerva McGonagall, a member of the faculty at Hogwarts School of Witchcraft and Wizardry, who is an Animagus, listed in a registry of such at the Ministry of Magic. Capable of transforming herself at will from human to animal form, Professor McGonagall in her cat form was indeed reading a map and a street sign—a sight that would seem perfectly commonplace in the wizarding world, but highly unusual to the world of Muggles (nonmagic folk).

As it turns out, cats (magical and otherwise) are quite common in the wizarding world. In fact, new students to Hogwarts are allowed to bring one pet: an owl, a toad, or a cat. Most choose owls because of their usefulness—they deliver the mail—but some, like Hermione Granger, choose a cat instead.

Part kneazle, Hermione's cat Crookshanks was purchased at the Magical Menagerie in Diagon Alley. As is soon apparent, Crookshanks is no ordinary cat, for he shows outward signs of intelligence that suggest he's more than what he seems.

Indeed, at Hogwarts, no cats can be taken for granted. Argus Filch, the cranky caretaker at the school, relies on his cat, Mrs. Norris, to help him in his never-ending pursuit to find trespassing students. Especially attentive, quick on her feet, and able to communicate with her master in ways that suggest a preternatural predisposition, Mrs. Norris is Filch's ally in keeping the students under constant surveillance.

Harry Potter trivia: J. K. Rowling said in an interview that the name for Filch's cat came from a Jane Austen novel, *Mansfield Park.*

Historically, cats have been around for at least ten million years, according to the *Encyclopædia Britannica,* and have enjoyed privileged status since their domestication five thousand years ago. The Egyptians were especially fond of cats; in fact, they had a cat-headed goddess named Bast. In their use of mummification—preserving dead bodies for entry into the afterlife—Egyptians mummified not only people, but their cherished cats as well. Cat cemeteries, common in Egypt, are known to house hundreds of thousands of cats, along with mummified mice, which were deemed essential as a source of food for the cats in the afterlife.

In sharp contrast to the reverence cats enjoyed in ancient Egypt, cats were often viewed with suspicion in the sixteenth and seventeenth centuries in Europe. It was a time of hysteria, when religious dogma held sway, and countless women, accused of witchcraft, were hung or burned at the stake, and their cats killed as well.

Witches were known to keep familiars, small demons disguised as animals who would do their bidding. Not surprisingly, black cats were singled out simply because of their color: Not merely considered

Scottish Town Pardons Executed Witches, Cats

The town of Prestonpans in Scotland took the unusual step of pardoning 81 people from the sixteenth and seventeenth centuries who had been accused of being witches, along with their cats. According to the news story, "More than 3,500 Scots, mainly women and children, and their cats, were killed in witch hunts. Many were condemned on flimsy evidence, such as owning a black cat or brewing homemade remedies."

Local historian Roy Pugh noted that it was a time of "hysterical ignorance and paranoia," a view shared by the town's court, who pardoned not only the accused Scots, but "the cats concerned" as well.

—*MSNBC News (Oct 30, 2004)*

unlucky, they were considered evil, and consorts of witches and even the devil himself.

By the 1800s, cats had shed their unsavory reputation and affiliation with witches, and were favorites in households all across Europe. (Queen Victoria of England, in fact, owned two.)

Today, cats (along with dogs) are the most popular pets owned by Muggles, and probably in the wizarding world as well.

Centaur

"Mars is bright tonight."

With that prophetic observation, voiced first by the centaur Ronan and repeated by the centaur Bane, both of whom look up at the vault of stars to see the planet Mars, the night sky reveals its prophecy—inescapable war is approaching—but in what form and when, the centaurs cannot say.

Hagrid, impatient to a fault, calls them "ruddy stargazers," but these centaurs know better than to interfere with fate. The destiny of what is foretold in the stars will be fulfilled, unless it is tampered with.

Intelligent half-man, half-horse creatures who keep to themselves in the Forbidden Forest, the centaurs are true seers.

Like the centaurs of Greek legend, those who dwell in the Forbidden Forest vary in temperament: Some, like Ronan, are helpful to the human race, whereas others, like Bane, are not.

In Greek legend, the half-man, half-horse creatures are slaves to their animal passions, and thus are known for their debauchery. Pulling the chariot of Dionysus (the wine god) or carrying Eros (the god of love), the centaurs' battles with humankind are inevitably the result of their inability to rein themselves in, so to speak. At Pirithous's wedding, for instance, the centaurs behaved so badly that a bloody battle ensued and they had to be driven away.

When a centaur, mindful of hospitality, had food and drink, including wine, on hand for Heracles, who was visiting the cave of Pholus, trouble ensued when the centaurs became drunk on the wine; the result was that some of them attacked Heracles, who defended himself with poison-tipped arrows.

One of the arrows struck the centaur Chiron, who was renowned for his wisdom, his healing powers, and his skills in prophecy; he eventually died and was set in the heavens as the constellation Sagittarius.

In the night sky, the southern constellation Centaurus can best be sighted in May.

Chimaera

From Greek mythology, the Chimaera is a female beast with the body of a lion (in front), a goat (in the middle), and a dragon (in the rear). A fire-breathing monster, she is an offspring of Typhon and Echidna (half woman, half dragon) whose other offspring include similarly fabulous, and deadly, beasts: the Hydra, the Sphinx, Cerberus.

Chizpurfle

Tiny magical parasites that infest wizards' homes.

Chiz: From the French, *chiz* means "at the home of."

Purfle: an obscure word meaning "to ornament the borders or edges."

These parasites have voracious appetites and literally make themselves at home. In size, design, and the damage that they create the chizpurfle reminds one of the termite, which is small with powerful jaws and capable of devouring the wood in a house.

Clabbert

A tree-dwelling creature resembling a hybrid between a frog and a monkey. Such a creature would be odd indeed, given its size.

In the Muggle world there is a tree-dwelling creature called the tree frog which has adhesive disks on its toes, but these frogs are smaller in size than other frogs. Monkeys, too, can travel through trees, but they use all fours to scamper across branches; only the spider monkey can swing like the apes, arm over arm.

Cockatrice

At a Triwizard Tournament in 1792, a legendary creature called a cockatrice that was supposed to be caught went on a rampage and injured the heads of the three European schools of wizardry: Hogwarts, Durmstrang, and Beauxbatons.

It's not surprising that a cockatrice could do so much damage, for this mythological beast of Hellenistic and Roman times is also known by its other name, a basilisk, which can kill with a single look. Its natural enemy was the weasel. Later, in the seventeenth century, elaborations on the legend gave the cockatrice another natural enemy, the cock, whose crowing could kill it. For this reason, wary travelers reportedly took cocks with them for self-protection, just in case a cockatrice (aka basilisk) was in the area.

Crup

A specially bred wizard-dog that resembles a Jack Russell terrier.

Looks can be deceiving. The small, friendly-looking Jack Russell terrier is an extremely intelligent dog known for its ability not only to hunt, but also to kill. These terriers were originally bred by an Englishman in the nineteenth century, the Reverend John (Parson Jack) Russell, specifically for hunting. These small but pugnacious dogs were also bred with bulldogs to create bull terriers. Specifically trained to fight in pits, this aggressive breed is termed the pit bull in the U.S.

Dementor

Seeking Sirius Black, an escapee from Azkaban prison, dementors are on the hunt, looking everywhere to reclaim him and give the dreaded Dementor's Kiss, a "kiss" that sucks the soul out of a person, leaving only an empty shell, alive but "gone."

On the Hogwarts Express, Harry Potter first encounters a dementor, a tall, spectral creature cloaked in black. When the sliding door to his train compartment is opened, the dementor appears and Harry feels intensely cold, chilling him not only to the bone but to his heart.

Demented (meaning crazy or insane) and *dementia* (a mental illness that impairs a person's ability to function normally, involving loss of memory and cognitive functioning) are the root words that are at the essence of dementors, whose spectral presence draws every good and positive thought from everyone nearby, creating a profound depression in them that deteriorates into insanity.

This is why incarceration in Azkaban prison, which is guarded by the dementors, is so feared: It's not the facility per se but its guards, whose presence eventually imprisons an inmate in his or her own mind, from which there can be no escape. In short, a dementor can drive someone crazy.

Unfortunately, within the walls of the wizard prison, the just and unjust have been incarcerated. As in Muggle history, where witch hunts were sanctioned by the church, the history of the wizarding world includes similar hunts in which innocents were hunted down, captured, or killed—a principal theme in the Harry Potter novels.

Soul-sucking entities are often found in popular culture, in the guise of

aliens in science fiction, but their roots in fantasy can perhaps be found in the English myth created by J. R. R. Tolkien, whose epic fantasy, *The Lord of the Rings*, prominently features Ringwraiths—tall, spectral creatures in black, who literally haunt Frodo Baggins as he makes his way to Mordor to destroy the One Ring. The Ringwraiths, fallen men who were seduced by the promises of power offered by the Dark Lord Sauron, are more spectral entities than men. In fact, when seen in their true form, the Ringwraiths are—in the film version by Peter Jackson—clearly men of proud lineage who were transformed into gaunt, skeletal figures.

The Ringwraiths serve only the Dark Lord, and all living creatures fear them for what they can do: The victim's flesh is stripped from the body, leaving only the mind intact, which is then subjected to an eternity of endless probing under the penetrating gaze of the Dark Lord himself. Death, most feel, would be preferable to this eternity of suffering.

With those things in mind, it's easy to see how Rowling, who admits to being a big fan of Tolkien's book, would find the notion of Ringwraiths an inspiration for her own dementors, who are similar in appearance, in their frightfulness, and in their spectral powers. When subjected to either a Ringwraith or a dementor, the end result is the same: The victim will suffer great and infinite pain.

Dementors, then, are a perfect symbol for the depression people suffer when all hope is gone, and despair sets in.

The closest cousin to a dementor is probably a Lethifold, which is described in Newt Scamander's *Fantastic Beasts & Where to Find Them*, which features an introduction by Albus Dumbledore.

In Scamander's book, we are told that the Lethifold (also known as "Living Shroud") is a creature who resembles a black cloak, glides over the ground at night, and usually attacks at night when its intended victim is sleeping. As its name suggests, it suffocates its victim by enfolding it in its thick, black cloak. The only defense, we are told, is invoking the Patronus charm, which is also used to repel a dementor.

Harry Potter fact: Rowling often comes up with dozens of names before selecting a final one. In this case, she was playing around with Latin words to come up with *dementor*.

It's well known that J. K. Rowling suffered from depression after returning to Scotland after a failed marriage and reentry into the workplace, where she was underemployed. The feelings of hopelessness that she experienced were likely instrumental in conjuring up the dementors, dispiriting creatures who leach all hope from their victims.

Demiguise

A creature with long, silky hair which is so fine that it is sought by wizards for making invisibility cloaks.

Rowling may have had in mind the gorilla, a species found in the rain forests of coastal West Africa. Weighing over 400 pounds and, at full stance, nearly seven feet tall, the gorilla is a formidable creature, but its apparent ferocity is more the stuff of popular fiction than fact: A vegetarian who is naturally disposed to gentleness, the gorilla almost never attacks people. A gentle giant with long, silky hair, the gorilla resembles humans in its genetic makeup more closely than does any other species.

Diricawl

This flightless bird can vanish and reappear suddenly.

The dodo bird and two other closely related species (the Réunion solitaire and the Rodrigues solitaire) are now extinct because of man. The dodo bird made its home on the island of Mauritius, located in the Indian Ocean. The size of a large turkey, the dodo bird had vestigial wings and breast structure that made flight impossible, so it could not escape its predator, man, which it had never seen before and therefore had not learned to fear. In short, this peaceful bird who led an otherwise peaceful existence was far too easy prey, which is why the Portuguese named it *dodo,* which translates as "simpleton."

Controversy surrounds the extinction of the dodo bird, since pursuing it and capturing it was hardly sporting, and its flesh was not palatable; in fact, it tasted so bad that Dutch settlers who followed the Portuguese in inhabiting this remote island called the dodo the *walgvogel,* which translates as "disgusting bird."

Dates vary as to its actual date of extinction—1662 to 1681—and the facts surrounding its demise remain a mystery.

Doxy

A creature that resembles a cross between a fairy and an insect.

Dragon

Hagrid, who has the disconcerting habit of befriending and harboring beasts of all kinds, won a dragon's egg in a card game. When the egg is hatched, a small dragon, a Norwegian Ridgeback whom he affection-ately named Norbert, emerges. Unfortunately, owning a dragon is forbidden under law, and so Hagrid reluctantly gives it up to Charlie Weasley, who is studying dragons in Romania.

The reason dragons are forbidden is their potential danger. Formidable beasts, dragons are the first obstacle that the Triwizard champions must face in their quest to win the tournament, recounted in *Harry Potter and the Goblet of Fire.* (Of the four champions, Harry fared best because of his ingenuity, though one of the judges, Karkaroff, upset at Hogwarts fielding two champions, gave him an unfairly low mark.)

In *Fantastic Beasts & Where to Find Them,* Scamander identifies the following ten species of dragons, one from South America, one from New Zealand, one from China, and the remainder from Europe. (For more detailed information on each, consult *Fantastic Beasts & Where to Find Them.*)

- Antipodean Opaleye (New Zealand)
- Chinese Fireball, aka Liondragon (China)
- Common Welsh Green
- Hebridean Black
- Hungarian Horntail
- Norwegian Ridgeback
- Peruvian Vipertooth (South America)
- Romanian Longhorn
- Swedish Short-Snout
- Ukrainian Ironbelly

The Komodo Dragon

Imagine a ten-foot, 300-pound lizard whose bite contains dozens of strains of deadly bacteria and that has been known to attack people. The Komodo Dragon, found only in the Lesser Sunda Islands in Indonesia, is the largest creature of its kind.

With a life expectancy of nearly a century, these lizards have almost been hunted to extinction but are now under the protection of the government and live in a preserve at the Komodo National Park.

In all of myth, legend, and folklore, the dragon reigns supreme as the fiercest, most formidable, and destructive creature ever imagined. In Western culture, dragons typically are large, heavily scaled (like a reptile), winged, with sharp claws, and can breathe fire. Typically, dragons prey on animals and people alike, lay up worldly treasures like gold and precious gems that they have no practical use for, and have near-human intelligence.

Derived from the Greek word *drakon* (meaning "large serpent"), the dragon is often referred to as a worm, snake, and sometimes firedrake.

J. R. R. Tolkien's depiction of the dragon Smaug, in *The Hobbit,* fits the general description perfectly. In addition, Smaug is excessively vain (which proves to be his downfall), loves riddles, and is greedy, knowing to the coin how much his dragon hoard is worth, though he has no use for his wealth.

Dragons show up in many cultures worldwide, but predominantly in European myth.

The dragon is represented in the heavens with the constellation Draco.

Dugbog

This creature lives in swamps and resembles a piece of floating wood.

Dug: "moved by pushing aside material."

Bog: wet, spongy ground; marshy.

The dugbog is aptly named. It lives in boglike environments and glides and slithers through marshy grounds.

Dwarf

Professor Gilderoy Lockhart, to everyone's surprise and dismay, announces over breakfast with his characteristic cheerfulness that because it's Valentine's Day, he's arranged a "little surprise," the first of many, which in this case turns out to be "a dozen surly-looking dwarfs" delivering Valentine's Day cards. Harry Potter is accosted—verbally and physically—by an aggressive dwarf who insists on singing the valentine, at any cost.

Outlandishly dressed with a pair of golden wings (to represent Cupid), the dwarf is carrying a harp as well.

In Norse mythology, the *dvergr* (dwarves) are an ancient race that resides deep in the bowels of mountains or in mines. Averaging three feet in height, dwarves are renowned smiths, crafting many beautiful treasures and objects for the gods, notably Thor's Hammer.

J. R. R. Tolkien, a college professor whose interest in philology was the principal inspiration for writing *The Lord of the Rings*, drew heavily from Norse mythology

to populate his imaginary Middle-earth. A contributor to the *Oxford English Dictionary*, Tolkien insisted that the plural of dwarf was not *dwarfs* but *dwarves*, perhaps making a distinction between stunted people in the real world (dwarfs) and his Norse-inspired dwarves. Tolkien's depiction of dwarves is consistent with Norse mythology: short in stature, aggressive in battle, fierce in loyalty to family and friends, renowned smiths, and at home deep in mountains and subterranean places.

Tolkien's famous dwarves included the great Thorin Oakenshield (in *The Hobbit*) and Gimli, son of Gloin (in *The Lord of the Rings*), who forged a friendship with the elf Legolas, to everyone's surprise, since dwarves and elves share a long history of enmity and war, and dwarves have long memories: Their sense of honor requires retribution, which is one reason why it's best not to pick a fight with a dwarf.

Dwarves have a certain skill with music, especially harps, and in Tolkien's *The Hobbit*, when they meet with the wizard Gandalf at Bilbo Baggins's home to discuss their plans to recover treasure from the dragon Smaug, one of the dwarves pulls out a harp and plays it with such skill that it takes Bilbo far away, instilling in him wanderlust, a desire to leave behind his exceedingly comfortable hobbit hole and get a walking stick to go where the road takes him.

Perhaps mindful of this memorable scene, Rowling, who undoubtedly read *The Hobbit*, tweaked the original inspiration for humorous effect—a rancorous, demanding singing dwarf with a harp, which was likely more a prop than a musical instrument. Rowling may also have had in mind the fact that dwarfs in Muggle history were pressed into service by those in power to be court jesters or entertainers solely because of their height. Indeed, the dwarf pressed into service by Professor Lockhart seemed put out to be wearing an outlandish getup and forced to be an entertainer—an assignment he clearly didn't relish.

Elf

In *Harry Potter and the Chamber of Secrets*, Harry Potter meets an elf for the first time in his bedroom at the Dursley residence, when a house-elf named Dobby visits Harry to warn him not to come back to school, no matter what. Despite Dobby's urgent pleas, Harry has no intention of not going back, and chaos results: Dobby does everything in his power—magical and otherwise—to put roadblocks up to prevent Harry from returning to school;

and even after Harry makes it to school after Herculean efforts, Dobby persists in hampering Harry at every turn.

A house-elf who serves the Malfoy family, Dobby is a pitiable creature

who is bound by honor to serve his assigned family, no matter how badly they treat him. Under normal circumstances, only death will release him from his eternal servitude, unless the master of the house releases him by giving him a gift, an article of clothing. Most house-elves, however, would be insulted with such a proffered gift; they take it as an insult.

At Hogwarts, a small army of house-elves willingly and gladly serve as housekeepers and cooks. To serve well is their chief goal in life, so when Hermione Granger takes a dim view of their enslavement and starts an organization called S.P.E.W. (a word redolent with meaning) to liberate them from themselves and their masters, the house-elves can't believe their batlike ears. They don't want to be party to Hermione's well-intentioned but poorly received plans for their eventual liberation, chronicled in *Harry Potter and the Goblet of Fire.*

In English folklore, there are references to several sprites—notably brownies and pixies—who can be alternately helpful or mischievous, depending on the treatment they receive. Brownies, for instance, are helpful until criticized, at which point they become mischievous. Both brownies and pixies accept food in payment, but are offended by other gifts and leave.

In popular culture, traditional elves are most like Rowling's, though more recent interpretations—notably Tolkien's high elves—imbue them with immortality, wisdom, courage, and a love for beautiful things, embodied in such characters as Legolas and Gil-Galad.

Erkling

An elfish creature indigenous to the Black Forest in Germany, this malevolent creature likes to lure children away and eat them.

This sounds similar to a malicious creature from German folklore, the Erl King (from *Erkkönig,* meaning "alder king"), who lives in the aptly named Black Forest and ensnares children for nefarious purposes.

Erumpent

A large African beast that resembles a rhinoceros and weighs as much as a ton.

The rhinoceros lives in Africa and Asia and is, in fact, an endangered species because of its prized 18-inch horn, which is ground into a powder and ingested for what are thought to be its healing powers and aphrodisiac qualities—neither of which it actually has.

The largest land mammal second only to the elephant, the White Rhino stands an impressive, and formidable, 6.5 feet tall, 13 feet long, and weighs up to 4 tons.

Fairy

This is the classical fairy, a small humanoid creature with wings. Professor Flitwick used them to decorate his classroom; and, for a Yule Ball at Hogwarts, these comely creatures were used to decorate a garden.

Creatures from English folklore, fairies—far from being benevolent, beautiful creatures of the forest—have traditionally been, for the most part, at odds with people. Known to ferry away children and leave behind substitutes in the form of changelings, and to take humans to fairyland, where they can be trapped forever if they partake of food or drink, the cruelty of fairies is legendary.

For an imaginative exploration of the fractious relationship between fairies and people, read *Jonathan Strange & Mr. Norrell*, written by Susanna Clarke, which delves into the traditional role of fairies. It's a masterful tale that not only uses as its premise the reintroduction of real magic in England during the time of the Napoleonic war in the nineteenth century, but highlights the plight of humans when trapped in fairyland.

Ferret

After a cowardly attack on Harry Potter by Draco Malfoy, Professor "Mad-Eye" Moody turns Draco into a ferret, bouncing him up and down on the stone floor, to the amusement of his classmates, until Professor McGonagall—horrified at the spectacle of a student being transfigured as a means of punishment—restores a bruised and bloodied Malfoy back to human shape.

Professor Moody's choice of a white ferret is especially appropriate in this instance, since they enjoyed such high popularity during the Middle Ages that only the well-off could afford one. Traditionally used as a hunting animal to flush out rabbits—a practice called *ferreting*—the ferret can be aggressive and, when provoked, will bite humans.

To *ferret* is "to hound or harry persistently," which is especially appropriate, since Draco Malfoy enjoys hounding and provoking Harry

The Wind In The Willows

One of the best-loved children's books of all time is Kenneth Grahame's *The Wind in the Willows.* This is the story of the boastful Toad who is cut down to size after a series of humiliating adventures in the real world and at the hands of the Wild Wooders who storm his beautiful home and take it over—weasels, stoats, and ferrets figuring prominently in the skullduggery—and anyone who enjoys a beastly good tale will find this story of the Badger, Mole, Rat, and Toad a literary joyride.

persistently, provoking him needlessly, just for the sport of it, just as Malfoy enjoys throwing sarcastic barbs at Harry's best friend, Ron Weasley.

Fire-Crab

This creature with a bejeweled shell resembles the tortoise.

In the Muggle world, the hard, bony shell of the tortoise, called the carapace, can be colorful and marbled with variegated designs, which is why it has always been in high demand as a material in jewelry. The use of tortoiseshell in the crafting of jewelry reached a high point in seventeenth-century France, when it was used for decorating many articles.

Fire Slug

Found in the Brazilian rain forest, fire slugs, about which little is known, are currently being studied by Newt Scamander.

Flesh-Eating Slug

Rubeus Hagrid shops in Knockturn Alley for a repellent for flesh-eating slugs, which are eating the cabbages on Hogwarts grounds.

Though several highly publicized reports of people being infected by a flesh-eating bacterium, a strain of *Streptococcus,* made the news in recent years in the United Kingdom, there is no such thing as a *flesh-eating* slug.

Flobberworm

After Professor Rubeus Hagrid introduces a hippogriff to his class (Care of Magical Creatures) with disastrous results, he second-guesses that he should have taught a more innocuous creature, like a flobberworm, which is a brown worm known only for eating vegetation.

The lowly earthworm, which ranges in size from one inch to eleven inches, is a welcome sight in gardens because its presence means that the soil is mixed up and aerated through a process of digestion and elimination, which is why the naturalist Charles Darwin, writing in *The Formation of Vegetable Mould through the Action of Worms* (London: John Murray, 1883), highly praised the worm: "It may be doubted whether there are any other animals which have played so important a part in the history of the world, as have these lowly creatures."

Fruitbat

Barny the Fruitbat is the official mascot of Ballycastle Bat Quidditch team. Capable of human speech, Barny has appeared in ads to promote butterbeer.

In the Muggle world, fruit bats are commonly found in Central and South America. These nocturnal creatures use bat radar (called echolocation) to orient themselves in flight. As its name suggests, the principal diet of the fruit bat is fruit.

With gray-brown fur and distinctive facial stripes, the Jamaican fruit bat smells like scented soap.

Furball

This is a small, furry, custard-colored creature for sale at the Magical Menagerie, a store in Diagon Alley. See "Puffskein."

Fwooper

A bird whose singing causes insanity.

In the Muggle world, the music of songbirds has principally two purposes: to establish territory and to attract a mate. The aural avians that fill the air with their unique sounds vary widely in their singing talents. The nightingale can sing more than 300 love songs, but the brown thrasher can sing more than 2,000. In sheer number, the chaffinch, in a single season, may sing more than 500,000 times. For sheer volume, the superb lyrebird can't be beat. But if there was a bird that might cause one to go insane, or at least a little batty, that dubious honor goes to the kakapo, also known as the owl parrot, a species of parrot in Australia with distinctive green plumage. It tramples a bowl-shaped depression in the ground, seats itself, self-inflates to the size of a football with its two air sacs, and then begins its loud booming sound, a sound that can be heard as far away as four miles. It engages in this practice daily for up to three months.

Ghost

Before Harry Potter and his classmates are sorted into their respective houses by the Sorting Hat, 20 ghosts suddenly appear out of nowhere, causing some students to scream in surprise. Arguing about Peeves the Poltergeist, the ghosts don't notice the students except in passing. One of the ghosts, named Fat Friar, chats amiably with the students and tells some of them that he hopes to see them in his old house, Hufflepuff.

We don't know how many ghosts reside at Hogwarts—this may have been just a small gathering, after all—but the ones we do know about are distinctive in their own ways: a melancholy ghost; a bloody ghost; an amiable ghost; an aloof, somewhat mysterious ghost; a disenchanted ghost; and a teacher who is a ghost. And there's a ghost who's not a ghost: Peeves.

The melancholy ghost is a former student who died suddenly. A permanent resident of the place where she died, Moaning Myrtle haunts a girls' bathroom.

The bloody ghost is appropriately named the Bloody Baron. The house ghost of Slytherin, he inspires fear in the students and the otherwise uncontrollable Peeves, who is obsequious in his presence.

The amiable ghost is the jolly Fat Friar, who frequently reminds students that he hails from Hufflepuff.

The aloof ghost—somewhat mysterious, since we know so little about her—is known only as the Grey Lady, who hails from Ravenclaw. Perhaps inspired by Lady Jane Grey, who has the unusual distinction of not only having been a Queen of England for a mere nine days, but also holding that position at the tender age of 15. She was beheaded, along with her father and husband.

The disenchanted ghost is Nearly Headless Nick—excuse me, I meant Sir Nicholas de Mimsy Porpington, as he prefers to be called—whose head liter-

ally hangs by a thread. A proud ghost whose head hangs low when he's rejected for entry into the Headless Hunt on a technicality (you see, he's not *really* headless), Sir Nicholas Porpington, who hails from Gryffindor House, doesn't celebrate his birthday but, more fittingly, his "deathday," at a party typically attended by other ghosts, with Harry Potter and Hermione Granger as the odd guests.

The ghostly teacher is Professor Binns, who died on the job, but that doesn't stop him from teaching classes. In death, as in life, Professor Binns drones on in an almost hypnotic tone of voice, boring his students to death: not literally, of course, but only in a manner of speaking.

The ghost who is not a ghost is Peeves, who is properly categorized as a poltergeist. We have Nearly Headless Nick's opinion that Peeves isn't *really* a ghost, so we can take him at his word. Peeves, living up to his name, is peevish in nature, and enjoys pesky activities designed to harass students. Peeves holds students in low regard, and it often takes his fear of the Bloody Baron to keep him in check.

Ghosts figure in many cultures and religions, with the general perception of them being that these paranormal entities live in two worlds; clearly, they are part of the netherworld, but they also live in the land of the living. Typically, ghosts haunt a specific place, usually where they suddenly died a violent death, or where they are tied to the past by a strong, emotional connection.

A free-floating spirit, the traditional ghost can't rest until old matters are reconciled, at which point the ghost vanishes and truly dies, going to where he or she should have gone in the first place: to heaven, to stand judgment for his or her life.

If seeing is believing, then a lot of people believe they've seen a ghost. Perennially popular, ghosts are now the centerpieces in walking tours around the country, where, by night, guides with lanterns take tourists to various places known to have harbored ghosts, in the hope of sighting one.

Ghosts are a mainstay of popular fiction, of literature, notably Shakespeare's *Hamlet* and Washington Irving's *The Legend of Sleepy Hollow* with its headless horseman, and especially of movies, like *Ghostbusters,* in which a trio of paranormal researchers try to rid the city of its ghostly inhabitants.

Ghoul

More mischievous than malevolent, a ghoul that haunts the Weasley house has taken up residence in the attic, just above Ron's room. Ghouls are slimy creatures that are considered harmless in the wizarding world.

Derived from Arabic *(Ghul)*, this demonic creature takes a female form to try and distract travelers, so it can kill and eat them. The only defense is to strike it hard with a single killing blow; a second blow brings it back to life.

In English folklore, the ghoul feeds not only on the living, on children, but on the dead as well. Neither male nor female in form, the ghoul haunts remote areas to lure unsuspecting travelers.

Giant

Having allied themselves with Lord Voldemort, giants were on the losing end of the war and suffered great casualties at the hands of Aurors, who hunted them down and killed them. The remaining giants sought refuge in distant mountain areas, far from Muggles and wizards alike.

Standing nearly 20 feet tall, an adult giant is a formidable opponent.

Rubeus Hagrid's mother, Fridwulfa, is a giantess.

In Greek mythology, giants were human, but sported "snake-like" legs. Frequently depicted as warring with the gods—the giants fought, unsuccessfully, against the Greek Olympians and the Norse gods—giants are staples in European culture, but often depicted as ungainly, dumb, and malevolent. Rowling's giant-sized mountain troll that runs amuck at Hogwarts in *Sorcerer's Stone* comes to mind, as do Tolkien's trolls.

In individual combat, giants tend to be bested not by brute strength but by cunning; David slays Goliath with a well-placed blow, and Jack the Giant Killer exercises brain over brawn.

Glumbumble

An insect that produces treacle.

Glum: meaning gloomy or moody. The treacle produced by this insect causes a state of melancholy.

Bumble: "to make a humming or droning sound." This is what an insect in flight would sound like.

Treacle comes from Middle English *triacle*, which means "antidote for poison."

Gnome

When Mrs. Weasley discovers that her garden is once again overrun with gnomes, she consults *Gilderoy Lockhart's Guide to Household Pests* to see what he has to say. The Weasley boys don't need to consult Lockhart's book to know what to do: They uproot each bulbous creature by hand, hold onto its legs, swing the protesting creature in circles, and let it fly. This creates such a commotion that other gnomes emerge from the holes to see what the ruckus is about, which is how they are captured and catapulted.

As Harry Potter finds out on his first attempt to toss a gnome, the creature has razor-sharp teeth and the unexpected bite causes Harry to launch the gnome a record 50 feet away.

Their name is derived from the Greek *gnosis,* meaning "knowledge." Gnomes are traditionally thought to guard mines or treasures, but they also treasure secret knowledge, hoarding it. In folklore, Gob is the king of the gnome race and wields a magic sword.

Goblin

Rowling's goblins are short and swarthy, with pointed heads and elongated fingers and feet. The bankers at Gringotts, the wizards' bank found in Diagon Alley, are all goblins and are exceedingly clever. At vault #713, a goblin named Griphook strokes its door, which causes it to open. Griphook remarks that if anyone except a Gringotts goblin had tried that, he would have been sucked in and imprisoned, which is a real concern since, according to Griphook, they do check to see if anyone has entered illegally, but only once a decade.

Their name is derived from the Greek word *kobalos,* meaning "rogue," in Western folklore. Goblins infest households and are frequently mischievous, like some of their magical cousins, brownies and imps. Elfin creatures, they stand about dwarf height (up to three feet tall).

Graphorn

A mountain beast with two horns which are highly prized for potions.

The graphorn seems to have much in common with the African rhinoceros, which has a horn prized for use as a dagger, and also prized in powdered form for its healing properties or as an aphrodisiac. The rhino's gray hide, with its many folds, resembles armored plates. Normally a docile animal, when provoked, this two- to four-ton animal can charge its foe at 30 miles per hour and use its single horn as a deadly weapon.

Griffin

Gryffindor House, one of four at Hogwarts, was founded by Godric Gryffindor. Its symbol is a lion, which is appropriate because Gryffindors are noted for their courage.

A mythological creature usually depicted with the head of an eagle and the body of a lion, the griffin is a favorite decorative motif.

The Griffin Family Crest heralds back to the Griffins of Scotland, dating from nearly two centuries ago. The Griffin family motto is "stand fast," which suggests steadfastness, loyalty, and courage—all qualities associated with the students of Gryffindor House.

Grim

In Divination class, Professor Trelawney looks in Harry Potter's teacup and, to the dismay of everyone, except the skeptical Hermione Granger, she reports seeing the image of a Grim. "The Grim, my dear, the Grim!" she tells Harry. She explains that it's the worst omen possible—a death omen—and that it's a "giant, spectral dog that haunts churchyards."

Previously, Harry, while shopping for required textbooks at Flourish and Blotts, sees a book titled *Death Omens: What to Do When You Know the Worst Is Coming*. The store manager tells Harry that it isn't a book he recommends because reading it puts one in the frame of mind where everything appears to be a death omen; as the manager explains, it's too suggestive.

It doesn't help matters that on the way to Diagon Alley, Harry sees what appears to him to be a large, spectral black dog, the symbol of the Grim, feared by virtually all in the wizarding community.

The word "grim," from Middle English, is most frequently used in association with the Grim Reaper, a death omen in the shape of a man in a black coat who is carrying a scythe, used for harvesting not grain but human lives.

See "Black Dog" for more information about the Grim's association with death.

Grindylow

Professor Lupin sees Harry Potter and invites him into his office, explaining that he's just taken delivery of some grindylows, which will be the subject of his next lesson. The grindylow, Lupin explains, is a water demon known for its tenacious grip.

The nearest equivalent to a grindylow is the Japanese kappa, which lives in and around water. Both are known to attack people. Both rely on their sharp teeth, but the grindylow has clawed limbs, whereas the kappa has webbed feet. See "Kappa."

H

Hag

Given Professor Gilderoy Lockhart's tendency for exaggeration, *Holidays with Hags* is likely not a reliable source of information on these women who, in appearance and behavior, closely resemble the traditional fairytale description of hags—old women, often bent over, of evil nature and with a taste for children.

At the Leaky Cauldron, Harry spots a hag whose choice of meal is a plate of raw liver.

A figure in European folklore, notably the Grimm's fairytale "Hansel and Gretel," the hag is typically characterized as an ugly woman who practices witchcraft. It's an enduring stereotype that has held sway since sixteenth-century Europe, when witch hunts began. Easy targets, old women unjustly accused of witchcraft were harassed, hounded, persecuted, and typically hung or burned at the stake in the name of Christianity, until the practice was abandoned and outlawed.

This kind of hysteria was not restricted to Europe, however. During six months in 1692, witch hysteria ran rampant in Salem, Massachusetts, when 19 innocent women were hung as witches, and dozens more were imprisoned awaiting trial, until the hysteria ran its course and abated.

To this day, the term "witch hunt" refers to groundless persecution of any person or group.

Note: Not surprisingly, the word "hag" has come to be associated with anything considered ugly, like the slime eel (brown in color, soft-skinned, and scaleless), more commonly known as the hagfish.

Hellhound

Once a secret package is removed by order of Albus Dumbledore from vault #713 at Gringotts Bank in Diagon Alley, it is taken to Hogwarts, where Rubeus Hagrid is entrusted to secure its protection. He does so by putting it beneath a three-headed dog ridiculously named Fluffy.

When Harry Potter, Ron Weasley, and Hermione Granger open a door and see a snarling Fluffy, only Hermione notices that the creature is guarding a trapdoor to an underground passage.

The hellhound, better known as Cerberus, stood guard at the entrance of Hades, the underworld, the place of the dead. A vicious beast, it had three heads, which made it impossible to evade his attention. Cerberus was the offspring of Echidna and Typhon, and his dual task was to bar the living from entering Hades and the dead from leaving.

In Roman and Greek mythologies, Cerberus is bested not by brute strength, but by cunning: Drugged honeycakes, water from the river Lethe (which induces sleepiness), and music all subdue the savage beast.

Hinkypunk

This is a one-legged wispy creature that uses a light to misdirect a lost traveler, who then sinks into a bog.

In English folklore, this malevolent creature performs its dastardly deed at night. Lighting a lamp to "guide" disoriented travelers, the hinkypunk leads them astray as they follow the trailing light to its end—and, often, their own.

In earlier times, people explained the eerie presence of colorful swamp gas, which hovers over bogs, by attributing it to the presence of hinkypunks; the unexplained lights, people thought, were really creatures with lamps. Following the "lamplight" resulted in unintentionally walking into a bog and sinking.

Produced by decomposing plants under water, methane (or swamp gas) looks like a very pale haze. If ignited, it burns with a bluish light.

Understandably, this phenomenon is misidentified as supernatural in origin.

Hippocampus

A cross between a horse and a giant fish.

Scamander's description of this mythical creature is consistent with Greek legend: the hippocampus (translated: "horse-like sea monster") has the torso of a horse but the fins of a giant fish, which allow it to pull Poseidon's chariot.

In biology, it is a sea horse, a small creature with bony plates that has a horselike head and a tail.

Hippogriff

In a Care of Magical Creatures class, the students have a close encounter with a hippogriff named Buckbeak, owned by the newest member of the teaching faculty, Rubeus Hagrid. A creature that looks like a cross between a horse and an eagle, the hippogriff looks fearsome and unapproachable, but a gentle and respectful manner will win it over, as Hagrid points out. An understandably nervous Harry Potter is initially reluctant to approach Buckbeak, but Hagrid urges him to approach the beast and bow, showing courtesy; Buckbeak responds in kind. Soon thereafter, Harry, sitting astride this magnificent, winged creature, goes on the ride of his life. Rocketing upward and soaring over the Hogwarts grounds, Harry feels, for one of the few times in his life, truly free.

Naturally, the detestable Draco Malfoy, with ill-concealed contempt for Hagrid, approaches Buckbeak and insults it, provoking it to attack him.

The hippogriff first made its appearance in Ludovico Aristo's epic poem *Orlando Furioso* (1516), which was very popular in Europe and had a significant impact on Renaissance literature.

An impossibility—crossing a filly (a female horse) and a griffin—the hippogriff came to symbolize something clearly impossible.

Unlike the griffin, which is untamable, a hippogriff could, according to legend, be tamed by a wizard or knight. In *Orlando Furioso* (Canto XVIII), the hippogriff is tamed by Atlante, a magician:

> No empty fiction wrought by magic lore,
> But natural was the steed the wizard pressed;
> For him a filly to a griffin bore;
> High hippogryph. In wings and beak and crest,

Formed like his sire, as in the feet before;

But like the mare, his dam, in all the rest.

Such on Piphaean hills, though rarely found,

Are bred, beyond the frozen ocean's bound.

Horklump

A tentacled creature that infests gardens.

Garden infestation is usually due to insects or mammals, such as the mole, which can burrow holes.

Horned Toad

Professor Snape, who delights in tormenting Neville Longbottom, forces him to disembowel a barrel of horned toads.

Up to five inches in length, the horned toad gets its name from spines on the top of its head, sides, and back. For this reason, it would be no easy, or pleasant, task to disembowel one of them, much less a whole barrelful. One could hardly imagine a more odious punishment, unless one has detention under Professor Dolores Umbridge.

Imp

The imp makes its home near bodies of water and delights in literally tripping people up.

Like other creatures of its kind, the imp is more mischievous than malicious. In common mythology, in the hierarchy of demons, the imp occupies the lowest rung. Small and usually male, imps often serve more powerful demons.

For a delightful fantasy about imps and demons, try Jonathan Stroud's *The Bartimæus Trilogy.*

Jarvey

A subterranean ferret-looking creature that can talk.

The only animals capable of mimicking human speech are birds such as mynahs and parrots. The ancient Egyptians, Greeks, and Romans prized parrots for their ability to talk. Of the parrot species, the African gray parrot is considered the most intelligent and rates high in animal cognition.

Most parrots simply mimic human speech and, if taught, will repeat rather rude comments to the surprise of unwary people.

Jobberknoll

When it dies, this otherwise soundless bird will finally scream, repeating everything it has ever heard in backward order.

At the moment of death, when the Jobberknoll shrieks, it would sound like a long string of nonsense, which brings to mind Lewis Carroll's nonsense verse "Jabberwocky," a poem comprised of mostly made-up words.

Kappa

Early on, Professor Lupin teaches the students about creatures that can catch them unawares, including kappas, which Scamander describes as "creepy water-dwellers that looked like scaly monkeys, with webbed hands itching to strangle unwitting waders in their ponds."

The kappa, as it turns out, is a mythical creature found exclusively in Japanese folklore. Scamander is right in noting that they look like "scaly monkeys" and have "webbed hands," but in Japanese legend these impish creatures, who lurk in rivers and ponds, aren't interested in luring and then strangling victims; in fact, these creatures' behavior ranks from mischievous to sinister, including eating young children—a delicacy to them. (You don't want to know *how* they prefer to serve humans because it's disgusting.)

Fortunately, kappas do speak Japanese, so it's possible to talk with them. They also have a sense of honor and observe etiquette, both of which can prove useful in dealing with them.

The top of a kappa's head is depressed, allowing it to hold water. But when the water is spilled, the kappa becomes immobilized. Therefore the easiest way to combat a kappa is to appeal to its sense of etiquette by doing it the honor of rendering it a traditional Japanese bow. Put your feet together, place your arms along the sides of your body, close your eyes, and bow deeply. The kappa feels duty-bound to return your politeness; when it bows, spilling water, it is weakened, sometimes to the point of death.

A kappa may also accept your gift or offering, which will obligate it to help you with its deep knowledge of medicine or farming. Even if tricked into helping, a kappa has no choice but to fulfill the oath, since its sense of duty is binding.

Above all, the kappa loves cucumbers—a gift it readily accepts—and from this ancient creature comes the name of a favorite form of sushi, kappa-maki: rice flavored with water and vinegar, wrapped in seaweed, with a cucumber core.

Kelpie

Though Rubeus Hagrid receives unsolicited advice from Professor Lockhart on how to keep this creature out of a well, Hagrid would be well advised to consider the source and pay no attention to the (likely) well-intended but erroneous advice. Better for Hagrid to consult *Fantastic Beasts & Where to Find Them*, which details exactly how to handle this dangerous creature and how to subdue it.

It is a shape-shifting water demon that typically takes the form of a horse.

Also known as a kelpy, this malevolent horse-shaped water spirit is from Scottish myth. The kelpie (or kelpy) causes drownings.

Knarl

Similar to a hedgehog, this creature will accept gifts of food only when the food is left on the premises; otherwise, it fears entrapment.

In England, hedgehogs are popular among gardeners who prize them for their ability to control pests in gardens. For this reason, gardeners frequently leave food on the premises, to lure them. It's best, though, to leave only a small amount of food, since the goal is to have the hedgehog eat the insects, slugs, and snails that typically plague gardens. This also explains why gardeners leave holes in their fences, large enough for a hedgehog to make its way through.

Principally feeding at night, the hedgehog has a unique method of self-defense by rolling itself into a tight ball and making loud noises. The hedgehog's spiny quills make it unpalatable as a meal and discourage its natural predators, ferrets and birds.

Kneazle

This catlike creature is highly intelligent, has an unerring sense of direction, and is a good judge of character.

Hermione Granger's orange cat, Crookshanks, is half kneazle.

Lacewing Fly

This flying insect is used in potion-making.

Despite its pretty name, the lacewing fly is more commonly known as stinkfly because of the odor it emits. Its larvae feed on soft-bodied insects, including aphids.

Leech

Used as an ingredient in making potions and as the principal ingredient for leech juice, this blood-sucking creature lives near water.

There are, in fact, land leeches and aquatic leeches. Depending on its elongation, the average leech can range up to eight inches, but the giant Amazon leech, which uses a retractable proboscis to suck blood, can reach 18 inches. The European leech *(Hirudo medicinalis)* produces an anticoagulant, which is why it was used in medieval times (and is having a resurgence today) for medicinal purposes for a wide variety of ailments, ranging from skin disease to mental illness.

Leprechaun

In *Harry Potter and the Goblet of Fire,* Ron Weasley is overjoyed to be paid in leprechaun gold—only to discover that the gold vanishes before his eyes.

If Ron were more familiar with Irish folklore, he wouldn't be surprised, since leprechauns are uncommonly clever and enjoy an ironic joke, especially at a person's expense.

Leprechauns are very short (three feet or less), usually old men with beards who wear a uniform conducive to their trade of making shoes. Though they are uncommonly good at it, they can't resist shortchanging their customers by giving only one shoe instead of a pair. (In fact, the word "leprechaun" means "one shoe maker.")

Ordinary folk with any knowledge of leprechauns are always on the lookout for them because leprechauns know where buried treasure is located. The easiest way to catch a leprechaun is to listen for the sound of shoemaking. The distinctive tap-tap-tap will give his position away, but that doesn't mean he's easy game, especially when it comes to revealing the location of his fabled pot of gold. Beware! An inveterate prankster, the leprechaun will trick the unwary human into looking away, albeit briefly, just as he's about to reveal the location of the treasure, which is all the time a leprechaun needs to make good his escape.

Lethifold

Known as the "Living Shroud," the creature smothers and then kills its victims.

At first glance, this appears to look like a dementor, which also has a thick black shroud. Defense against a dementor is also the Patronus charm. Perhaps the Lethifold is a distant cousin of the dementor?

Lethe, a Latin word from the Greek *lethe,* meaning "forgetfulness," means oblivion or forgetfulness.

Lobalug

This aquatic creature secretes a poison which is used in potions.

The name "Lobalug" suggests an insect, since "lob" is an archaic word for spider, in which case the sac spider comes to mind. *Chiracanthium inclusum* has a venom poisonous to humans.

Even more deadly is the arrow-poison frog, a brightly colored frog found in South America whose poison glands produce an extremely deadly toxin that affects the nervous system. The poison of the most deadly species, the *Phyllobates terribilis,* is so potent that local hunters capture and subsequently release the frog after scraping the tips of their blowgun darts across its skin.

Mackled Malaclaw

It's literally unlucky to be bitten by a malaclaw, since its bite will make the victim unlucky for up to a week. It resembles a lobster.

Unlike the Mackled Malaclaw, the lobster—especially the Maine Lobster, or American Lobster—is a delicacy, with firm, sweet-tasting meat found in its claws and tail. Normally brown in color, but red when boiled or broiled for consumption, the average lobster weighs up to two pounds. (The record is a 22-pounder caught off the east coast of Canada.) Because a dead lobster forms bacteria quickly, it must be boiled alive or killed and then immediately cooked. The easiest way to tell if the lobster is fresh is to inspect its tail, which should be curled up beneath its body.

Manticore

This Greek beast is *extremely* dangerous because its scorpion tail produces a fatal sting.

Scamander's physical description of the beast is consistent with legend: the head of a man (sometimes with horns), the body of a lion, and the tail of a scorpion (or tiger). A symbol of the devil in medieval times, the manticore is a creature of Persian origin. Ranging from lion to horse size, the manticore is said to have a beautiful voice.

From Pausanias's *Description of Greece:*

> The beast described by Ctesias in his Indian history, which he says is called "martichoras" by the Indians and "man-eater" by the Greeks, I am inclined to think is the tiger. But that it has three rows of teeth along each jaw and spikes at the tip of its tail with which it defends itself at close quarters, while it hurls them like an archer's arrows at more distant enemies; all this is, I think, a false story that the Indians pass on from one to another owing to their excessive dread of the beast.

Merpeople

Harry Potter attempts his second task and encounters grasping grindylows and sees merpeople in front of their homes, as a crowd of them are singing to Harry and the other champions competing in the Triwizard Tournament.

In the Copenhagen harbor, the Little Mermaid—the symbol of Denmark—is eternally seated on a rock, viewed by more than a million tourists annually. It was inspired by Hans Christian Andersen's story "The Little Mermaid." Created by sculptor Edvard Eriksen and installed in 1913, the statue is a national landmark and treasure.

Mermaids are the stuff of legend: The upper half is a young, beautiful woman; and the lower half is the body of a fish. Less commonly cited: the merman, with the upper half a man and the lower half a fish. Together, mermaids and mermen comprise a community of merpeople.

In European folklore, mermaids love music and enjoy long lives, though they lack souls. Typically, mermaids comprised a danger to sailors, luring them into the water to drown or serving as evil omens: Seeing a mermaid during a voyage meant a shipwreck was imminent.

Despite countless assertions, usually by sailors, that mermaids have been spotted in the oceans, there are no known instances on record. There are, however, countless documented cases of sailors who have mistaken the manatee or the dugong (found in coastal areas from eastern Africa to Australia) for a mermaid.

Moke

A lizard that can shrink at will.

Professor Martin Wikelski, who studies ecology, ethology, and evolution at the University of Illinois at Urbana-Champaign, made an unusual discovery when researching the Galápagos marine iguanas, located on the remote island in the Pacific Ocean west of Ecuador: To adapt to the El Niño weather patterns, these iguanas can shrink in size by as much as 20 percent, losing more than one-third of their weight.

Professor Wikelski states, "We hadn't really believed it. You'd think it's a measurement error. For vertebrates, it's sort of a dogma that 'they don't shrink'" (ABCNews.com story, 2000).

Mooncalf

This creature leaves "intricate geometric patterns behind in wheat fields."

If you have a conversation with a cerealogist, what do you think you'd be discussing?

If you think breakfast food, you'd be wrong. A cerealogist studies the formation of crop circles.

Though crop circles have been around since the time of Isaac Newton, the modern era of crop circle research began in England in the 1970s. Crop circles are circular and geometric patterns in farmers' fields where crops grow.

Though some are clearly human-made, others are of more dubious origin, which gives rise to the notion that the patterns are created by little green men, or aliens, with big feet marching precisely to create patterns in wheat fields. Scamander is having fun with the notion of aliens stomping around at night, creating intricate patterns in farmers' crops.

Mummy

At first glance, it would seem ridiculous to fear a mummy. After all, aren't these merely the preserved remains of long-dead people? True enough, but imagine how horrific it would be if a mummy came back to life to stalk the living.

It's the greatest fear of Hogwarts student Parvati Patil, who, in a class taught by Professor Lupin (Defense Against the Dark Arts), must confront a boggart in the form of a mummy.

The boggart, capable of assuming any shape, is closeted in a wardrobe chest. When released in the classroom, the boggart shape-shifts into one's worst fear. The only defense is to utter, with conviction, the charm "riddikulus," followed by laughter.

In Patil's case, the lurching mummy—its bandaged arms outstretched—becomes entangled in its own bandages, tripping itself, causing its head to roll off. A ridiculous sight indeed!

To those in Ancient Egypt who practiced mummification, the task of preparing the dead for an afterlife was anything but ridiculous; in fact, they were dead serious about the process and its implications, for the mummification process, if done right, was essential in preparing the body for safe passage to the netherworld.

The process of mummification is necessarily grisly:

1. Wash and ritually purify the body.

2. Remove the internal organs.

3. Wrap the organs carefully in linen cloth and place in sealed canopic jars for safekeeping.

4. Stuff the body with natron, used as a preservative.

5. Cover the body with natron.

6. Prepare the body for bandaging.

7. Hold a funeral ceremony.

If you want a more detailed (and grisly) explanation, with cartoons, everything you'd want to know can be found in *You Wouldn't Want to Be an Egyptian Mummy,* by David Stewart, published by Franklin Watts. (This is one in a series of similar books, which include *You Wouldn't Want to Be a Roman Gladiator* and *You Wouldn't Want to Be a Slave in Ancient Greece.*)

Interestingly, not only pharaohs were given the body-wrap treatment; cats (and, for their sustenance, mice) were mummified as well, since they were held in highest regard.

The practice of mummification was eventually abandoned when Christianity took hold. Unfortunately, the ancient tombs with their treasure troves were systematically plundered by grave robbers, chronicled in popular culture in movies like *The Mummy.*

In the Middle Ages, mummies were ground up and used not only for medicinal purposes, but also in magic potions. And later, in the 1800s in England, whole mummies were sought after as collector's items and curiosities.

Murtlap

The growth on this ratlike creature's back resembles a sea anemone.

Named after the flower, the brightly colored sea anemone, like the murtlap, can most commonly be found in coastal waters. The sea anemone immobilizes its prey by stinging it.

The growth on the murtlap, in contrast, has medicinal purposes, enhancing resistance to curses and jinxes.

Niffler

As a prank, after Fred and George Weasley make their dramatic escape from Hogwarts on brooms, they leave nifflers with their friend Lee Jordan, who lets them loose in Professor Dolores Umbridge's office, utterly trashing it. The nifflers, attracted to bright, shiny objects, also go for the rings on her fingers.

There is a mammal who is also fond of shiny objects—the wood rat, more commonly called the pack rat. Nearly ten inches long and weighing over a pound, these rats collect shiny metal objects or discarded human items to add to their varied collections, called middens.

Because the wood rat's urine has a high mineral content, ecologists have found deposits that date back many thousands of years, giving them a time capsule, as it were, of what they had collected.

Nogtail

This demon resembles a piglet. When it suckles an ordinary pig, it brings bad luck to the farm.

Nundu

A gigantic leopard with toxic breath.

Obviously, there's no leopard whose breath is as toxic as the nundu's, but leopards are nonetheless first-class predators that can clear out a village when one is on the loose. In Rudraprayag, a leopard killed 125 people; and the Panar Leopard reportedly killed 400 people, chronicled in Jim Corbett's book *The Man-Eating Leopard of Rudraprayag.*

A leopard can be weigh up to 200 pounds, range up to seven feet in length (excluding its tail), and is so strong that it can carry its prey, three times its own weight, up into a tree.

O

Occamy

A winged creature with a serpentine body.

Before dragons evolved into fire-breathing behemoths, they were called worms, or serpents, and had scaly bodies and the ability to fly. So the occamy is likely a distant relative of the dragon.

It's likely that, despite its connection in name only, occamy is a reference to a well-known principle called Occam's razor, which states that all other things being equal, the simplest explanation is the most likely one.

Owl

When Harry Potter first goes to Diagon Alley with Rubeus Hagrid to pick up school supplies, the list states that one is allowed to bring a pet—a toad, a cat, or an owl.

Few Hogwarts students choose a toad, since its likely to make the owner subject to needless ridicule, though some choose a cat (as does Hermione Granger, though her cat, which is part kneazle, is very likely something more than an ordinary cat), and Ron Weasley is allowed to bring his pet rat, which clearly isn't on the list.

The overwhelming majority of students wisely choose owls for one practical reason: Owls can carry mail—airmail, as it were. Available in Diagon Alley at Eeylops Owl Emporium, owls of all shapes, sizes, and colors are popular, and useful, choices. This is why Hagrid gives Harry a snowy white owl, whom Harry names Hedwig—a generous and welcomed birthday gift.

Owls in the wizarding world are also affectionate and playfully nip their owners, or tug insistently to get paid when making a delivery; they carry little leather pouches strapped to one leg, which act as cash depositories.

In legend, an owl is revered and is a symbol of wisdom, but it is not suited to be a family pet because it is a natural predator and therefore cannot be domesticated. Requiring room to fly, noisy to a fault, and needing a steady diet of (preferably) whole mice, owls are solitary creatures.

The child who desires a snowy white owl (like Hedwig) or an elf owl is doomed to disappointment because, in most countries, it's illegal to own one; beyond that, it makes no practical sense, since owls—born free—don't take well to captivity in small, confined places, like an oversized bird cage.

Harry Potter fact: Hedwig was named after Saint Hedwig of Andechs (1174–1243).

Phoenix

A scarlet-colored, swan-sized bird decked out in gold, the phoenix lives to a ripe old age, at which point it bursts into, and is consumed by, flame, only to be reborn as a new hatchling. Its feathers are used as cores for wands. Indeed, Harry Potter's wand and Lord Voldemort's wand have one thing in common: The two feathers at the heart of their wands were the only two yielded by Fawkes, the phoenix owned by Professor Dumbledore.

Appropriately, the phoenix is the symbol of the Order of the Phoenix, a secret organization comprised of witches and wizards organized by Dumbledore who believe Lord Voldemort must be opposed at every turn.

One of the most magnificent mythical creatures, the Egyptian phoenix is scarlet in color, with gold plumage. Reputed to live at least 500 years, this male bird, at the end of its long life, will burst into flame and then be reborn from its own ashes. It reportedly has a beautiful, melodious voice.

A symbol of immortality, the phoenix can be seen in the southern hemisphere as the constellation Phoenix.

Pixie

The pixie is small, wingless, blue in color, and mischievous by nature, and its high-pitched speech is intelligible only to others of its kind.

Professor Gilderoy Lockhart gets a well-deserved round of laughter when, during his class, he dramatically points to a bird cage containing blue Cornish pixies and says they are dangerous. He foolishly opens the cage and the pixies fly out, creating mayhem, as Lockhart dives beneath his desk for cover. The pixies hail from Cornwall, England; hence their name: Cornish pixies.

The favorite pastime of pixies is to lead travelers astray. Prominent in the folklore of southwestern England—especially Devon and Cornwall—pixies are mischievous by nature, but not malevolent.

Plimpy

This round fish with long, rubbery legs is a bottom-dweller.

Note: The name is likely a combination of "blimp" and "plump," suggesting a round object.

Pogrebin

A Russian demon that pounces on its victims when they are in utter despair.

The Russian word *pogrom* means "riot." It refers specifically to a mob attack on a minority people on racial or religious grounds. The first Russian pogrom took place in 1881 after Tsar Alexander II was assassinated. Because there was a Jew associated with the Tsar's attackers, angry mobs in 200 cities attacked Jews in anger and in retribution.

The worst pogrom took place in 1903 in Kishinev, when dozens of Jews were killed, hundreds injured, and thousands of Jewish homes were looted.

Poltergeist

Unlike the ghosts who haunt Hogwarts, Peeves the Poltergeist is an oddity. He's more mischievous than anything else, delighting in dropping things on students and misdirecting them, especially when they're late for class. He doesn't listen to anyone but fears the Bloody Baron, who haunts (naturally) Slytherin House; however, when Fred and George Weasley make their dramatic escape from Hogwarts, to the frustration of Professor Umbridge, they task Peeves to serve in their absence, and he does. Otherwise, he is pretty much on his own, delighting in endlessly teasing students.

Peeves is aptly named. To be peeved is to be annoyed or be irritated, which precisely describes this pesky poltergeist.

The German word *poltergeist* ("racket" plus "spirit") specifically refers to a ghost who is rarely, if ever, seen, but manifests itself physically by making noise, throwing furniture, breaking dishes, and so on. More than simply annoying, it can also be destructive. Traditionally, a poltergeist focuses its attention on a child, perfectly captured in the first *Poltergeist* movie.

Peeves is visible to students and annoying, and sometimes engages in wanton destruction, but he does not focus his attention on any one student—he's an equal opportunity offender.

Harry Potter fact: "Peeves isn't a ghost; he was never a living person" (from J. K. Rowling's website, www.jkrowling.com).

Porlock

A shy horse-guardian that mistrusts humans.

The town Porlock is found near Somerset and Devon, England, in an area called Exmoor, known for its grounds where ponies and other animals graze.

Puffskein

This cuddly round ball is a scavenger with an indiscriminate appetite. In fact, it has a fondness for sticking its long, thin tongue up the noses of wizards to eat . . . well, it's not for me to say!

The word *puffskein* ("fluffy" plus "wound yarn") suggests a small, round object. Rowling may have had in mind a powder puff, which is a pad used to apply cosmetics to one's face. A cream puff comes to mind as well: a small, round dessert usually filled with custard or whipped cream.

Writer David Gerrold's tribbles—small, furry creatures that overrun the starship Enterprise in *Star Trek* (episode airdate: December 29, 1967)—are the closest fictional equivalent; however, Gerrold's furballs know better than to pick trouble by probing people's nostrils.

Quintaped

This is a carnivorous beast—actually, a transfigured member of the MacBoon wizard clan—with a taste for human flesh. It lives on the Isle of Drear off the northernmost tip of Scotland, and is said to have finished off the McClivert clan members.

Though there are many islands off the coast of Scotland, mostly on the western side, there is no northernmost island named the Isle of Drear. Scamander may have had in mind the Isle of Man, located northwest of England, with Ireland to its west. The name of the warring wizard clans—the McCliverts and the MacBoons—reinforces this supposition, since those are distinctly identifiable as Scottish names.

Ramora

A magical fish prized by the wizarding community for its ability to anchor ships and act as a guardian for sailors.

In the marine world, the remora is also known as the suckerfish because of its ability to adhere to ships, other fish, and large predators (such as sharks) with a sucker-like organ on top of its head. Ranging in size up to three feet long, these warm-water ocean fish can be found worldwide. They are helpful scavengers that sometimes clean the exterior of whatever they attach to, so the relationship can be symbiotic.

In earlier times, a remora was known as a "ship-holder" because it could stop a sailing ship, which is why Rowling likely made her Ramora capable of anchoring ships. Obviously, it would have to be very large and very strong to do so, on the order of a giant squid or mythological kraken (Scandinavian sea monster), which was thought to have been powerful enough to drag ships under the water.

Rat

On the Hogwarts Express, Harry Potter shares a compartment with Ron Weasley, who is painfully aware that among wizarding families, his is short of money, though rich in love; as the youngest boy in the family to attend Hogwarts, he gets his brothers' hand-me-downs, including Scabbers, the family rat.

For first-year students, the approved pets include owls, cats, and toads, but not rats, which makes one wonder: Why was an exception made in Ronald Weasley's case? Be that as it may—perhaps it's petty to even bring it up—Scabbers, Ron's pet, is a constant companion, until the owner-pet relationship doesn't experience further growth, but, instead, peters out.

The witch or wizard in search of a rat will find plenty of them at the Magical Menagerie in Diagon Alley.

As a slang word, a "scab" is someone who is regarded as contemptible, and the word "rat" has many unsavory meanings. To rat out someone is to fink or sell them out—a traitor. As a noun or a verb, the word "rat" is not a term of endearment; in fact, it's insulting, though sometimes appropriate.

Therefore, to name a rat "Scabbers" suggests that it's a traitorous and treacherous rat, and a defector, to boot.

Raven

A witch or wizard wanting to buy a raven will find them for sale in Diagon Alley at the Magical Menagerie, which Ron Weasley, Hermione Granger, and Harry Potter visit.

We know nothing about ravens and their role in the wizarding world, except that we are told they are noisy.

A large black bird with glossy feathers, the raven is a symbol of dark prophecy. A noisy bird, capable of gurgling and guttural sounds, it can actually mimic human speech, with a few learned words, if taught as a nestling, a baby bird.

Red Cap

In Defense Against the Dark Arts, taught by Professor Lupin, the students study Red Caps, malevolent creatures who haunt battlefields, dungeons, and other places where blood is shed with the intent of bludgeoning their victims.

Haunting castles on the Scottish border, the Red Cap—so named because of the human blood-soaked cap he

wears—is short and stocky, but moves remarkably fast. Because he is exceptionally strong, the only defense against this awful creature is to quote a few words from the Bible or bear a cross or cross-handled sword.

Re'em

A re'em is a giant ox whose blood gives the drinker enormous strength . . . *if* you can catch one.

The mighty ox figures prominently in many cultures and religions for its use as an oblation: a sacrificial offering. The sacrifice of the life-blood of the animal pleased or appeased the gods.

Runespoor

This three-headed snake can be as much as seven feet in length and is colored vivid orange with black stripes; of its three heads, one is extremely venomous.

A coral snake, though it has only one head and its length is no more than 2.5 feet, has vivid black, red, and yellow bands, and can be deadly. Its poison affects the nervous system and causes paralysis, resulting in a high mortality rate among those bitten.

Salamander

The white-colored salamander is literally fueled by fire, created by flames, and lives only as long as the flames that produced it.

Scamander may have had in mind the fire salamander, which is black with yellow markings (spots or stripes), and can be found in southern and central Europe.

Note: Fire salamanders—some of which have red and orange spots—do not enjoy being around fire; in fact, they prefer water, for laying larvae, and are active on rainy days.

Sea Serpent

The sea serpent has been wrongly considered a dangerous creature. A legendary aquatic beast that crops up in numerous legends, the sea serpent is characteristically considered a monstrous, malevolent, and evil omen. Despite exhaustive searches—especially for the Loch Ness monster—there has not been one verifiable sighting.

In this case, behind the fiction is a fact: The fifty-foot giant squid is most likely what has been sighted and misidentified as a sea serpent. The evidence for a real sea serpent remains elusive, not unlike the serpent itself.

Shrake

This is a spiny fish that destroys Muggle fishermen's nets.

The spiny dogfish, so named because of the spines on its dorsal fins and because it hunts in "dog" packs, is an average 39 inches in length. A hunter of other fish, the dogfish will actually bite through fishermen's nets to get to other fish. The principal danger to people is in its handling, since the spines can produce a nasty wound if touched. When caught in commercial nets used to haul in fish, the spiny dogfish can damage the nets.

Commonly used for "fish and chips," a favorite British treat, the spiny dogfish has seen its numbers greatly decreased due to heavy sea harvesting. Currently, this North Atlantic fish is on the "Endangered" list.

Snake

On a family outing to the reptile house at the zoo, Harry Potter encounters a snake for the first time, but not in a fashion he expected. Winking at him knowingly, the boa constrictor communicates with Harry who is a Parselmouth—someone who can speak in Parseltongue, a language used to communicate with snakes. When it's clear that the snake, which was bred in captivity, yearns to go to Brazil, Harry unknowingly causes the plate glass window separating them to disappear. The snake slithers off, offering his thanks.

The keeper of the reptile house is astounded, wondering what happened to the plate glass.

The enchanting episode gives us forewarning that we can likely expect unusual, if not great, things from the fledgling boy wizard, Harry Potter.

Also called serpents, snakes inhabit every corner of the world, except the frozen wastelands near the north and south poles. Widely misunderstood and generally feared by the population at large—a popular misconception is

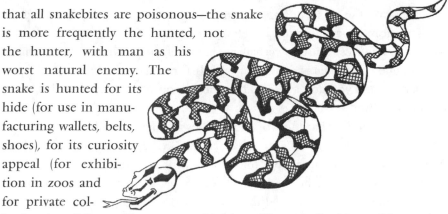

that all snakebites are poisonous—the snake is more frequently the hunted, not the hunter, with man as his worst natural enemy. The snake is hunted for its hide (for use in manufacturing wallets, belts, shoes), for its curiosity appeal (for exhibition in zoos and for private collections), and for tourist traps—snake farms. The only "legitimate" harvesting of snakes is their collection for medical research and for milking them for venom to create antivenin.

Snake meat is prized by some cultures in Asia. According to the BBC News online (Dec 6, 2001), a whopping 10,000 tons of snake meat are served every year in restaurants and at dinner tables in China, in stir-fry dishes and in soups. At the same time, reports the BBC, the hunt for vipers and cobras—prized for their venom—is depleting the snake population in China.

Ever since the snake reared his head in the Garden of Eden and tempted Eve with an apple, it has figured largely in myth and legend worldwide, most notably in the Norse myth in which a giant snake (serpent) encircles Midgard (earth). The snake has also figured prominently in cultures and religions worldwide from ancient to modern times, from the Aztecs to the American Hopi Indians.

Of the estimated 2,700 species of snakes, most are not poisonous; of the 20 percent that are, most belong to the pit viper family, which include the adder, asp, copperhead, rattlesnake, and water moccasin.

The best way to avoid getting bitten by a snake is to avoid the areas where you are likely to find them (notably tall grass and rocks) and, if you see a snake, leave it alone. (Remember, it *will* attack when provoked.)

Not surprisingly, in the Harry Potter universe, Slytherin House—one of four at Hogwarts—is where most of the shady students reside. The name alone is suggestive not only of duplicity ("Sly"), but also snakes ("Slytherin" equals "slithering"). Interestingly, one of the star pupils, as it were, of Slytherin House is Draco Malfoy, whose first name, from the Latin *draco*, means "serpent."

Interestingly, *draco* also means "someone baneful," which precisely describes Malfoy, a sneering, contemptible coward—a snake in the grass whose venomous attitude toward Harry Potter and "Mudbloods" (a derogatory term he loves to use to verbally assault Hermione Granger, referring to her Muggle parentage) is consistent with his true nature. He's truly a viperous person, and you don't have to be a Parselmouth to converse with a snake the likes of him!

It's no wonder that most of the witches and wizards who go bad come from Slytherin House, founded by Salazar Slytherin, whose firmly held belief was that only those from pureblood wizarding families should attend Hogwarts. Salazar Slytherin would have found a kindred soul in Draco Malfoy, whose parents instilled in him the wrong set of core values, including bigotry.

Snake: Nagini

A 12-foot (or longer) snake belonging to Lord Voldemort, she is milked for her venom by his handservant, Wormtail, since in order to survive, the Dark Lord needs a drink every few hours of an elixir of snake venom and unicorn blood.

Considering Nagini's length, one would think she is a reticulated python, which can grow up to 26 feet in length, but she's not. Nagini doesn't kill by constriction, by squeezing her victim; she kills by venom.

When Nagini, who can communicate with her master, the Dark Lord, tells him that a Muggle is standing outside the door to his room, the Dark Lord kills him with the Killing Curse, though Nagini could have bitten him and killed him instead.

Snidget

An amazing aerodynamic bird that can fly fast and, because of its unique rotational wing joints, can change direction in flight. It was initially used in Quidditch, until it faced extinction.

The orange-throated sun angel hummingbird, sometimes called the golden hummingbird for its color, may be the inspiration for the Snidget, which is the same color and shares other characteristics. The unique structure of the hummingbird's wings, connected only at the shoulder joint, allows it to hover like a helicopter, able to move up and down, front and back, and from side to side.

The hummingbird is visually beautiful, with iridescent, metallic-colored feathers, and its long bill is ideally suited for harvesting nectar from flowers.

Sphinx

In *Harry Potter and the Goblet of Fire,* Harry, in pursuit of the Triwizard Cup, uses his brain, not brawn, to best beasts and merpeople; the final obstacle is a female sphinx that, like others of her kind, poses what seems to be an inscrutable riddle. If Harry fails, she will make a fatal attack.

Riddle me this: What creature walks on four feet in the morning, on two at noon, and on three in the evening?

If you happened to be on the road to Thebes in Egypt and were asked that riddle by a sphinx, as was Oedipus, you can bet your life that if you answered incorrectly, your life would be forfeit: The sphinx would simply devour you.

If you answered correctly—a man in his infancy is on all fours, a man in midlife is upright on two, and a man in old age with a cane uses three—you could pass, and know, too, that you were probably as clever as a witch, in which case your journey could continue instead of coming to an abrupt and gruesome end.

A mythological creature from both Egyptian and Greek cultures, a representational Egyptian sphinx dating back to 2465 B.C. can be seen in Giza, Egypt. With a human head and a lion's body, the Great Sphinx of Giza is a portrait of a pharaoh, King Khafre.

In Greek culture, the sphinx is a symbol of bad luck; a demon of destruction with a woman's head and a winged lion's body, the sphinx is a fearsome and formidable beast indeed.

Fortunately, during the Triwizard Tournament, when confronted with such beast, Harry did not tarry; he answered correctly and was allowed to pass to retrieve the coveted Triwizard Cup.

Squid (Giant)

The students at Hogwarts enjoy the use of a lake on its grounds for recreational purposes, even if one of its inhabitants is a giant squid. Fortunately, this giant squid is benign and not only allows Fred and George Weasley and their friend Lee Jordan to tickle its tentacles but also swims with students; in one instance, it rescues Dennis Creevey from certain death.

Ancient mariners feared the giant squid, which they called the kraken, immortalized in Alfred Lord Tennyson's poem "The Kraken":

> Below, the thunder of the upper deep,
> Far, far beneath in the abysmal sea,

His ancient, dreamless, uninvaded sleep
The Kraken sleepeth: faintest sunlights flee
About his shadowy sides; above him swell
Huge sponses of millennial growth and height;
And far away into the sickly light,
From many a wondrous grot and secret cell
Unnumber'd and enormous polypi
Winnow with giant arms the slumbering green,
There hath he lain for ages, and will lie
Battening upon huge sea-worms in his sleep,
Until the latter fire shall heat the deep;
Then once by man and angels to be seen,
In roaring he shall rise and on the surface die.

Imagine a creature measuring up to 43 feet in length, with eyes the size of basketballs, and 16-foot tentacles with hundreds of suction cups. It would indeed be a fearsome sight if seen in its natural habitat, but it's a deep-sea creature that never comes to the surface, unless it dies and its body is washed ashore. With its eight arms and two long feeding tentacles, it grasps its prey in an unbreakable grip and brings it to its parrotlike beak and mouth, which tear apart its catch.

Though the giant squid is carnivorous and could easily feed on people, its diet is mostly marine fish and smaller squid. Its only known predators are the sperm whale and sleeper shark.

Understandably, ancient mariners feared the prospect of a kraken arising from the depths to attack their ships. Old-time drawings depict a capsized ship in the grip of a giant squid, but it's just fanciful imaginings, the stuff of nightmares, perhaps brought on by a sailor's excessive love for rum.

Streeler

A giant snail whose secretion burns all vegetation it passes over.

Snails are indeed destructive to gardens because of their love of fresh plants and crops, but they are nowhere near as damaging as their cousin, the giant slug *(Limax maximus)*, which is even more of a devourer. In any case, the snail, when crossing a garden, moves at the proverbial snail's pace, inching along on its "foot" with a gland that secretes a silver-colored mucus, which quickly hardens.

The snail comes out mostly at night or on cloudy days to feed; otherwise, it prefers to withdraw into its hard shell, shielding itself from sunlight. During cold weather, it simply hibernates.

Tebo

This warthog prefers to conceal itself from wizards who seek it for its hide and can make itself invisible.

The warthog isn't invisible, but then again, it doesn't need to be for purposes of self-defense. Standing up to five feet tall and weighing as much as 330 pounds, with two pairs of tusks, including razor-sharp short ones, the warthog can be a formidable beast in combat, though it is herbivorous by nature.

Thestral

Distinctive in appearance—skeletal, black, with distinctive white eyes and a dragonlike face—these winged creatures are seldom seen, for only someone who has witnessed a death can see them. (Among Hogwarts students, Luna Lovegood and Harry Potter are two of the few known to be able to see thestrals.)

Because of its specterlike form, a thestral is considered a bad omen—especially by those who have never seen one—but it's an undeserved reputation. Rubeus Hagrid is quick to point out that they are useful creatures, which in fact they are: Dumbledore uses one as alternative transportation because it is exceedingly fast in flight.

Toad

Hogwarts, it seems, is more than a school; it also is a menagerie, harboring a variety of student pets, including rats, cats, owls, and . . . toads?

Though owls, cats, and toads are on the approved list, the question arises: Why would anyone *want* a toad for a pet? An owl, after all, is beautiful and useful, since it can carry mail (airmail, of course). A cat, at least, is suitable for stroking and can be affectionate in its own way, but a toad is, well, just a toad.

At one point, toads were probably very popular at Hogwarts, but that must have been a long time ago, because any student foolish enough now to bring a toad as a pet is ridiculed.

Neville Longbottom, unfortunately, has a toad named Trevor, which was given to him by his Great Uncle Algie. Neville has a problem keeping Trevor in his possession; on Neville's first trip on the Hogwarts Express, the toad runs amuck on the train, prompting Hermione Granger, among others, to help look for it. On top of that, the mere possession of Trevor has singled Neville out for ridicule, which is unfortunate because, on his own, he is frequently the butt of jokes from students of Slytherin House; and even among the students of his own house, his bumbling, yet endearing, ways always seem to land him in trouble.

Clearly, toads have a certain commercial value. Large purple toads, for instance, are available for sale at the Magical Menagerie in Diagon Alley. But Trevor's toad seems to be of the ordinary garden variety: large, warty, stout-bodied, with poison-secreting glands for self-protection.

Among those who practice witchcraft, the toad has special significance. Sometimes used as a familiar, the toad is said to have in its head a jewel called a toadstone, which, when set in a ring, will become warm in the presence of poison and thus alert its owner

As for Trevor's name, the origin may be found in an Irish writer named William Trevor, whose works include *The Old Boys,* his first successful novel, in which he recounts unhappy schoolboy experiences and the effect they had on those boys as adults. Indeed, a frequent theme of his work is the exploration of people whose trying circumstances must be overcome to achieve understanding—a description that exactly fits Neville Longbottom.

Troll

At a Halloween feast, when Professor Quirrell dramatically bursts in and gasps, "Troll—in the dungeons—thought you ought to know," and then faints dead away, pandemonium results. It takes Professor Dumbledore to restore silence by exploding several purple firecrackers, at which point the prefects are in charge of taking the students in their respective houses back to their dormitories.

Ron Weasley and Harry Potter spot the troll—a smelly, gray, 12-foot-tall creature armed with a club—heading into a girls' bathroom, where a cornered and understandably terrified Hermione Granger is soon under attack. Ron and Harry are soon face to face with an adult mountain troll, an encounter few have survived.

In addition to the mountain troll, there are also forest and river trolls.

Note: *Travels with Trolls,* by Professor Gilderoy Lockhart, is available at the bookstore Flourish and Blotts, but keep in mind that it may be a bit, ah, fanciful.

Prominent in Scandinavian literature, a troll is characteristically large, ugly, and stupid. He is difficult to kill; the easiest way is to trick and expose him to sunlight, if possible, which will turn him to stone. (This is how Gandalf fools three trolls—forever known as the stone trolls—into bickering over dinner until the sun comes up, in *The Hobbit.*)

In an encyclopedia published in 1908, the entry for trolls reads:

> Trolls are dwarfs of Northern mythology, living in hills or mounds; they are represented as stumpy, misshapen, and humpbacked, inclined to thieving and fond of carrying off children or substituting one of their own offspring for that of a human mother. They are called hill-people, and are especially averse to noise, from a recollection of the time when [the Norse god] Thor used to fling his hammer at them.

Unicorn

It didn't occur to me for quite a while that I was writing fantasy when I'd started "Harry Potter," because I'm a bit slow on the uptake about those things. I was so caught up in it. And I was about two thirds of the way through, and I suddenly thought, This has got unicorns in it. I'm writing fantasy!

—*J. K. Rowling, interviewed by Malcolm Jones*
in Newsweek *(July 10, 2000)*

A hauntingly beautiful creature—pure gold when born, then silver at two years old, and finally white at age seven, when fully grown the unicorn described by Rowling closely matches the one popularized in fifteenth century Europe.

Difficult to catch, the unicorn is sought by many, for various reasons, according to Rowling. This powerfully magical beast is prized for its tail hairs, which are used as a core element in wands, its horn (a costly 21 Galleons at the Apothecary in Diagon Alley), and its silver blood. The latter grants its slayer life, no matter how close the slayer is to death, but at a terrible cost: The slayer will have but a half-life, the price paid for killing a pure and defenseless creature, according to Firenze, a centaur who lives in the Forbidden Forest.

In *Harry Potter and the Sorcerer's Stone*, Hagrid is in the Forbidden Forest and shows Harry and his friends a pool of silver blood "shining on the ground"—unicorn blood. This is the second time in a week, notes Hagrid, that a unicorn has been injured or killed.

But by whom—and, just as important, why?

A mythical creature from Greek literature, the unicorn (from the Greek word *monokeros*) may have had its real-world origins in the Indian rhinoceros, though the historian Ctesias cited the wild Indian ass because of its singularly notable feature: a long horn protruding from its forehead.

Because of their swiftness, it was nearly impossible

to catch unicorns, whose horns were greatly prized for their ability to neutralize poisons, as well as for other medicinal purposes. It was commonly held that there were only two ways to capture a unicorn: The more risky method was to provoke it to charge, and then leap out of the way, so the beast's horn became embedded in a tree and the beast itself was stuck, or possibly knocked unconscious, or killed. The safer, and more reliable, method was to use a virgin girl to entrap the beast, which would lay its magnificent head on her lap and fall asleep, at which point hunters could capture it.

Medieval art is replete with images of the unicorn, notably the tapestry known as "The Lady and the Unicorn," which dates back to the late fifteenth century. Not surprisingly, the unicorn shows up in the art of other cultures as well, including the Islamic world and in China.

The Constellation Monoceros

In *Harry Potter and the Sorcerer's Stone*, when the centaur Ronan—a stargazer—looks up to the heavens for answers, a frustrated Hagrid urges him to be more specific and answer more directly, though Ronan is clearly in no hurry.

If Ronan were looking up in the night sky in winter from a vantage point of the northern hemisphere, and directed his attention to a right ascension of seven hours and a declination of minus five degrees, he'd see the constellation Monoceros, more commonly known as the Unicorn. Identified by Jakob Bartsch in his star chart of 1624, *Unicornu* (Unicorn) is clearly visible with eight points comprised of stars that form a profile of the legendary creature.

Vampire

Though it's required reading for students, *Voyages with Vampires* is probably more fiction than fact, considering its author, Professor Gilderoy

Lockhart, who passes off these books as based on his own experience, when, in fact, he usually mines other people's memories for his books—a reverse form of ghostwriting.

Those in the wizarding world have no great love for vampires; in fact, in an attempt to impress the veela at the Quidditch World Cup, one young man asserts that he's a famous vampire hunter—a patently false assertion, of course. Though there are tours available for the danger-seeker who wishes to encounter a vampire, most people in the wizarding world would just as soon give them a wide berth, and for good reason: They live up to their bloody heritage.

Pale, gaunt, blood-sucking fiends, vampires are studied in Defense Against the Dark Arts class, and their treatment is regulated by the Ministry of Magic. Hailing from Romania and Transylvania, high up in the Carpathian mountains, the vampires have few, if any, friends or allies. (Interestingly, at Honeydukes, a candy is made especially for them: a blood-flavored lollipop.)

The truly adventurous, those who have an unquenchable taste for adventure, might want to stop by Terrortours at 59 Diagon Alley. This tour company offers the wizarding community "Transylvanian castles for rent, with the host a guaranteed vampire." (Important safety tip: According to the ad that appeared in the *Daily Prophet*, "Terrortours accepts no responsibility for death or injury.")

To protect yourself against a vampire, wear a wreath of garlic. It will reek, but it may prevent an encounter with a vampire—a draining experience that will leave you with a nasty neck bite, to boot.

Creatures of the night, vampires as we know them are firmly rooted in European tradition, popularized in 1897 by Bram Stoker, whose epistolary novel *Dracula* tells the tale of the undead Count Dracula, who lives in Transylvania.

For nearly a century, the bloodsucking vampire has been modeled after this famous count, but times change, and so did our perception of the vampire. Though Stephen King's *Salem's Lot* hews close to *Dracula*, Anne Rice's vampires—decadent, elegant, and glamorous, with their own society—restored new life to an aging classic. In *Interview with the Vampire*, the bloodsucking fiend, the undead, is very much alive indeed.

More recently, in the movie and television series *Buffy, the Vampire Slayer*, the vampires are depicted along the lines of Stoker's original imaginings. Despicable creatures of the dark, the vampires are ugly but powerful;

fortunately, Buffy's adversaries soon get the point, usually in the chest, with a sharpened wooden stake.

At Hogwarts, in Defense Against the Dark Arts, defense against vampires is one of the subjects taught. If the professors stay close to the traditional methods, here's what they will likely recommend:

1. The classic approach: impale the vampire with a sharpened, wooden stake, preferably made of hawthorn or ash wood. (Be sure to decapitate the vampire, as well.)

2. Trick the vampire so that he is in a situation where he's exposed to sunlight, which will burn and kill him.

3. If your purpose is simply to discourage him from attacking, have a silver object and garlic or holy water on hand, and carry a cross and a Bible.

Keep in mind that vampires *cannot* enter your house until invited, so keep the doors and windows locked, and the vampire-repelling paraphernalia handy.

Werewolf

A self-proclaimed expert on all things magical, Professor Gilderoy Lockhart is not quite what he seems. Far from being an expert in the Defense Against the Dark Arts, the position for which he was hired, Lockhart and his books are more fiction and bluster than nonfiction and fact.

One of the books Lockhart assigns to his students, one of several books he authored, is *Wanderings with Werewolves*. It's doubtful that Lockhart ever wandered anywhere with a werewolf, which means that the Hogwarts students who do their homework would do well to consult another book in the school library, written by someone with more credentials and firsthand experience.

Students would be wise to fear the werewolf. Unlike some of the other

Hypertrichosis and Porphyria

A genetic disorder, hypertrichosis—an excess of body hair—marks a person for life. It would be bad enough to suffer from hypertrichosis in our time, but imagine how much worse it would have been in centuries past when people afflicted with this rare disease were sometimes taken for werewolves. You can imagine how people in fifteenth century Europe reacted when they heard rumors of a werewolf running loose near their town and saw an excessively hairy person that may have resembled a beast more than a man.

Porphyria, another genetic disorder, marks a person as well. With this condition, the afflicted are very sensitive to light and, curiously, may have red fingernails and teeth. At first glance, it might appear that they are werewolves, since wolves like to feast at night and they look as if they've just consumed their latest, clearly bloody, meal.

creatures they face—notably the boggart, who can be bested by the spell "riddikulus" accompanied by loud and sustained laughter—the werewolf is an ancient beast that has its origin in Greek mythology, when Zeus, hearing of the tyrant Lycaon, went to see for himself and discovered, in fact, that Lycaon was a monstrous beast of a human. After Lycaon attempted to serve up human flesh at a banquet at which Zeus was present, the outraged god harnessed thunderbolts to destroy Lycaon's house. Fleeing his own house in fear, and realizing that the visitor was indeed who he claimed to be, one of the gods, Lycaon found himself way out in the countryside, transforming from man to beast, a fitting incarnation for a man that was, in truth, more beast than man.

In fact, there's a mental disorder termed lycanthropy, which is derived from the Greek words *lykos* (wolf) and *anthropos* (human being), hence *wolfman*. These people fancy themselves wolves and, in fact, have wolfish appetites, preferring flesh (sometimes human) over other forms of food.

Long a staple in popular culture, the werewolf emerged as a formidable creature of darkness in the folklore of fifteenth century Europe, as a figure who is a man by day and, by the light of a full moon, a wolf at night. Clearly mortal, werewolves when wounded would revert to human form, with the wounds clearly visible—the only way to discern their true identity.

Zombie

For those with stout hearts and a taste for adventure, perhaps the ad in the *Daily Prophet* caught your eye: Come "face to face with the living dead!" as you travel down "Zombie Trail." Stop by Terrortours (59 Diagon Alley) and make reservations. Important safety tip: As with their tours to meet a vampire and their cruise through the Bermuda Triangle, "Terrortours accepts no responsibility for death or injury."

A zombie is a person who has been resurrected from the dead for purposes of enslavement, usually heavy labor, or for committing evil deeds. Revived by a voodoo witch doctor (a mambo or houngan), the zombie literally has no free will. He is simply a slave who takes orders from the witch doctor who reanimated and brought him back to life. (Voodoo has its origin in Haiti and West Africa, and is still practiced today in some parts of the southern United States, notably in the Louisiana bayou.)

If defense against zombies were taught in Defense Against the Dark Arts, the professor would likely suggest either destroying his brain or dismembering him. (To be on the safe side, burn the body, as well.)

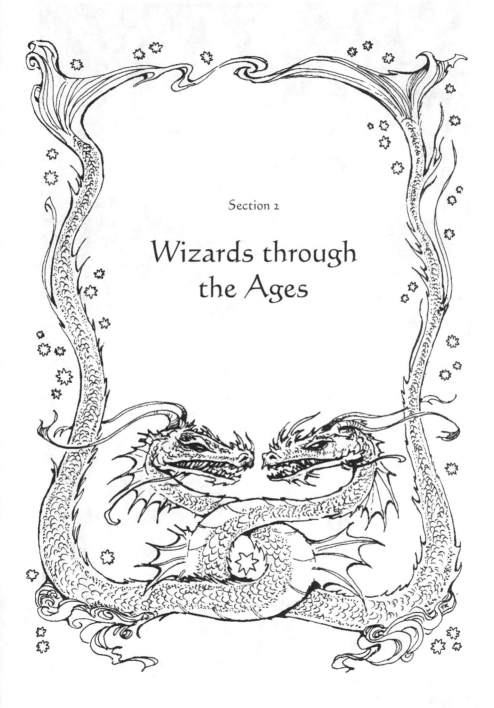

Section 2

Wizards through the Ages

A comprehensive list of every witch and wizard mentioned in the Harry Potter novels would necessarily be exhaustive, both in scope and to the hapless author. The named witches and wizards found in the novels, on the Chocolate Frog trading cards, and in passing reference—drawn from Muggle history—would be a pretty big book in itself!

I've therefore reluctantly restricted my selection to the witches and wizards I feel are distinctive in name or deed. Often the name itself suggests the personality or character, which is one reason why reading the Harry Potter novels is so much fun.

Falco Aesalon

An Animagus is someone who can transform him or herself into an animal at will. A rare ability requiring advanced magical skills, this powerful magic can be misused; hence the Ministry of Magic keeps a registry of all known Animagi.

As an Animagus, this ancient Greek could transform himself into a falcon, a bird of prey. Like his namesake, Rowling's Falco Aesalon could do the same.

Of the 35 species of falcons, not all are known for their swiftness. The caracara, for instance, is a scavenger and is somewhat sluggish in its habits, in sharp contrast to the Merlin falcon, known for its speed, which is why it's bred for falconry.

Cornelius Agrippa

The first wizard to be profiled on a Chocolate Frog trading card, Cornelius Agrippa was imprisoned by Muggles for his writing, according to the text on the card.

An expert on the occult—among his many talents—Heinrich Cornelius Agrippa von Nettesheim, born in 1486, had a colorful career, frequently at odds with the church and the government, in France and especially in Germany.

Denounced in the town of Metz for defending a woman accused of witchcraft, and after a contentious battle with the Inquisitor of Cologne, von Nettesheim was subsequently banned from Germany.

The author of *De Occulta Philosophia,* von Nettesheim was jailed twice: once for criticizing royalty, and once for his published attacks on occultism and what then passed for science, which enraged Charles V, to whom he was once a court secretary.

 B

Ludovic "Ludo" Bagman

Once the head of the Department of Games and Sports at the Ministry of Magic, Ludo Bagman left that position under a shadow in June 1995. A compulsive gambler who borrowed money from goblin bankers to bet on the Quidditch World Cup, Bagman took bets, but paid off the winners with leprechaun gold, which soon vanished.

The eternal optimist and incorrigible gambler, Bagman borrowed heavily and placed a large bet on the outcome of the Triwizard Tournament, hoping that as a judge he could influence the outcome in his favor. Placing his faith, and money, on the underdog Harry Potter, Bagman was surprised when the tournament was declared a draw, forcing Bagman to flee once again from his creditors.

Once held in high regard for his athletic abilities—he was a Beater for the Wimbourne Wasps—the now heavy-set, ruddy-faced Ludo Bagman is, because of his gambling, held in low regard. More a misguided soul than an evil one, Ludovic Bagman lives up to his unsavory namesake.

Bagman: "a racketeer assigned to collect or distribute payoff money."

Musidora Barkwith

This composer is best known for her composition the "Wizarding Suite," which was banned because it featured an exploding tuba that took out the roof of the Town Hall of Ackerly in 1902.

Musidora: a multitalented woman who was a celebrated star in the French silent cinema in the early 1900s, whose "acting career ended with the advent of sound" (Sandra Brennan, in *All Movie Guide*).

There's also a work of classical music titled "Musidora," composed by Adrien Talexy (1821–1880).

Barnabus the Barmy

This wizard is more than a little nuts. In Hogwarts, on the seventh floor, directly opposite the Room of Requirement, a moving tapestry hangs on the wall. The tapestry shows Barnabus's vain attempt to train ungainly trolls for the ballet.

Barmy: "eccentric, daft."

Oswald Beamish

Oswald Beamish (1850–1932) was a pioneer of goblin rights.

Beamish is the name of a village in County Durham, England.

According to www.answers.com, "well-known ghosts of Great Britain . . . are the ones of Warkworth Castle, Stirling Castle, Auckley, Lancaster's Grand Theater, Beamish Hall, and Denbigh Castle."

Professor Binns

Among the colorful characters found on the faculty at Hogwarts, Professor Binns has a singular distinction: He's a ghost. Dying in front of a fireplace in the staff room, Binns hadn't noticed he was dead and went off to class, leaving his body behind.

Rather than come through the classroom door, like everyone else, this chalk-like ghost simply appears through the blackboard.

Unfortunately, Professor Binns can't make the history of magic, an inherently interesting topic, come alive; in fact, his flat, droning voice and preoccupation with details combine to make him perhaps the most boring teacher—the kind who could bore you to death.

That's why his name is so ironic, for *binns* is Old Irish for "sweet, melodious." As any of his students will attest, Professor Binns's voice may be music to his own ears, but to the drowsy students falling into stupors, this ghostly teacher's dry recitation of the facts is what makes his class one of the least popular at Hogwarts.

Beatrix Bloxam

Bloxam is the author of a series of children's books called *The Toadstool Tales*. The books were subsequently banned because of their side effects, which included vomiting, a symptom of fungi poisoning.

"Beatrix" is likely a reference to Beatrix Potter, the English author and illustrator who published 23 books, many of whose titles began with *The Tale of . . .* , including her first, and most famous, book, *The Tale of Peter Rabbit*, published in 1902.

A little known fact about Beatrix Potter was that she was an amateur botanist and not only wrote about lichens (used for food and for making medicine and dye), but also spent a decade making careful, scientifically accurate paintings of them.

Bloxam is a village in Oxfordshire in central England.

Broderick Bode

An Unspeakable, an employee of the Ministry of Magic who worked in the Department of Mysteries, Bode attempted, and failed, to retrieve Harry Potter's prophecy *(Harry Potter and the Order of the Phoenix)*, after Lucius Malfoy placed him under the Imperius Curse, turning him into an unwilling servant. Sustaining spell damage during the ill-fated attempt, Bode was taken to St. Mungo's Hospital to recuperate. Lucius Malfoy sent him an innocuous-looking potted plant, which strangled him; the plant was the Devil's Snare.

Bode is the past tense of "bide," a word with multiple meanings:

1. "to wait for," which characterizes Malfoy's patience in waiting to strike at the most opportune time.

2. "to continue in a state or condition," which characterizes Bode's stay at St. Mungo's.

3. as "to bode," "to predict; foretell," which ties into the Harry Potter prophecy.

Pierre Bonaccord

He held the title of First Supreme Mugwump of the International Confederation of Wizards.

An advocate of trolls' rights, Bonaccord lives up to his name.

Bon: from the French, meaning "good." Bonaccord tried unsuccessfully to put in a good word for the trolls.

Accord: "to bring into agreement" or "to grant or give especially as appropriate, due, or earned." This characterizes Bonaccord's attempts to reconcile the race of trolls with the wizarding community.

Libatius Borage

He wrote *Advanced Potion-Making*.

Libatius: from the word "libation," meaning "an act of pouring a liquid as a sacrifice (as to a deity)," and "a drink containing alcohol."

Borage: "a coarse hairy blue-flowered European herb used medicinally and in salads."

Mr. Borgin

The proprietor of Borgin and Burkes in Knockturn Alley is an unctuous man who pretends to play up to Lucius Malfoy; he is clearly contemptuous of Malfoy after the latter's departure from his store.

Borgin: a name recalling the Italian noblewoman Lucrezia Borgia (1480–1519), who earned a reputation—some say undeserved and unsubstantiated—for treacherous ways.

Barberus Bragge

Now a protected species, Golden Snidgets were nearly hunted to extinction for the sport of it. The popularity of Snidget hunting continued unabated, however, and when Barberus Bragge offered a kingly reward at a Quidditch match for anyone who could catch the Golden Snidget, a reward equivalent to a million Galleons today, it resulted in all the players abandoning their posts in hot pursuit of the defenseless bird. Complaining to Chief Bragge that this was not sporting, Madam Rabnott used a summoning charm to bring the poor bird to her, and then ran away.

Notwithstanding Rabnott's good-hearted gesture, Golden Snidgets soon became an integral part of Quidditch, as 150 points (equal to the 150 Galleons he originally offered) were awarded to anyone who could catch the Golden Snidget. In time, the dwindling population of Golden Snidgets forced a change, and a substitute, the Golden Snitch, was invented by Bowman Wright of Godric's Hollow.

Barberus Bragge earns his name. As the good Madam Rabnott pointed out to him, hunting and catching the defenseless Golden Snidget is barbaric.

His surname, Bragge, is also appropriate because anyone who catches the Golden Snidget has earned his bragging rights.

Mr. Burke

A principal of Borgin and Burkes, a retail store in Knockturn Alley.

The name "Burke" recalls an infamous pair of scoundrels, William Burke and William Hare, who did their grisly business in Edinburgh.

In the mid 1690s, when Edinburgh's College of Surgeons found itself with a growing student population, the demand for bodies for dissection was so urgent that some of the citizenry turned to grave robbing. The buyer was Dr. Robert Knox, who not only paid in cash, but also never asked any questions.

The infamous pairing of William Burke and William Hare began when both men arrived in the city to work on a construction site. A friendship ensued and, at the boarding house that Hare owned, when a boarder died of natural causes, the two went into the grisly business of providing corpses to the medical school through Dr. Knox.

In the end, the two were caught, but only William Burke was convicted; William Hare agreed to turn in evidence sufficient to convict his former colleague, and though Hare went free, Burke was hung, witnessed by a large crowd (25,000) and then publicly dissected.

Sir Cadogan

At Hogwarts, there are pictures on the wall, as you'd expect in any school. At this one, however, those depicted within the picture frames are alive and, when they wish, can move from frame to frame, as well.

In *Harry Potter and the Prisoner of Azkaban*, the Fat Lady, whose picture guards the entrance to Gryffindor Tower, runs away and hides in another picture frame because of her fear of killer-on-the-loose Sirius Black. A knight named Sir Cadogan temporarily occupies her frame, to the students' dismay.

Though clearly stout of heart, Sir Cadogan is somewhat daft, and enjoys bedeviling students not only with complicated passwords, preventing them from entering, but also challenges to unprovoked duels.

Though there is a prominent Cadogan in English history (the first Earl of Cadogan, who was an outstanding staff officer who rose to the rank of lieutenant general), the more likely inspiration for Sir Cadogan may have been drawn from literature, notably the White Knight in Lewis Carroll's children's classic *Through the Looking Glass*. In this story, when a Red Knight charges up to Alice to claim her as a prisoner, a White Knight rides up and proclaims that he is rescuing her, and the two knights fight, after agreeing to observe the Rules of Battle. The White Knight is triumphant. As he escorts Alice to the edge of the wood, she gets a close look at him and thinks that she's never seen such a strange-looking soldier.

Though he is brave and of stout heart, with a kind and gentle face, the White Knight is also a little addled—perhaps as a result of too many blows to the head during combat—and his curious actions and circumlocutory explanations exasperate Alice, who says, "It's too ridiculous!"

Such an observation would also hold true for Sir Cadogan, who doesn't exactly cut an inspiring figure, but is full of bluster and, in the end, a buffoon.

Circe

Older Muggles will fondly remember a time when baseball cards came packed in waxy paper with a flat piece of bubble gum that measured just slightly less than the size of the card itself—a practice that began in 1951 when Topps introduced two 52-card sets. (A complete set in fine condition will set you back $52,000; in fact, one card alone is worth $15,000—that of Mickey Mantle.)

The practice, however, has fallen by the wayside, but in the wizarding world, the Famous Wizards Cards still include a chocolate frog; the cards themselves are collectible, of course, but no reliable price guides are available on their worth, calculated in Galleons, Sickles, or Knuts, or for that matter, dollars, Eurodollars, or pounds.

But if you have a yen for collecting Famous Wizard Cards, it makes sense that the more famous the witch or wizard, the more collectible the card, which is why the Circe's card may be a good investment.

Circe was a powerful witch who lived on an island populated with animals. When men—mostly sailors who were shipwrecked or lost—came to her for help, she granted it, but not in a way they had hoped. Though Circe fed her victims well at the dinner table, afterward she used her wand to transfigure, or bewitch, them. The swinish sailors would soon become rooting pigs, eternally doomed (or damned, depending on your perspective) to live out their lives on all fours.

One of the pigs (a man named Eurylochus), however, escaped and made his way back to Odysseus, who then set out to liberate his men who had been blown off course to Circe's island. Carrying a moly (a mythical herb with magical powers), Odysseus dined at her dinner table, hoping pork wasn't on the menu. When Circe waved her wand to transform him into a pig, the magic failed. The holy moly protected him; the use of the moly was a pearl of wisdom given to him by Hermes, who knew that, otherwise, Odysseus would have to cast his lot with the swine.

When Circe realized that the gods had intervened, she agreed to transform the pigs back into men, as long as Odysseus agreed to remain on the island as her consort. He met the condition and freed his men.

Cliodna

An Irish druidess and Animagus who could take the form of a bird; she had three magical birds that could heal the sick.

It's not surprising that Cliodna's Animagus form is a bird, for in Irish legend, she is said to take the form of either a wave or a wren. Eating magic apples, the three birds in question can indeed heal the sick with their sweet songs.

Cliodna is a goddess of beauty, whose name translates, roughly, as "Shapely One."

Vincent Crabbe

One of two associates of Draco Malfoy—the other being Gregory Goyle—who do double duty as his enforcers and bodyguard. Vincent Crabbe is the brighter of the two, but probably not by much. With his long arms and beefy build, Crabbe has a simian appearance.

Not surprisingly, Crabbe follows Malfoy's lead and lives up to his namesake "crab," which means "to interfere with and ruin; spoil," "to find fault with; complain about," and "to make ill-tempered or sullen."

Just as Draco is intent on continually harassing Harry Potter and all of his friends, Crabbe follows suit and joins in with the criticisms.

Like the crustacean that bears his name, Crabbe is a king crab, a predator who uses his intimidating bulk to full effect.

Fleur Delacour

Part veela, Fleur Delacour competes in the Triwizard Tournament, recounted in *Harry Potter and the Goblet of Fire*. With blue eyes and platinum blonde hair, Fleur Delacour is the center of attention because of her beauty. Because of her veela blood, she is, at least temporarily, irresistible to any boy who meets her. Not surprisingly, Hogwarts girls, feeling somewhat outclassed, are less impressed.

Delacour is initially off-putting because of her constant putdowns of Hogwarts while, at the same time, praising her own school, Beauxbatons ("beautiful sticks," i.e., beautiful wands), from which she graduates. She later takes a job at Gringotts Bank (to improve her English), where she meets, and begins dating, Bill Weasley.

Fleur: "flower."

Delacour: "of the court."

In an interview on America Online, J. K. Rowling explained that the origin of the name translates as "noblewoman."

Sir Patrick Delaney-Podmore

The leader of the Headless Hunt, this ghost denied membership to Nearly Headless Nick on a technicality: All members must be headless, and not *nearly* headless, as is Nick, whose head literally hangs on by a thread. This prompts Nearly Headless Nick to disparagingly call him "Sir Properly Decapitated-Podmore."

Podmore: Frank Podmore (1856–1910), as an undergraduate at Haileybury and Pembroke College, developed an interest in psychic phenomena and, though he later rejected spiritualism, he continued to embrace extrasensory perception (ESP). Along with Edward Reynolds Pease, Podmore helped found the Fabian Society, which advocated a gradual approach to socialism.

Dedalus Diggle

Considered by Professor McGonagall not to have much sense, Dedalus Diggle is one of the first wizards to meet, and acknowledge, Harry Potter in the Leaky Cauldron, during Harry's first visit to Diagon Alley. In fact, Diggle had met Harry earlier, in the Muggle world, and had bowed to him in public—an act so unusual that Harry remembered seeing him. At formally meeting Harry Potter in the flesh, Dedalus Diggle is excited almost beyond words.

We know little of substance about Diggle, except that he served as a member of the Order of the Phoenix against Voldemort, which suggests that there's more to him than meets the eye.

In Greek mythology, Daedalus was a craftsman and inventor who, at the order of King Minos, built the labyrinth for the Minotaur. King Minos, however, refused to let Daedalus leave, so the inventor was forced to escape with his son, Icarus. Together, they flew on wings made of feathers and wax, but Icarus flew too close to the sun and fell to his death; Daedalus made his escape to Sicily.

Daedalus is considered a symbol of inventiveness, so Dedalus Diggle, in spite of his silly-sounding surname, may yet have a part to play as a member of the Order of the Phoenix in the next encounter with Lord Voldemort.

Professor Albus Dumbledore

Albus Percival Wulfric Brian Dumbledore is the current headmaster at Hogwarts. A decorated wizard ("Order of Merlin, First Class, Grand Sorc., Chf. Warlock, Supreme Mugwump, International Confed. of

Wizards"), Dumbledore downplays his considerable wizarding skills, though it's clear that he's likely the most powerful wizard in the world, and the only one to give Lord Voldemort a run for his Galleons. He showed promise even as a student; when he was taking his N.E.W.T.s at Hogwarts, Griselda Marchbanks observed that he "did things with a wand I'd never seen before. . . ."

Previously a professor at Hogwarts who taught Transfiguration and a head of Gryffindor House, Dumbledore is the "Wise Old Man," of psychologist Carl Jung's archetype. (Another "Wise Old Man" is Gandalf the wizard from J. R. R. Tolkien's *The Hobbit* and *The Lord of the Rings*.)

In fantasy literature, the naming of names—especially one's true name—is taken very seriously, most notably in Ursula K. LeGuin's *Earthsea* novels about a boy named Sparrowhawk who didn't know he was destined to become the most powerful wizard in the world and prematurely showed powers to classmates with unforeseen, and catastrophic, consequences.

A look at Professor Dumbledore's name is very revealing. Whether by accident or deliberate design, his name speaks volumes. The explication of his name:

Albus: *Albion* is an ancient literary name in Britain for "white," and *albescent* means "becoming white," according to www.dictionary.com. Both words suggest that Dumbledore is a wizard who practices white (i.e., good) magic.

Percival: Known for his virtue, he is, at least in the original telling, the only knight of King Arthur's Round Table who finds the Holy Grail; he's also the knight who, in pursuit of the Holy Grail, kills the Dark Knight (known as mortal sin) and the Red Knight (known as death).

Dumbledore, a dark wizard slayer, defeated the Dark Wizard Grindelwald in 1945 and will likely confront Lord Voldemort, and his followers, the Death Eaters, in the near future.

Wulfric: A Catholic saint born in 1154, Saint Wulfric was known for his miracles and prophecies, not unlike Dumbledore, whose wizardry is nothing short of miraculous, and whose deep knowledge of the future is integral to helping Harry Potter plan for what is inevitable: a showdown with Lord Voldemort.

Brian: Of Celtic origin, this word means "strong," which certainly describes Dumbledore.

Dumbledore: Rowling has gone on record saying that she liked this archaic name because it suggested the professor's easygoing, happy-go-lucky nature; she imagined him walking through Hogwarts' halls, humming to himself, like a bee.

This obscure word, also spelled *dumbledor,* means "bumblebee."

All of which perfectly describes Professor Dumbledore.

Ethelred the Ever-Ready

We know little about this wizard, other than he was well known for frequently taking umbrage at the remarks of others, and eventually died in jail.

Likely named after Ethelred II, who, according to the *Encyclopædia Britannica,* "was an ineffectual ruler who failed to prevent the Danes from overrunning England. The epithet 'unready' is derived from *unraed,* meaning 'evil counsel.'" Ethelred was also known as "Ethelred the Unready," not because he was unable to prevent the Danish invasion, but because he prematurely assumed the throne as a child, at age ten. Even after paying tribute to the Danes, he could not prevent them from attacking again, which is why he was considered a weak king; he never came up with a workable strategy to defend his country.

Argus Filch

The caretaker at Hogwarts, Argus Filch is a squib, a person born in a wizarding family who has no natural talent for magic. Frustrated by his lack of innate magical talent, Filch lives for the moment when he can catch a student breaking the rules, no matter how small, and is quick to report it.

Though Hogwarts has been around for a millennium, and though Filch has been its caretaker for some years, his age is unknown. He does say that he preferred the good old days when students were manacled and chained for infractions. Lamenting the passage of such strict measures—if, indeed, they were true—Filch is prepared to reinstate the old ways, and thus keeps his collection of chains properly oiled to protect them from rusting.

Aided by a preternatural cat named Mrs. Norris, Filch is always on the prowl, looking for misbehaving students. In his small room, he keeps records of all the students and their infractions, as well as contraband confiscated from students in a drawer intriguingly titled, "Confiscated and Highly Dangerous." It is from this drawer that George and Fred Weasley liberate the Marauder's Map, which they use to sneak in and out of Hogwarts unde-tected. (They later make a gift of it to Harry Potter, since he is more in need of it; unable to get permission from a guardian to go to Hogsmeade with his classmates, Harry goes off on his own, using this map and his invisibility cloak.)

Filch, says J. K. Rowling, has a singular distinction: When the school closes for summer, all the students and professors leave, but only Filch remains (J. K. Rowling, in an interview by the South West News Service, 2000).

Argus Filch lives up to his namesake. *Argus* is Greek for "all seeing" and *filch* means "to appropriate furtively."

Argus: In Greek mythology, this giant was the faithful servant of Hera. Slaying the cave-dwelling monster Echidna, Argus let little escape his gaze, since he had 100 eyes, and only a few would be closed in sleep at any given time.

Hera tasked him to guard a heifer, who in fact was a young girl named Io, claimed by Zeus. Unable to speak, the unhappy, transfigured girl used a hoof to write her name in the river mud, at which point the River god, her father, realized it was his own daughter. Seeing her distress, Zeus sent his son, the trickster Mercury, to kill Argus. Knowing he could not sneak up on Argus, Mercury employed a more effective weapon. Playing a melodious flute until all of Argus's eyes were closed, he then killed the faithful Argus, whose eyes were then immortalized forever by Hera when she put them on the feathers of peacocks.

Even though Argus Filch has the usual two eyes, they are always looking everywhere, in every nook and cranny of Hogwarts, and few escape his vigi-lant and knowing gaze.

Filch: This word has a double meaning in reference to Argus Filch.

Because it means "to appropriate furtively," it refers to students who are always stealing things, which he later must confiscate. Also, Argus Filch himself is furtive, sneaking about and showing up unexpectedly, to the dismay of generations of Hogwarts students.

Nicholas Flamel (1330–1418)

> Most of the spells are invented, but some of them have a basis in what people used to believe works. We owe a lot of our scientific knowledge to the alchemists!
>
> —*J. K. Rowling, interviewed by Amazon.com (no date)*

A fifteenth-century French alchemist, Flamel has the singular distinction of reputedly being the only person to have successfully achieved what fellow alchemists in his time considered impossible—making the Philosopher's Stone. This stone conferred not only wealth (by transmuting base metals like lead into gold) but immortality.

Legend has it that the search for the Philosopher's Stone took Flamel more than two decades. By traveling extensively and consulting masters, Flamel was finally able to decode a mysterious book that held the key to how to make the Philosopher's Stone.

The truth is that Flamel was indeed wealthy and became a philanthropist, though in some circles it is believed that his wealth was a result of his financial dealings and investments, and not due to the transmutation of worthless metals into precious metals.

Living an astonishing 88 years—the average lifespan in the fifteenth century was a mere 35 years, at most—Flamel clearly did not achieve immortality, though his legend lives on, fueled by the curious fact that his tomb is empty.

In the wizarding world, Nicholas Flamel is celebrated as a famous wizard because he not only made the Philosopher's Stone but was also a partner of Professor Dumbledore.

Mundungus "Dung" Fletcher

Mundungus Fletcher is a colorful wizard, to say the least. On one hand, he's a member of the Order of the Phoenix and is very loyal to Dumbledore, who bailed him out on at least one occasion. On the other hand, he's not above lining his own pockets with illicit gains when an opportunity arises.

For instance, at the Quidditch World Cup, Fletcher claimed reimbursement for a 12-room "tent" with fabulous furnishings, when, in fact, he slept on the ground, with a cloak propped up by sticks. Fletcher also tried to hex Arthur Weasley when he wasn't looking.

Fletcher is a bedraggled-looking wizard who has seen better times, and his loyalty to Dumbledore is unquestioned; but even when tasked with the important assignment of watching Harry Potter, he abandons his post to pursue a shady cauldron deal, which opens up a window of opportunity for Dolores Umbridge to send dementors to attack Harry near his Muggle home.

Despite Fletcher's faults, the fact remains that he's good at heart, and his ability to mix in with a rougher crowd—the kind that frequent Hog's Head Inn or Knockturn Alley—will likely provide useful information to the Order of the Phoenix.

Wreathed in green smoke from his foul-smelling pipe, Mundungus has the nickname "Dung," which means "something foul or abhorrent" as well as "manure."

Mundungus: an archaic word for foul-smelling tobacco.

Cornelius Fudge

When Cornelius Fudge first assumed the duties of the Minister of Magic, he was so unsure of himself and his capabilities that he constantly sent owls to Professor Dumbledore for advice, which the good professor willingly gave. It was an omen, a telling sign, that Fudge was simply not qualified for the job.

Whether he's simply obtuse or in denial, the fact remains that Fudge makes a mess of things. For instance, when the Chamber of Secrets is reopened, he's quick to blame Rubeus Hagrid, and sends him off to Azkaban, until Hagrid is cleared, which casts doubt on Fudge's leadership abilities.

Those abilities are tested again when Fudge adamantly refuses to accept the fact that Lord Voldemort has returned to wage war once again in the wizarding community. Rather than believe the simple fact, acknowledged by Professor Dumbledore and like-minded wizards and witches, Fudge mistakenly thinks the *real* reason Dumbledore is saying that Voldemort is back is that Dumbledore is making a move on Fudge's job. Fudge therefore begins a campaign to discredit Dumbledore; but in the end, Fudge reluctantly admits, in the face of overwhelming evidence, that Lord Voldemort is indeed back.

Prizing loyalty above all else, Fudge installs Dolores Umbridge at Hogwarts and nearly brings the institution to ruin. A career bureaucrat with evil intentions, Umbridge has her own agenda and expects to climb up the ladder at the Ministry of Magic by sacrificing anyone who stands in her way.

An incompetent leader and manager, Cornelius Fudge has from the start shown a complete lack of skills in the job he holds, to the detriment of the wizarding world.

In *Harry Potter and the Half-Blood Prince,* Cornelius Fudge is thankfully replaced as the Minister of Magic (J. K. Rowling, World Book Day online chat, March 2004).

The word "fudge" has many meanings, all appropriate, all shedding light on the nature of Cornelius Fudge: "fudge the issue" means "to dodge, to fail to come to grips with." This certainly reflects his inability to admit that Lord Voldemort is back.

To "fudge" is "to exceed the proper bounds or limits of something." This is what happens when he presumes Dumbledore is making a power play for his job, at which point he tries to discredit him.

Most telling of all, the word "fudge" means "to fail to perform as expected." This is the key consideration: Cornelius Fudge has simply never risen to the challenge. The job, in truth, is beyond him. It would take someone with the wisdom and humanity of Professor Dumbledore to do the job justice—a job, by the way, that he turned down. The default candidate for the job, a grasping ladder-climber, Cornelius Fudge is simply out of his element.

Gregory Goyle

A Hogwarts student from Slytherin House, Gregory Goyle is one of Draco Malfoy's lackeys, the other being Vincent Crabbe. Of the three, Goyle is clearly the least intellectually gifted (okay, he's just plain dumb), and if it were not for his intimidating size, he couldn't play the role of bodyguard for Malfoy, who is full of bluster and threats and ready to pick a fight—so long as Goyle and Crabbe are at his side.

Goyle's physical appearance can best be described as unfortunate. No "pretty boy," Goyle, in fact, looks like he's one step up the evolutionary ladder from his simian ancestors. He also is completely lacking in wit.

Goyle: His surname recalls gargoyle, which was a sculpture used as a waterspout in medieval Europe. Gargoyles typically were fashioned in the shape of squatting demons or spirits, their faces leering and their mouths open.

The word "gargoyle" has two meanings that fit this character: "a grotesque ornamental figure or projection," and "a person of bizarre or grotesque appearance."

Hermione Granger

A Hogwarts student from Gryffindor House, Hermione Granger is the academic standout of her class. The daughter of two Muggles—her parents are dentists—she immediately gains a reputation as a "swot" (a British slang word meaning "someone who studies hard"), which is well deserved. After purchasing the first-year textbooks from Flourish and Blotts in Diagon Alley, she spent part of her summer reading them from cover to cover, which gave her an advantage over her classmates, most of whom merely skimmed, or ignored, the textbooks until class time. Predictably, Hermione's hand is usually the first up to answer questions in any class.

A pragmatic person by nature and initially bossy to the point of putting off Ron Weasley in their first year, Hermione mellows and, though still a stickler for the rules, realizes there's a time to do things by the book and a time to toss the book out the window and trust your friends. As a result, she earns the respect of Ron Weasley and Harry Potter.

In her fifth year, both she and Ron are chosen as prefects, which is a role that suits her perfectly. Ron is less comfortable with the attendant responsibilities, notably enforcing the rules, especially when it comes to his older brothers, pranksters who make it clear that they still expect to be able to use their seniority to their personal advantage.

Academically, if she continues on her current course of action, she will likely be the valedictorian of her class: some magic, mostly hard work, which is her style. Eschewing classes she considers "wooly," like Divination, she prefers classes like Arithmancy, which deals with numbers. She is, in fact, so assiduous in her studies that Professor McGonagall loans her a Time-Turner that allows her to double up on her academic class load, until it's clear that even she can't keep up that pace.

The faculty at Hogwarts acknowledges her academic excellence, though Professor Snape does so begrudgingly and treats her dismissively—as he does her fellow Gryffindor students Harry Potter and Neville Longbottom.

A witch with a social conscience, she starts an organization humorously called S.P.E.W. (Society for the Protection of Elvish Welfare), in which she wants to free the house-elves at Hogwarts. She persists in her efforts, although she doesn't get much support from her fellow students or from the elves themselves, who prefer to remain in servitude.

Exceedingly clever, she figures out Professor Lupin's dark secret, after Professor Snape substitutes for him in class. She also hexes a list of students, who surreptitiously attend a Defense Against the Dark Arts class, to reveal anyone who betrays their cause of secret study. Substituting logic and brainpower for guesses and brute strength—the latter characteristics shared by Crabbe and Goyle, who are Draco Malfoy's constant companions—Hermione Grainger is mum about her future goals, but it doesn't take a crystal ball to see that she'd make a fine addition to the Hogwarts faculty, if she gets her teaching certification.

As Hermione matures, she's begun to notice boys, notably, and briefly, Viktor Krum. She shares a platonic friendship with Harry Potter, but is now starting to think of Ron Weasley a little differently.

Hermione: J. K. Rowling has said in interviews that she wanted to give this character an unusual and distinctive name. It's a rare name, drawn from a character in a William Shakespeare play *A Winter's Tale*, though, as Rowling points out, "my Hermione bears very little relation to that Hermione" (from a talk at the National Press Club, 1999).

Hermione has a lot in common with Rowling. In a radio interview in the U.S. on WBUR in 1999, Rowling said that she was Hermione at age 11. Later in life, Rowling got a reputation as a "swot" and was a head girl, as well.

Gregory the Smarmy

This medieval wizard invented a potion that, when drunk, fooled the drinker into thinking that whoever gave him the drink was his best friend. The potion is called Gregory's Unctuous Unction.

Smarmy: "hypocritically, complacently, or effusively earnest."

Unctuous: "characterized by affected, exaggerated, or insincere earnestness."

In medieval times (at least until the Battle of Hastings in 1066, when people were given Christian surnames), people's surnames were descriptive, intended to help identify a person in his village or town: by paternity, geography, topography, occupation, vocation, or nickname. Thus Harry Potter might have been known as Harry son of James, or Mundungus Fletcher might have been known as Mundungus the Foul.

In the case of Gregory, "smarmy" refers to his character, so we know he was an ingratiating sort of person, like Borgin of the retail establishment Borgin and Burkes. (Borgin is obsequious and simpers to Lucius Malfoy, but only in his presence; when Malfoy leaves, Borgin's contempt for Malfoy manifests itself.)

The Grey Lady

She is a Ravenclaw ghost at Hogwarts.

In English society, a "lady" is a general title to designate the wife of a baronet or a knight, or for any peeress below the rank of duchess, according to the *Encyclopædia Britannica*.

"The Grey Lady" is used specifically to designate a female ghost, usually associated with English castles and places. According to Answers.com, "The most famous Grey Ladies are the ones of Warkworth Castle, Stirling Castle, Auckley, Lancaster's Grand Theater, Beamish Hall, and Denbigh Castle."

Davy, Galvin, and Gladys Gudgeon

The surname is telling. It means to be a "chump, dupe, fall guy," according to the *Encyclopædia Britannica*.

In Davy's case, he foolishly tries to get past the Whomping Willow, and it nearly costs him an eye.

In Galvin's case, he's a Seeker for the Chudley Cannons, but is not up to the task. For instance, in a game with the Appleby Arrows, he misses the Golden Snitch by a nose—his own, when the Snitch bounces off it twice. One definition of gudgeon is "pivot," with a specific meaning, "a key player or position," which describes Galvin's job as a Seeker.

In Gladys's case, she is duped by Professor Gilderoy Lockhart, to whom she writes weekly fan letters.

H

Rubeus Hagrid

> *Hagrid* is also another old English word meaning if you were hagrid, you'd had a bad night. Hagrid's a big drinker and has had a lot of bad nights.
>
> —*J. K. Rowling, interviewed on "The Connection" on WBUR Radio (October 12, 1999)*

The offspring of the giantess Fridwulfa and a wizard, Rubeus Hagrid is a half-blood giant standing seven or eight feet tall, literally and figuratively a giant among men.

Hagrid is inextricably linked to Hogwarts, first as a student (who was framed by Tom Riddle and expelled, though subsequently exonerated), then as the Gamekeeper and Keeper of the Keys, and later as a professor teaching Care of Magical Creatures. Hagrid lives on the Hogwarts grounds in a small but cozy hut. An endearing, and physically imposing, figure, Hagrid is a softie and cares for the students—especially Harry Potter—as if they were his own children.

Despite having a rough life—abandoned by his mother at three, seeing his father die when he was a teenager, and being sent briefly to Azkaban prison for a crime he didn't commit—Rubeus Hagrid has maintained a cheery disposition and holds steadfast in his allegiance not only to Professor Albus Dumbledore, but also to Hogwarts, the institution he's known and loved, along with its students, excepting (understandably) Draco Malfoy.

A gentle giant who harbors the most dangerous beasts imaginable and gives them cute names that belie their true natures (a vicious three-headed dog named Fluffy, for instance), Hagrid's imposing size and intimidating looks (long, black hair and scraggly beard) are in sharp contrast to his true nature: a steadfast friend with a heart as big as the world.

Harry Potter fact: J. K. Rowling said that because Hagrid is now a professor at Hogwarts, he can perform magic (J. K. Rowling, in an interview by the South West News Service, 2000).

Rubeus: Rube is a nickname for Rubeus. A rube is a rustic, an awkward, unsophisticated person. This is the perfect characterization of this half-giant, half-man.

Hagrid: To be "hagridden" is to be tormented or harassed, "especially with worry or dread" (www.dictionary.com). This is an accurate characterization of Hagrid, since he's tormented by the past, and as a half-giant, he's well aware of the persecution his kind (giants) suffered at the hands of wizards, who hunted and killed them, after forming an early alliance with Lord Voldemort. As Hagrid once admitted to Harry Potter, "I am what I am, an' I'm not ashamed."

Others, notably Lucius Malfoy, think Hagrid's differences single him out for discrimination and persecution, a view held by his son, Draco.

With a realistic viewpoint on life ("No good sittin' worryin' abou' it. . . . What's comin' will come, an' we'll meet it when it does"), Rubeus Hagrid remains essentially optimistic, good-natured, and resilient in spirit.

Hengist of Woodcroft

A medieval wizard seeking refuge from Muggle persecutors, Hengist founded the magical village of Hogsmeade.

Woodcroft may be a geographic reference to Woodcroft Castle, near Peterborough, in Cambridgeshire, located in eastern England.

In English history, according to historian Saint Bede the Vencrable, the brothers Hengist and Horsa were leaders of the first Anglo-Saxon settlers; they fought for King Vortigern against the Picts.

According to the Mysterious Britain Gazetteer (www.mysterious britain.co.uk), Woodcroft Castle is said to be "haunted by the clash of steel and cries for mercy, said to originate from a civil war skirmish." The castle was a guerilla base for Dr. Michael Hudson, whose men fought Cromwell's troops: "The doctor, retreating to the roof of the castle fell from the top and managed to hang on to the ramparts with his fingertips. One of the round-heads promptly sliced through his fingers with a sword and he fell to his death below."

Madam Hooch

Teaching the fine art of flying at Hogwarts, Madam Hooch is also the Quidditch coach and acts as a referee for Quidditch matches. Resembling a bird of prey—short hair, piercing eyes, and an accomplished flyer—Madam Hooch is no fly-by-night witch.

Little else is known about Madam Hooch; in fact, we don't even know her first name. Unfortunately, her surname is not suggestive; the definition of "hooch" (bootleg liquor) is not helpful. This is likely a case in which Rowling simply liked the sound of the name and used it.

Inigo Imago

He is the author of *The Dream Oracle*.

"Imago," which is an idealized portrait of a person usually formed in childhood that persists into adulthood, is a key component of psychology, notably the study of archetypes, which Carl Jung developed:

> As a boy Jung had remarkably striking dreams and powerful fantasies that he had developed with unusual intensity. . . . He studied [dreams] scientifically by keeping detailed notes of his strange experiences. He later developed the theory that these experiences came from an area of the mind he called the collective unconscious, which he held was shared by everyone. This much contested conception was combined with a theory of archetypes that Jung believed were of fundamental importance for the study of the psychology of religion *(Encyclopædia Britannica)*.

Ingolfr the Iambic

A Norwegian poet (circa 1400) whose verses include references to Quidditch.

Muggle history records that Ingolfr Arnarson of Norway settled in Iceland in 874.

"Iambic" is a reference to a form of verse, a metrical foot. It's not surprising that Ingolfr would use iambic; in fact, he likely wrote in "iambic pentameter," which is a line of ten syllables with an accent on every second beat, a metrical form so versatile that it's the mainstay of English verse. Shakespeare, in fact, wrote his plays in iambic pentameter.

Arsenius Jigger

He is the author of *Magical Drafts and Potions*.

Arsenius: similar to the word "arsenious," which means "containing arsenic," a highly poisonous metallic element that was used in medicine.

Jigger: a small measure for liquor.

For someone dealing with measurements of drafts and potions, Arsenius Jigger's name is properly descriptive.

Igor Karkaroff

A former Death Eater who betrayed his own in order to evade a certain life sentence at Azkaban, Karkaroff subsequently took the post of headmaster at Durmstrang, one of the three schools of wizardry in Europe, where, unlike Hogwarts, only purebloods are admitted and, reputedly, dark arts are taught.

During the Triwizard Tournament, Karkaroff was alerted to Lord Voldemort's return because the Dark Mark on his arm began to burn black. Karkaroff, knowing Voldemort's retribution would be swift and deadly, went into hiding. Karkaroff's current whereabouts are unknown.

Montague Knightley

A wizard chess champion, Knightley has a last name that recalls the name of a crucial chess piece, the knight, an armored soldier.

From the Old English *cniht*, meaning "boy" or "lad," the knight in chess is unusual because of its ability to jump over pieces—especially useful when the chessboard is crowded—and because it can play on either white or black squares. In chess, its value is considered equal to the bishop's.

Viktor Krum

Early on, as a student at Durmstrang, Krum was well known in Quidditch circles because of his exceptional skills as a Seeker; in fact, he was so formidable that he earned a slot as a Seeker on the Bulgarian team at the 1994 Quidditch World Cup. Not surprisingly, Krum was selected by the Goblet of Fire as the representative from his school, competing with students from Beauxbatons and Hogwarts in the Triwizard Tournament.

He was romantically linked to Hermione Granger—he was her escort at a Yule Ball—but their relationship eventually ran its course and cooled off.

Viktor: This sounds the same as "victor," the winner of a contest, which describes him perfectly.

Krum: The inspiration for Viktor's surname may have come from the highly regarded Krum, a Bulgarian Khan who ruled from 808 to 814 A.D.

Morgan le Fey

Known as Morgana, she was a dark sorceress and King Arthur's half-sister. An Animagus, she takes the form of a bird. She appears on a Chocolate Frog trading card.

A healer and shapeshifter, Morgan le Fey was said to be a fairy enchantress. According to Geoffrey of Monmouth, who wrote *Vita Merlini (The Life of Merlin)*, she ruled Avalon, an island also called the Isle of Apples or the Fortunate Isle. It was there that King Arthur was healed of his wounds. Morgan le Fey learned magic not only from Merlin, but also from books.

The mirage Fata Morgana can be seen in the Strait of Messina (located between Italy and Sicily).

Bellatrix Black Lestrange

A pureblood witch married to Rodolphus Lestrange, she is a Death Eater, and related to Sirius Black (cousin) and Narcissa and Andromeda Black (sisters).

Convicted for using the Cruciatus Curse on the Longbottoms (Frank and Alice, Neville's parents), she was sentenced to Azkaban prison, but later escaped in a mass breakout to rejoin Lord Voldemort.

Bellatrix: Named for the Greek mythological hunter, Bellatrix is a major star in the Orion constellation.

Lestrange: Likely inspired by the French-derived word "estrange," which means "to make hostile, unsympathetic, or indifferent; alienate."

The surname Lestrange is telling. This dark witch is certainly estranged from the wizarding world. She was also estranged from her family.

"Dangerous" Dai Llewellyn

The most famous Quidditch player for a Welsh team, the Caerphilly Catapults, Llewellyn earned his nickname for his reckless sense of play. In fact, at the end of each Quidditch season, the "Dangerous" Dai Commemorative Medal is awarded to the player who takes the most risks during game play. (A ward at St. Mungo's is named in his honor.)

Rowling appears to have invented this name.

Professor Gilderoy Lockhart

How Gilderoy Lockhart got the job as Defense Against the Dark Arts teacher at Hogwarts is something of a mystery. Clearly, a thorough job interview would have exposed him for what he is: a strutting peacock whose only "achievement" that rings true is being a five-time winner of *Witch Weekly's* "Most Charming Smile" award.

From Hermione Granger to Molly Weasley, Lockhart has his admirers. Taken in by his charming ways, they swallow the bait . . . hook, line, and sinker.

When Hermione and the Weasleys are at Flourish and Blotts to pick up the required texts—most of them written by Lockhart—for the new term, Lockhart is there and spots Harry Potter. He immediately embraces him, for it's a photo opportunity he can't pass up: the famous author and the famous boy wizard. Understandably, Harry, like Ron, is underwhelmed by Lockhart and his grandstanding ways.

It soon becomes obvious that Lockhart's not quite the wizard he appears to be. Though he takes every opportunity to announce his past accomplishments, from encounters with formidable beasts to writing numerous bestsellers, gilding his own lily, so to speak, Lockhart shows his true colors time and again when confronted with real danger. He always has a ready excuse for his failings, but he knows deep down that he's a fraud.

Gilderoy: This word perfectly encapsulates the excessively vain Professor Gilderoy Lockhart, whose outward appearance is flashy and eye-catching, and needlessly draws attention to himself. To "gild" is "to give an attractive but often deceptive appearance to" something or someone.

Additionally, to "gild the lily" means "to add unnecessary ornamentation to something beautiful in its own right." This phrase ironically rings true, for Gilderoy, a handsome man, is constantly wearing outfits that enhance his appearance. He doesn't need to do so, but he can't help himself.

According to J. K. Rowling, "Gilderoy" can be found in one of her favorite reference works, *Brewer's Dictionary of Phrase and Fable*.

Lockhart: J. K. Rowling is famous for getting names from any and every source; in this case, from a World War I memorial. When asked where she gets her names, she replied, "War memorials, telephone directories, shop fronts, saints, villains, baby-naming books—you name it, I've got names from it! I also make up names" (J. K. Rowling's website, www.jk rowling.com).

Neville Longbottom

A student in Gryffindor House, Neville Longbottom is best known for his poor memory, which is why his grandmother gave him a Remembrall, a large marble that turns red when its owner has forgotten something. Born with the proverbial green thumb, Neville is an outstanding student in Herbology but, unfortunately, a mediocre one in Potions, which is why he fears Professor Snape, who delights in terrorizing and humiliating him in class. (In one of Professor Lupin's classes, at which students were taught how to combat a boggart, a shape-shifter that takes the form of one's worst fears, Neville's boggart was, predictably, Professor Snape.)

Neville is a pureblood, and his parents are Frank and Alice Longbottom, who sadly are permanent residents of St. Mungo's Hospital for Magical Maladies and Injuries, after a devastating attack by a Death Eater, Bellatrix

Lestrange. Frank and Alice are permanently mad, with no hope of recovery, which is why Neville is being raised by his grandmother.

Significantly, Neville may yet have a part to play in Harry Potter's life, beyond simply being a classmate, since he is one of two wizards—the other is Harry Potter—who could be the subject of a prophecy regarding Lord Voldemort.

Longbottom: Purely speculative on my part, the only possible linkage that comes to mind is Rowling's knowledge of, and appreciation for, Tolkien's *The Lord of the Rings,* in which there is a rural area of the Shire called "Longbottom," known for its pipeweed (tobacco).

Luna "Loony" Lovegood

> Luna is the anti-Hermione because Hermione is so logical and so inflexible whereas Luna is the one who is prepared to believe a thousand mad things before breakfast.
>
> —*J. K. Rowling, in an interview conducted by Robert Fry at a public talk at the Royal Albert Hall in London (2003)*

Luna Lovegood is a Hogwarts student from Ravenclaw, whose father edits the *Quibbler,* the alternative newspaper published in the wizarding world. A decidedly odd witch, Luna is the mirror opposite of Hermione Granger: Luna's beliefs are faith-based, whereas Hermione's are fact-based; Luna dresses oddly and calls attention to herself, whereas Hermione is conventional and conservative in her dress; and Luna is gullible, swallowing whole beliefs that Hermione would consider absurd, like the existence of a Crumple-Horned Snorkack (Luna and her father plan a trip to Sweden with the purpose of catching this elusive beast, although it is generally believed to be a mythical creature).

Though she cares little for the comments and criticisms that her fellow students heap on her—her first name suggests her derogatory nickname—she cares very much for her father and his newspaper.

Though misguided and gullible to a fault, she is nonetheless a good-hearted person.

She is a member of Dumbledore's Army.

Luna: an obvious reference to the moon, which was thought in ancient cultures to cause periodic insanity in people. In later years, people believed that shape-shifters, notably werewolves, would turn from human to animal form at the sight of a full moon.

Figuring largely in world mythologies, the moon is linked to both male and female deities, including the Greek goddesses Selene, Phoebe, and Artemis, to name a few.

Loony: The archaic definition of being loony is "intermittent mental derangement associated with the changing phases of the moon." The modern definition is "insanity, especially insanity relieved intermittently by periods of clear-mindedness."

Professor Remus J. Lupin

By all rights, Professor Remus J. Lupin, who taught Defense Against the Dark Arts, should have been a howling success at his job, since he is clearly knowledgeable in the subject and quickly earns the respect of his students and his fellow professors, as well. Unfortunately, Lupin is tormented, haunted by the prospect of a full moon. . . .

Harry Potter first meets Lupin in his third year, when he, Hermione Granger, and Ron Weasley share a compartment with him on the Hogwarts Express. At first glance, Lupin's disheveled appearance doesn't inspire confidence, but looks can be deceiving; in fact, he quickly proves himself to be a formidable wizard, and wards off a dementor who boarded the train to look for an escaped convict, Sirius Black.

Harry soon learns to trust Professor Lupin, who is a bridge to his own past: Lupin was a good friend to Harry's parents, James and Lily Potter.

Soon, however, Harry learns much more about Professor Lupin and discovers his darkest, well-kept secret.

Remus: Along with his twin brother Romulus, Remus is one of the legendary founders of Rome. As infants, Romulus and Remus floated in a small boat down the Tiber River, finally resting at a place where the future city of Rome would be built. Both infants were suckled by a she-wolf.

In Rome, at the Capitoline Museums, a bronze statue of the she-wolf was erected in homage to the historic founding of the city; later, statues of Romulus and Remus were added.

Lupin: The word "lupine" means "characteristic of or resembling a wolf" and "rapacious; ravenous" (www.dictionary.com). Both obviously describe Professor Remus J. Lupin.

Malécrit

He is a playwright who wrote a book published in French, its title translating as *Alas, I Have Transfigured My Feet.*

Mal écrit is French for "bad writing." The title of the book suggests Malécrit's ineptness as a wizard—at least regarding his transfiguration skills—and the book's contents suggest a book with poor focus, that is, a badly written book.

The Malfoy Family: Lucius, Narcissa Black, and Draco

As recounted in *Harry Potter and the Chamber of Secrets,* when Lucius Malfoy visits a dark arts retailer in Knockturn Alley, the fawning Mr. Borgin (of Borgin and Burkes) says to Malfoy, "The Ministry wouldn't presume to trouble you, sir, surely?"

Malfoy's response: "I have not been visited yet. The name Malfoy still commands a certain respect, yet the Ministry grows ever more meddlesome."

The name Malfoy does indeed command a certain respect, but mostly it commands fear and distrust. A dark wizard, Lucius Malfoy is a pureblood and is supercilious, holding anyone who isn't a pureblood to be beneath him. But then again, being pureblood is no guarantee of Malfoy's respect. Arthur Weasley, who works at the Ministry of Magic, is a pureblood, yet Malfoy, later in the aforementioned conversation, makes a reference to "that flea-bitten, Muggle-loving fool Arthur Weasley."

The head of the Malfoy household, this former Death Eater hates not only those whom he derisively calls "Mudbloods" (witches and wizards whose blood isn't pure), but many magical creatures and Muggles (non-magic folks) as well. Truth be told, this sinister wizard has his own agenda, and it's hard to know what's really on his mind.

Well connected, Lucius Malfoy makes generous donations of Galleons to the Ministry of Magic, by which means he has simply bought his influence.

Malfoy reminds one of the evil wizard Saruman from J. R. R. Tolkien's *The Lord of the Rings.* Saruman, once a white wizard, takes pride in telling

Gandalf, another wizard of his order, that he's now a wizard of many colors, including white—a clear inference that he's also a wizard of the color black, which turns out to be accurate. Saruman used to seek out Treebeard, who knows the history of Middle-earth, for long talks with him, but they were mostly one-way. As Treebeard observed, Saruman's mind is like a shuttered window, closed to all.

Likewise, Lucius Malfoy uses everyone as he sees fit to promote his agenda, the dominance of purebloods in the wizarding world, though there are, as Sirius Black pointed out, few pureblood families, since their numbers are so few that only intermingling saved the wizarding population.

An imperious and powerful dark wizard, Lucius Malfoy owes allegiance only to Lord Voldemort, whose return to power is what Lucius Malfoy most desires, since he wants to take his place as Voldemort's instrument to further his own ends.

Lucius Malfoy is a Machiavellian schemer with an evil nature, whose misguided values are shared by his wife, Narcissa (née Black), who hails from a prominent wizarding family. The union of these two purebloods produced a son, Draco, who unfortunately is the image of his father.

Little is known about Narcissa Malfoy, a tall, blonde witch who, as it has been pointed out, has a permanent look on her face as if she's smelled something disagreeable—a visual sign of her contempt for everyone that doesn't meet her favor.

Her first name is telling: Narcissus was the handsome boy of Greek myth who would live forever if he never saw a reflection of himself. The goddess Nemesis, however, took pity on all the girls who pined and wasted away wanting him, and so forced the issue: She manipulated events so that he looked in a lake to see his own reflection, and thus died.

Narcissa, we are told, would be considered attractive, if it were not for the look of disdain that seems to be a permanent affliction.

Interestingly, the narcissus plant is beautiful, with a trumpet-shaped central crown in white, yellow, or pink, and long leaves, but its bulbs are poisonous: a beautiful but deadly flower.

Also of interest, in the second century A.D., a Roman athlete named Narcissus would later assassinate the Roman emperor while the latter was asleep. This may be an important clue as to Narcissa Malfoy's true nature.

As for Draco Malfoy, to paraphrase an old adage, the poison fruit doesn't fall far from the tree. Our first encounter with Draco does not bode well. Draco happens to be at Madam Malkin's Robes in Diagon Alley getting outfitted for his first year (recounted in *Harry Potter and the Sorcerer's Stone*) and meets Harry, who is also getting his robes. Not knowing he is talking to Harry Potter, Draco makes it clear that he is confident of being placed in Slytherin House (true), thinks Hagrid is a "savage" (not true), and that he thinks only pureblood wizards should attend Hogwarts.

In short, what we see is what we get; and what we see, we know we won't like. In fact, not long thereafter, when the first-year students arrive at Hogwarts, Draco Malfoy realizes he had met *the* Harry Potter, who was already well known in the wizarding community, and attempts to strike up a power-based relationship, which Harry wisely turns down, on the basis that he can choose who his own friends should be, thank you very much.

It's the first shot in what will be an ongoing war between the two boys, Harry and Draco: the white wizard against the dark wizard, and Gryffindor versus Slytherin.

Malfoy: The family name is resonant with multiple meanings. "Mal" comes from the Latin *malus,* meaning "bad," which is certainly descriptive of all three members. It means, literally, "bad, abnormal, or inadequate." And *mal foi* is French for "bad faith."

All three Malfoys are clearly bad people. In terms of personalities, though we don't know Narcissa well enough to speak of her, we do know that father and son are psychologically impaired, twisted, and warped individuals who are predestined to follow the dark arts, and everything that suggests.

The root word "mal" recalls several words: malformed, to describe both father and son in terms of their development as people; malodorous, to describe Narcissa's facial expression; and malevolent, which means "baleful, sinister." (Harry Potter, on the other hand, is its exact opposite: benevolent, which means predisposed to kindness.)

The root word "foy" is similar in sound to "foil," which again is descriptive of the entire family: an obsolete (meaning: not in general use) definition of "foil" is "trample," which is what the Malfoys want to do to anyone who stands in their way. It also means "to prevent from attaining an end" and to "defeat," which are both very appropriate, especially since the father and son work toward their own ends, which means having to thwart others from achieving theirs, another definition of the word "foil."

Lucius: sounds similar to "Lucifer," one of the many names of the devil.

Draco: from the Latin meaning "dragon," a species well known for its ferocity and evil. It is also the root word of "draconian," which means "cruel" and "severe."

No matter from which perspective the Malfoys are viewed, this is a family whose names and deeds bode ill for any who cross their paths. Like father, like son, Lucius and Draco are human instruments of evil who will stop at nothing to achieve their contemptible goals.

Madam Malkin

She is the store owner of Madam Malkin's Robes for All Occasions in Diagon Alley. This is the store where, significantly, Harry Potter meets Draco Malfoy for the first time. It is where Harry gets outfitted and refitted for his school robes.

Malkin: from the Middle English, meaning "servant woman." In British dialect, it means "an untidy woman." A synonym for the word is *slattern*, probably from the German word *schlottern*, which means "to hang loosely," a description of how a robe fits—it hangs loosely on a person's frame.

The surname is deliberately ironic, since Madam Malkin is obviously not an untidy woman, but, in fact, deliberate and precise, as one would have to be to be a clothier. She is not, in any sense of the phrase, a "servant woman," which in England had a very specific meaning. (For information on English life, go to www.printsgeorge.com.)

Olympe Maxime

A half-giant who denies her heritage, she simply claims (as oversized Muggles also do) to be "big-boned." The counterpart of Albus Dumbledore at Beauxbatons Academy, she is an elegant dresser. In her spare time, when she isn't running the academy, she breeds the Abraxan winged horses, which (like her) are large and powerful. (A team of Abraxan horses draws the Beauxbatons Academy's carriage to Hogwarts for the Triwizard Tournament.)

Olympe Maxime is the apple of Rubeus Hagrid's eye, though it's not clear to what extent she feels the same way. For now, she's a friend, but there's a possibility of a closer relationship.

Olympe: This word directly refers to Mount Olympus in Thessaly, in Greece, the home of the gods. It also means "befitting or characteristic of an Olympian," which describes the woman. She is not only a spirited competitor in her own right, but is the headmistress of her school who takes her students to the Triwizard Tournament, which is the students' Olympics.

The word "olympic" also is connected to the word "lofty," which refers not only to an elevated character or spirit, but also "rising to a great height."

Maxime: Her surname recalls the word "maximum," which means "the greatest quantity or value attainable or attained" and "the period of highest, greatest, or utmost development," both of which reflect on her involvement in the Triwizard Tournament.

Professor Minerva McGonagall

The Head of Gryffindor House, Professor Minerva McGonagall is a severe-looking witch who teaches Transfiguration. An Animagus, she is capable of turning herself into a tabby cat. Not one to play favorites like some other professors—notably Severus Snape, who favors Slytherin students to the point of indulgence—McGonagall has high standards, and expects those in her house to be model students. Not surprisingly, she is fond of Hermione Granger, whom she befriends; the loan of a Time-Turner, a powerfully magical device that allows the wearer to slip in and out of the timestream, enables Granger to double up on her classes.

Especially fond of Quidditch, the stern McGonagall rarely lets a smile escape, though occasionally it does, showing that beneath her hard exterior is a soft heart.

Though a harsh taskmistress to her students, she knows that to have high standards and enforce them will ultimately serve her students well. Not surprisingly, she holds her fellow professors to an even higher standard, and is quick to voice her criticisms when dealing with the likes of Professor Gilderoy Lockhart (an egocentric incompetent), Professor Sibyll Trelawny (a ditzy seer), and especially Professor Dolores Umbridge (a malicious busybody who is pure poison to all at Hogwarts), with whom she is constantly at war. A strong ally and a determined enemy, Minerva McGonagall is clearly not one to suffer fools gladly; in fact, she doesn't suffer them at all.

Minerva: A Roman goddess of wisdom and also war, Minerva is the daughter of Jupiter and Juno, and is frequently depicted in battle gear, with a helmet and chain mail, and carrying a spear. Minerva, unlike Mars, favored defensive, not offensive, operations in war. Minerva's Greek equivalent is Athena, who is strongly associated with owls. (In Athens, the symbol of the owl was stamped on the drachma, the currency of that day.)

These goddess qualities fit Minerva McGonagall perfectly: The head of Gryffindor House, she is not only wise, but also compassionate in her own way, giving a hoot for her students and for her love of Quidditch, as well. In fact, when Umbridge and her underlings attack Hagrid, she defends him and gets struck with multiple stunning spells (recounted in *Harry Potter and the Order of the Phoenix*).

The association of owls with her Greek equivalent is telling, as well. Owls are traditionally celebrated for their studious intelligence and wisdom.

The name "McGonagall" came from a "very, very, very bad Scottish poet" (J. K. Rowling, in an interview aired on WBUR, 1999). According to www.ScotlandVacations.com, "William McGonagall (1830–1902) is Dundee's best remembered nobody. He was a man without talent who thought he was a great poet and tragedian and only needed an opportunity to prove it. . . . All his poems have been published and so are there to be judged: they have, if nothing else, the quality of inimitability."

Merlin

A famous magician of medieval times whose face appears on a Chocolate Frog trading card, he created the Order of Merlin to protect Muggles. (The Order of Merlin prohibits using magic against Muggles.)

In Muggle history, Merlin (as Merlin Ambrosius) first makes his appearance in Welsh tales, but Geoffrey of Monmouth inextricably linked Merlin to the King Arthur legend in his three books: *Prophetiae Merlini, Historia Regum Britanniae,* and *Vita Merlini.* In Geoffrey's accounts, Merlin was initially an advisor to the British king Vortigern; in *Vita Merlini,* Merlin had the powers of divination which he used to advise King Arthur's father, Uther Pendragon, and King Arthur, as well.

Told and retold by numerous others, with changes and embellishments, the Merlin legend survives today with Merlin as a powerful and worldly wizard, a loremaster, who served King Arthur as his principal advisor.

In popular fiction, Merlin—again, with changes and embellishments—crops up in Mark Twain's *A Connecticut Yankee in King Arthur's Court* and, very prominently, in T. H. White's *The Once and Future King.* In contemporary fantasy, Marion Zimmer Bradley, Mary Stewart, and Bernard Cornwell have written books in which Merlin figures prominently.

Alastor "Mad-Eye" Moody

A member of the Order of the Phoenix, a retired Auror, and a Hogwarts professor who was hired to teach Defense Against the Dark Arts, Alastor Moody is known for his gruff manner and is readily identifiable because of his prominent magic eye, which can not only see through solid objects, but also render the invisible visible. Considered to be the best Auror ever in the history of the Ministry of Magic, Moody is a one-of-a-kind wizard who commands respect.

Moody is a scarred and grizzled veteran with many quirks (one is an obsession with wand safety), and his understandable catchphrase is "Constant Vigilance!"

Alastor: an avenging deity or spirit—most notably, in Greek legend, the goddess Nemesis, who personified indignant disapproval.

Moody: "subject to depression." From the word "mood," which is "a distinctive atmosphere or context: Aura," which is suggestive of "Auror."

This well-named character is in fact an avenger. A successful dark wizard hunter who has put more of them in Azkaban than anyone else, the battle-scared Moody has seen a lot of action.

Given his aptitude as an Auror and the dark world in which he must travel, it's not surprising that he would be, in temperament, moody. Nonetheless, he is a steadfast friend and loyal supporter of Professor Dumbledore, and has earned the respect of Arthur and Molly Weasley, and many others in the wizarding world.

Moaning Myrtle

Probably the only ghost haunting Hogwarts who died as a student, Moaning Myrtle was the object of prolonged teasing from her then-fellow student Olive Hornby. Seeking privacy and refuge from the teasing, she hid in a girls' bathroom, where she died after inadvertently gazing at the basilisk that hid in the Chamber of Secrets beneath the school itself.

She earned her nickname from her never-ending lamentations. Sensitive to every slight, whether real or imagined, she fancies Harry Potter, probably because he is polite to her, which is a far cry from how she remembers being treated as a student.

Lamenting the fact that she's not corporeal, that she's unjustly a ghost, Moaning Myrtle lives up to her nickname.

Moan: "a low prolonged sound of pain or of grief."

The word "moan" is also associated with the word "complaint," which is "a bodily ailment or disease," an ironic definition because she obviously doesn't have a body to speak of.

Paracelsus

If you're at Hogwarts and find yourself wanting to take the shortest route to the Owlery from the Gryffindor Common Room, you will pass a bust of this famous wizard who is immortalized on the first-numbered Chocolate Frog trading card.

Philippus Aureolus Theophrastus Bombastus Von Hohenheim, who called himself Paracelsus (above Celsus) because he considered himself above the first-century Roman physician Celsus, is justly celebrated in the annals of medicine. Holding that "knowledge is experience" and realizing that much of what was being taught as modern medicine was likely doing no good at all, or doing more harm than good, Paracelsus, who received his doctoral degree in 1516, abandoned the current body of medical knowledge to forge his own path to discover new truths.

Paracelsus discovered that natural cures (i.e., nature-based) were more effective in treating wounds than the traditional salves, ointments, and lotions foisted on the public by "doctors." During those medically unenlightened times, apothecaries stocked such "useful" medicinals as dried dung, a popular salve.

At the center of controversy, Paracelsus was admired and respected by students who challenged contemporary medical thinking, though he was at odds with the medical establishment at the time. Paracelsus's groundbreaking study of the curative powers of chemical medicine and his theory of the relationship between nature and medicine, which formed the basis for homeopathic remedies, made him a pioneer.

Pansy Parkinson

The perfect female counterpart to Draco Malfoy—the two, in fact, attend the 1994 Yule Ball as a couple—Pansy Parkinson is a student in Slytherin House. Described by Harry Potter as "hard-faced," she is no English Rose, with whom she shares only one trait: her thorny nature, mostly against Harry Potter and all of his friends.

Also described as having the face of a pug, Pansy Parkinson—if the description is accurate—is an object of pity. A pug is a kind of dog known for its sturdy build and squarish body, with a wrinkled face and a snub nose: not the kind of girl who is going to get a lot of compliments for her appearance. In short, an unfortunate-looking girl.

This dog breed is especially known for its intelligence and stubbornness.

The word "pug" is also a slang word for a fighter, which is certainly true of Pansy Parkinson, who is quick to pick a fight with Harry and company.

Pansy: a garden flower with beautiful varieties that are favorite show plants. The word "pansy" comes from the French *pensée*, which means "thought." The flower earned this name because of its resemblance to the human face.

The name is somewhat ironic, since Pansy Parkinson's looks don't suggest thoughtfulness, nor can she be considered a beautiful flower like Beauxbatons graduate Fleur Delacour, an attractive blonde with an exotic French accent.

Madam Irma Pince

An unsavory character who prizes the books in her library more than anything else, Madam Irma Pince reluctantly allows a copy of *Quidditch Through the Ages* to be loaned to Muggles by way of Albus Dumbledore, who literally has to pry the book from her fingers. Afterward, Dumbledore has to remove the "usual library spells" from the book, and warns that she has a well-deserved reputation for putting jinxes on books. In short, this librarian is a real witch when it comes to her tender tomes.

Described as having a shriveled face and looking like an underfed vulture, this gaunt librarian is especially suspicious of students and is quick to brandish her characteristic feather duster as a weapon.

With an irritable disposition and a general wariness regarding the loan of library books, Madam Irma Pince is particularly vengeful when she discovers that a book has been mistreated. In that case, according to Dumbledore, in his foreword to *Quidditch Through the Ages*, expect to pay the price.

Madam Pince's name is suggestive of her temperament. A pince is a pair of "eyeglasses clipped to the nose by a spring," which suggests an object that is held tightly. In fact, a pincer is a tool used to grasp and squeeze an object, which suggests her proclivity for holding onto books with a tenacious grip, like a lobster. Furthermore, this is the characteristic eyeglass worn by bookish types, like librarians.

Moreover, the description of her being vulturelike is telling as well, since a vulture has exceptionally well-developed eyesight; in Madam Pince's case, all the better to keep an eye on those pesky students and the way they mishandle her precious books. A vulture is also solitary by nature, which describes Madam Pince, who is very much a person unto herself; she likely has few, if any, friends among the faculty. The most common image of a vulture is one perched on a tree overlooking a carcass, a dead body.

Painted in the most unflattering physical terms possible, Madam Pince is the stereotypic librarian, a type that contemporary librarians rail against because it paints them as draconian figures. In fact, on an episode of *Family Feud,* a television game show, the contestants, when asked to describe the top five characteristics of a librarian, cited: quiet, mean or stern, unmarried, stuffy, and wearing glasses. This certainly describes Madam Irma Pince, who is the stereotypic librarian, with a nasty twist.

Madam Poppy Pomfrey

In the Muggles' world at a school's infirmary, the nurse will likely tend to minor medical matters, such as dealing with the scrapes and bruises of most students and the sports accidents of the athletically inclined. At Hogwarts, however, the school's infirmary has to be prepared for virtually anything. For instance, if a boneheaded professor suddenly takes it upon himself to repair your broken arm and, by using the wrong incantation, takes all the bones out of it, leaving it rubbery, what should you do? (You should rush to Madam Pomfrey, who will use the nasty-tasting Skele-Gro to regrow your bones and restore your arm to its natural form.) Or let's say your teeth have suddenly grown like a beaver's, jutting out from your mouth, after a poorly aimed spell strikes you instead of the intended victim. This happened to Hermione Granger, who got hit with the Densaugeo (from the Latin, "tooth" plus "grow") curse. Fortunately, Madam Pomfrey knows exactly what to do.

The list of ailments that afflicts the student body is long. Fortunately, Madam Pomfrey's knowledge and expertise are extensive, so there's likely little she hasn't seen in her years at Hogwarts.

Fussing like a mother hen over her brood, Madam Poppy Pomfrey is the classic nurse: imperturbable, efficient, and highly effective, with a well-stocked store of potions, herbs, and other ointments. In addition, she has a mastery of curing spells, which comes in handy when all else fails.

Poppy: Madam Poppy Pomfrey's first name is drawn from a plant, harvested for purposes both legal (medicinal) and illegal (opium).

Harry Potter

When Rubeus Hagrid meets a young Harry Potter at a broken-down shack by the sea (a place as remote as possible, which suited Uncle Vernon just fine, since he wanted to escape the blizzard of letters arriving for Harry), he says, "Harry—yer a wizard."

It's the turning point in young Harry's life. Then 11, Harry realizes why he never quite fit in with his adopted family, the Dursleys, who are Muggles (non-magic folk).

Hagrid gives Harry a quick update on who and what he is—a famous figure in the wizarding world—because together they leave for Diagon Alley, so Harry can begin to fulfill his destiny.

The door to the hut, smashed down by Hagrid, is symbolic of the last Muggle barrier that stood between Harry and the wizarding world in which he truly belongs. No longer ignored and treated as a third-class citizen, Harry gradually comes to realize that the Muggle world in which he's lived for all of his young life is, happily, not his lot.

Even before he gets to Hogwarts, he begins to realize he's not just another student selected to attend the prestigious Hogwarts School of Witchcraft and Wizardry. A brief walk-through of the Leaky Cauldron, the gateway in London to Diagon Alley, makes it clear that even though he knows virtually no one except Hagrid—and him only recently—everyone certainly knows him: He is "the boy who lived." He is the only person ever to have survived the deadly Killing Curse, and at the hands of the most powerful dark wizard in the world, Lord Voldemort.

Deliberately isolated from his wizarding heritage, he is dazed to find out on the train to Hogwarts that, as Hermione Granger points out, he's listed in *Modern Magical History, The Rise and Fall of the Dark Arts,* and *Great Wizarding Events of the Twentieth Century.*

Though it's clear that he is oblivious to the ways of magic, unlike some of his classmates who grew up in the wizarding world, he doesn't take long to get up to speed. Like his father, James, he becomes an outstanding Quidditch player, a Seeker for his house, Gryffindor.

While his fellow students worry only about classes, about fitting in, and about what to do during their summer vacations and school breaks, Harry has much more on his mind: His first year at Hogwarts, especially outside the classroom, is an education in itself. Like Alice, who falls down a rabbit hole to discover a world bereft of logic, Harry negotiates his way to a chamber where he meets a dark figure from his past—Lord Voldemort.

Though his parents died when he was an infant, Harry, with each passing year, discovers how bound he is to the past, to his parents (especially his mother) and their friends, and has to come to grips with the incontestable fact that he must be either the hunter or the hunted, that Lord Voldemort neither gives nor expects mercy. As the Dark Lord lusts after power and regains his strength, gathering his followers, the Death Eaters, back to him, Harry must prepare himself in every way possible, since a final showdown is inevitable: It is, in fact, foretold in the stars.

For far too long, the wizarding world, misled by the inept Minister of Magic, Cornelius Fudge, has played a foolish game of "see no evil" and thus has ignored the incontestable fact that Lord Voldemort has indeed returned, and those in the wizarding world will once again do battle with him.

In *Harry Potter and the Half-Blood Prince,* it is likely that events will build to a climax with the reemergence of the Dark Lord, now more powerful than ever, and the boy wizard who must make hard decisions. Hard times and difficult choices are in Harry Potter's future.

Clearly the standout student in Defense Against the Dark Arts, Harry Potter would, after his seventh year at Hogwarts, graduate and be allowed to practice magic. Given his temperament and talents, he would likely make an outstanding Auror, a hunter of dark wizards.

Harry Potter: On her website, J. K. Rowling categorically states that the inspiration for the name "Potter" came from a family she knew when she was a young girl, and that Harry himself was drawn wholly from her imagination: "Once more I put fingers to keyboard to state wearily that Harry is a completely imaginary character."

It's an important distinction, because Rowling's cousin Ben asserts, to the point of taking a polygraph test, that he was the inspiration for the Harry Potter character. Said her cousin Ben, "When I read the first Harry Potter book, my jaw dropped. It was uncanny, far more than a coincidence. I know Jo based Harry on me. I can see so much of the young me in his character."

Truth be told, Harry Potter is an archetype and, as such, a lot of disenfranchised young boys who seek empowerment will identify with the character—Rowling's cousin Ben included.

On this matter, polygraph test notwithstanding, we can take J. K. Rowling at her word, since she's proven, time and again, to be straightforward and honest with her readers.

Ernie Prang

The Knight Bus provides emergency transportation for stranded witches and wizards. Its driver is an elderly man named Ernie Prang, who wears thick-lensed glasses and whose driving skills are suspect; objects in his path magically leap out of the way to avoid what looks to be an inevitable collision.

Prang: This British word means "to crash" or "to damage by colliding with a car."

Demetrius J. Prod

Argus Filch is a squib, which means that, though he was born into a magical family, he has no magical talent whatsoever. To correct this deficiency, he enrolls in a mail-order (that is, via owl) correspondence course called Kwikspell, the literature of which features endorsements from various satisfied customers, including D. J. Prod, whose sneering wife made fun of his inadequacies, notably his inability to cast charms. But, Prod enthuses, ". . . one month into your fabulous Kwikspell course I succeeded in turning her into a yak! Thank you, Kwikspell!"

Some time later, after a noisy argument with his wife, Prod dies. (It is not known whether she was restored to human form or remained a yak.)

That his wife was turned into a yak may be relevant. Her constant yakking (i.e., complaints) about his shortcomings might have been the cause of his ultimate demise.

Curiously, the yak is domesticated and is not known to be violent. Also, a female yak is called a *nak*, so Prod may have used the wrong spell.

Demetrius: This word is similar in spelling to the word "deletrius," which is a spell used in the wizarding world to make something disappear; the word "deleterious" is telling, for it means "having a harmful effect."

Prod: "To jab or poke" and "to goad to action; incite" are both telling. My speculation is that the constant verbal jabs resulted in her transfiguration into a yak, which in turn was the reason she was likely goaded into action and killed her husband.

Professor Quirrell

When Harry Potter first meets Professor Quirrell at the Leaky Cauldron, the professor doesn't cut an imposing figure. Exceedingly nervous and stuttering, Quirrell seems nice but essentially harmless. Explaining Quirrell's jittery behavior, Hagrid tells Harry that Quirrell's had a rough time in recent years. "Poor bloke. Brilliant mind. He was fine when he was studyin' out of books but then he took a year off ter get some firsthand experience. . . ."

What Quirrell experienced firsthand during his year's absence from Hogwarts proved to be more than he had bargained for.

An experienced professor who taught Defense Against the Dark Arts, Professor Quirrell displays erratic behavior after his return that is noticed but essentially disregarded, except by Professor Snape, who consequently confronts Professor Quirrell.

As Professor Quirrell discovered, book learning is one thing and confronting evil outside the classroom is quite another matter. The latter proved to be Professor Quirrell's ultimate undoing.

His surname sounds similar to "squirrel" and, indeed, his behavior is squirrelly, which means "eccentric" or "cunningly unforthcoming or reticent." This certainly describes Professor Quirrell, who strikes the students and staff at Hogwarts as eccentric, with his new turban; he is certainly cunning as well, careful not to reveal something, as Harry Potter discovers.

The definition of "squirrelly" as "nutty" doesn't quite fit Professor Quirrell. The poor professor, a victim of circumstance, is decidedly odd, but hardly crazy.

Professor Quirrell's name also sounds like "quarrel," which means "an angry dispute; an altercation" (www.dictionary.com). This is certainly descriptive of the professor, who finds himself in an altercation with Professor Snape, who realizes that Professor Quirrell's behavior invites suspicion; as a result, Professor Snape warns Professor Quirrell that he doesn't want to make an enemy of him.

R

Augustus Rookwood

A spy for Lord Voldemort, Augustus Rookwood is an Unspeakable, a wizard who worked in the Ministry of Magic's Department of Mysteries. After another Death Eater betrayed him by giving his name to the Ministry, he was sent to Azkaban, where he spent five years. Rookwood subsequently broke out of Azkaban with other dark wizards in a mass breakout.

Augustus: The root word, *august,* means "marked by majestic dignity or grandeur." Related words include awful, fearful, and overwhelming. Since he worked in the Department of Mysteries, this first name is certainly suggestive—even more so as he's a spy for Lord Voldemort.

Rookwood: The root word, *rook,* is very descriptive in this instance, for to rook someone is "to obtain something valuable from or by improper means." This spy certainly tried to rook his employer, obtaining and delivering information to Lord Voldemort. Rookwood obtains this information by any and all means possible, since the demanding Voldemort exacts the ultimate price for failure.

Evan Rosier

He is a Death Eater hunted down and killed by Aurors.

Rosier: According to *The Devil: A Visual Guide to the Demonic, Evil, Scurrilous, and Bad,* by Genevieve and Tom Morgan: "The patron devil of seduction, Rosier tempts humans to fall in love. He puts syrupy words of love in the mouths of mortals and causes them to act like fools. His adversary in Heaven is Basil." The authors point out that Rosier is, along with the other demons cited, one of "the more well-known and significant of the fallen angels, those comrades the Devil relies on most heavily to run his kingdom who, in turn, preside over millions of lesser demons."

Kingsley Shacklebolt

A tall, black Auror who is a member of the Order of the Phoenix, Kingsley Shacklebolt is an imposing figure who speaks with a "calming" voice, as Harry Potter characterizes it. His is the voice of authority, resonant with wisdom.

Part of the Advance Guard sent to retrieve Harry Potter to the headquarters of the Order of the Phoenix, Shacklebolt took on two Death Eaters in the battle at the Department of Mysteries, as recounted in *Harry Potter and the Order of the Phoenix.*

Kingsley: Rowling may have had the British writer Charles Kingsley in mind. He was an advocate of social reform, whose most popular novels included *The Water-Babies* and *Hypatia.* Answers.com characterizes Charles Kingsley as "tall . . . swarthy . . . with flashing scorn and indignation against all that was ignoble and impure." This would serve to describe Kingsley Shacklebolt as well.

Shacklebolt: To shackle a bolt is to secure it through a U-shaped piece of iron used to bind a prisoner's legs or wrists—the preferred method of restraining criminals.

Stan Shunpike

The conductor of the Knight Bus, Stan Shunpike has a distinct Cockney accent. He is contemptuous of Muggles, as recounted in *Harry Potter and the Prisoner of Azkaban:* "Never notice nuffink, they don'."

Later, during the Quidditch World Cup tournament, Stan embellishes himself in hopes of impressing a veela. He says he's going to be the youngest Minister of Magic ever—an absurd claim that makes Harry Potter snort with laughter.

Shunpike: a side road used to avoid the toll on a turnpike. An appropriate name for someone who is a conductor of a magical bus that careens through Muggle England, traveling off the beaten path.

Professor Sinistra

Little is known about this Hogwarts professor who heads the astronomy department, suitably located in the tallest tower at Hogwarts. This is curious, since astronomy is taught every year to all students, which makes it a high-profile class.

So little is known about this professor that only the careful reader will catch a reference to her in *Harry Potter and the Goblet of Fire,* in which this professor is dancing at the annual Yule Ball with a male wizard.

Even without the confirmation of the temporary pairing at the Yule Ball, the name is feminine in form; a male form would be Sinister, Sinistro, or something similar, like Sam versus Samantha, or Oliver and Olivia.

Sinistra: "Sinister" is the Latin word for left, and the left hand is considered unlucky. The word also has several other meanings that may be significant, including "singularly evil or productive of evil," "presaging ill fortune or trouble," and "accompanied by or leading to disaster."

Because so little is known about this character, it's impossible to speculate as to whether this teacher is sympathetic toward the dark or the light side. In truth, she could be either, but if the name is telling, she may lean toward the dark.

Rita Skeeter

A tabloid journalist, Rita Skeeter is an unregistered Animagus who can transform herself into a beetle, which is how she was able to listen in on conversations to reword and rephrase them in a story to suit her.

The distinction between a journalist and a tabloid journalist is one of intent: A journalist is one who reports the facts and writes a story in an objective manner; a tabloid journalist is one who takes the facts and twists them to write a subject story with a specific angle, usually unflattering.

Before Skeeter was "found out," she mingled with Hogwarts students to do research for her stories; understandably, Professor Dumbledore banned her from the school grounds. So she transformed herself into a small beetle, virtually undetectable, at least until Hermione Granger figures out the truth, captures Skeeter in a jar, and strikes a deal with her: The price of freedom is for her to put down her poison pen for a year.

Skeeter, whose byline usually appears in the *Daily Prophet,* writes a revealing, and accurate, story about Lord Voldemort's return in that paper's competition, *The Quibbler,* which fans the flames. Harry Potter is telling the truth about Lord Voldemort's return, Skeeter insists. The Ministry, through its embedded henchwoman at Hogwarts, Dolores Umbridge, unsuccessfully tries to ban the paper, which merely adds fuel to the fire.

J. K. Rowling's relationship with the media, especially newspaper reporters, is, at best, strained. Though she concedes that they have a job to do, which requires them to be intrusive, she also feels they've crossed the line too many times, to the point where she's been forced to erect barriers between them and her. The result is that she gives very few interviews and universally shuns the persistent reporter who shows up unannounced at her residence to demand an interview.

Whether this character is a deliberate parody of these reporters or not is a moot point. The fact is that a skeeter is southern U.S. dialect for "mosquito," which is a small, noisy, buzzing insect that sucks blood for its sustenance. This is a perfect characterization of Rita Skeeter, who flits around virtually unseen as a beetle and, with her enchanted quill, writes stories that draw blood: a bloodsucker, in other words.

Professor Severus Snape

The Potions Master at Hogwarts and head of Slytherin House, Professor Severus Snape has a hooked nose, a sallow complexion, long, black greasy hair, and yellow teeth. He is almost vampiric in appearance, suggesting a creature of the night. Indeed, his arm bears the mark of a Death Eater, a follower of Lord Voldemort, but he has recanted and turned to the white side, joining the Order of the Phoenix and providing information to Dumbledore.

Exceptionally skilled at potion-making—a difficult, exacting art—Professor Snape has the professional respect of his colleagues, including Dumbledore, who tasks him to teach Harry Potter the difficult art of Occlumency, which is a form of mental self-protection against intrusion from another person's mind.

Severe in appearance and in manner, Professor Snape is especially hard on students outside his own house. Gryffindor, especially, seems to take the brunt of his sharp-edged sarcasm: Neville Longbottom quite properly is fearful of Professor Snape; Hermione Granger is frequently belittled or cruelly dismissed; and Harry Potter seems, from the beginning, to be targeted for no other reason than blood relations. Indeed, there's bad blood between Professor Snape and the Potters—father and son, James and Harry—that doesn't appear to lessen with age.

Despite outward appearances and a cold and calculating manner,

Professor Snape has the best interests of Hogwarts at heart, and will likely play an important role in the final confrontation between Harry Potter and his arch nemesis, Lord Voldemort.

Severus Snape's name is very suggestive of the man himself.

Severus: Latin for "severe." The following are its meanings:

1. "strict in judgment, discipline"
2. "rigorous in restraint, punishment, or requirement"
3. "strongly critical or condemnatory"
4. "maintaining a scrupulously exacting standard of behavior or self-discipline"
5. "sober or restrained in decoration or manner"
6. "inflicting physical discomfort or hardship"

The dictionary citation notes that "SEVERE implies standards enforced without indulgence or laxity and may suggest harshness."

Snape: This is similar in sound to snipe, which means "to make malicious, underhand remarks or attacks." A snipe is "a contemptible person."

Taken together, Severus Snape suggests a person of inflexibility, a person who is quick to condemn and deliberately attack with cruelty when he so desires.

Harry Potter fact: J. K. Rowling says that Snape is the name of an English village. For more information on the town, go to www.snapevillage.org.uk.

Phyllida Spore

She is the author of a book called *One Thousand Magical Herbs and Fungi*.

Phyllida: Considering her surname is Spore, the first name, which has been feminized, has as its root *phylum*, which is a taxonomic grouping developed by Carolus Linnaeus. From top to bottom, these include: Domain, Kingdom, Phylum (for animals) or Division (for plants), Class, Order, Family, Genus, and Species.

The linguistic humor here is that given her last name, her first name should have as its root "Division" (because it's the proper grouping for plants), but perhaps Divisia would have sounded too exotic.

Spore: "A small, usually single-celled reproductive body that is highly resistant to desiccation and heat and is capable of growing into a new organism, produced especially by certain *bacteria, fungi, algae,* and nonflowering plants" (emphasis mine).

Since spores are intrinsic to fungi, and considering the title of her book, she is appropriately named.

Professor Sprout

The Herbology professor and the head of Hufflepuff House, Professor Sprout likes to get her fingers dirty. In fact, she has plenty of opportunity to do so, since she can usually be found in the greenhouses at Hogwarts, where she teaches her classes. With a patient manner and a gentle demeanor, Professor Sprout enjoys the respect of both students and colleagues.

Dealing with both commonplace and dangerous plants, she is exceptionally skilled. When students are petrified, as recounted in *Harry Potter and the Chamber of Secrets,* she prepares a draught of Mandrake to revive them.

Sprout: "To grow, spring up, or come forth" and "to send out new growth," this word accurately describes the good professor. Obviously, not only does she deal with plants that sprout out of the ground, but the students under her charge must grow in their knowledge of herbology if they are to become competent witches and wizards.

Felix Summerbee

He is a wizard (1477–1508) who invented the Cheering Charms.

Felix: His first name is suggestive of his work. *Felix* is the root word, meaning "the Lucky One."

Summerbee: A name coined by Rowling, who delights in inventive and whimsical wordplay.

Emeric Switch

This wizard is the author of *A Beginner's Guide to Transfiguration,* a required textbook for first- and second-year students at Hogwarts.

Switch: To switch is to "exchange," which describes the physical process of transfiguration: to switch a person or thing from one form to another.

Janus Thickey

This wizard faked his death to his wife so he could be with another woman, the landlady of the Green Dragon.

Janus: This Roman god, the spirit of doorways and archways, is also considered the god of all beginnings. Visually represented by a two-faced man, he has come to represent someone who is duplicitous: a person who hides his true face behind the face he presents to the world.

Thickey: The root word is *thick*, which is suggestive in this case, since he got into the thick of things by perpetrating a fraud and being found out. The word "thicken" means "to make or become more intense, intricate, or complex," which is certainly the case here: He fabricated a fanciful story about being killed by a fabulous beast called the Lethifold, in order to escape his marriage and enter into a relationship with another woman.

Nymphadora Tonks

A colorful character whose wonky nature and personality belies her serious intent (she's an Auror), Nymphadora Tonks has no idea why her mother gave her such an embarrassing first name, but she prefers it not to be used in conversation.

A half-blood, she is the daughter of Ted Tonks and Andromeda Black. She is also one of the very rarest in the wizarding world—a Metamorphmagus, she was born with the ability to change her appearance at will without resorting to spells or potions. This gives her a tremendous advantage as an Auror when it comes to cover and concealment in *Harry Potter and the Order of the Phoenix*.

She is an endearing witch, whose most obvious personal trait is her clumsiness and a penchant for changing her hair color as frequently as she changes her face, which entertains Harry Potter and his schoolmates during dinner at the headquarters of the Order of the Phoenix. Tonks is injured in battle as the Order confronts Lord Voldemort and his Death Eaters.

Nymph: In Greek mythology, a nymph was characteristically a young, beautiful female with an amorous nature. Personifications of nature, nymphs were omnipresent in water (lakes, streams, rivers, and oceans) and on land (trees, forests, and mountains). The common usage of the word "nymph" is a seductive woman; more to the point, she has an insatiable appetite, to put it mildly, which is why Tonks wants to be called by her surname only, at least until she gets a nonoffensive nickname.

Alberta Toothill

This witch defeated the favored Samson Wiblin at the All-England competition of 1430 by using a Blasting Charm. She is on a Famous Wizard card.

Toothill: The root word *toot* is suggestive. It means "to sound a short blast" or "to cause to sound." Since she used a Blasting Charm, she obviously made a sound.

Professor Sibyll Trelawney

Living and teaching in the North Tower at Hogwarts, Professor Sibyll Trelawney is an oddity, even among a faculty known for its odd professors, past and present. With glasses that magnify her eyes, dressed in gauzy clothing, and bejeweled, Trelawney speaks in a hushed tone, as befitting someone who can pierce the veil and see into the future.

Interviewed by Professor Dumbledore in 1979 at the Hog's Head in Hogsmeade, Sibyll Trelawney, during the interview, falls into a trance and makes a prediction, now on record at the Department of Mysteries at the Ministry of Magic. It is one of two prophecies by her that ring true: both deal with the Dark Lord, Voldemort. Other than these two predictions, Professor Trelawney's track record hasn't been impressive. Still, she holds the post of Professor of Divination, and spooks impressionable students with her dramatic ways and eerie predictions.

Whether "wooly" (as Hermione Granger characterizes Divination) or predictively accurate, Sibyll Trelawney has seer blood in her. A very famous seer, Cassandra Vablatsky, can be found in her family tree; Sibyll is Cassandra's great-great-granddaughter. Though Sibyll is, in terms of predictive powers, no match for her talented ancestor, she may yet play a part in Harry Potter's future, since the Dark Lord Voldemort has, over the years, been building up his strength, gathering his followers, and planning a final assault against all who oppose him in the wizarding world, with Harry Potter as his principal target.

Sibyll: properly called Sibylla, a Greek seer who, in a frenzy, would utter her cryptic predictions, which could not be understood until the events came to pass. Later, other women, known as sibyls, carried on the seer tradition. Legend has it that the predictions of the sibyls were collected in nine books, of which only three remain, since the original customer, a Roman king, Tarquinius Superbus, offered only partial payment. These precious three books, which were consulted on an occasional basis during times of emergency, were kept in the temple of Jupiter.

Cassandra: a famous seer from Greek mythology who reneged on her promises to Apollo, who had bestowed the gift of prophecy. Apollo avenged himself by ensuring that no one would believe her prophecies. Consequently, though she accurately predicted the death of the Greek king Agamemnon and the fall of the city of Troy, her prophecies were disregarded, and her doom was sealed: After the city fell, she and Agamemnon were both killed.

U

Professor Dolores Umbridge

Professor Dolores Umbridge is, among the Hogwarts faculty, one of a kind, which in this case is not a compliment. A toady whose only allegiance is to the Minister of Magic, Cornelius Fudge, Umbridge has risen rapidly to the heights of power at the Ministry due to her well-placed connections. She uses them to jockey for position, allowing herself to be inextricably embedded at Hogwarts, first as professor, then as a High Inquisitor, and finally as headmistress, to the dismay of all and the detriment of Hogwarts itself.

From her first appearance, recounted in *Harry Potter and the Order of the Phoenix,* Umbridge takes offense at a Ministry of Magic hearing at which Harry Potter takes center stage. Harry uses magic to defend himself and his cousin Dudley Dursley; Harry's only defense is the truth and, of course, the imperturbable Professor Dumbledore, whose assertion was that the dementors who attacked Harry and Dudley were, in fact, under the control of the Ministry of Magic.

Not only does this assertion prove to be true, but the finger inescapably points to Umbridge, who bears full responsibility.

Rotten to the core and tenacious in her belief that Professor Dumbledore is a meddling, old wizard whose time has come, Umbridge gets a foothold at Hogwarts by filling a vacancy as teacher of Defense Against the Dark Arts.

It becomes clear that Umbridge's sanitized, theoretical knowledge of Defense Against the Dark Arts simply won't prepare the students for the reality of dealing with dark wizards, but it's also clear that Umbridge will brook no criticism.

Taking umbrage at Harry Potter's increasingly vocal objections to her teaching methods, she assigns him to detention, where he is forced to write, over and over, with a magical quill pen, "I will not tell lies." The pen, cutting into his flesh, makes the point: Dolores Umbridge will not stand for criticism, even when she's wrong and needs to be held accountable.

In short order, Umbridge convinces the Ministry that Hogwarts has, due to the bad leadership of Dumbledore and the ineptness of certain teachers, strayed far afield from its original charter, to prepare young witches and wizards for entry into the wizarding world. As a result, she gets herself assigned as a High Inquisitor with unparalleled powers over students, and teachers as well. The situation rapidly deteriorates as Professor Dumbledore is then removed as headmaster and, in his place, Dolores Umbridge is appointed headmistress, to the dismay of almost all the students, except (predictably) some of those in Slytherin, who recognize a kindred spirit.

Aided by the handpicked students who join her Inquisitorial Squad, Dolores Umbridge is on a witch (and wizard) hunt, and fires Professor Trelawney; when she goes after Rubeus Hagrid as well, Professor MgGonagall rushes to his defense, but is injured in the resultant fracas.

A nasty, contemptible person who is characterized by Rowling as "pure poison," Professor Dolores Umbridge more than lives up to her unsavory name.

Dolores: *Dolor* is from the Latin, meaning "pain, grief." A synonym for dolor is "sorrow," which means "mental suffering or anguish." Clearly, Dolores Umbridge is the instrument of pain, grief, and mental suffering at Hogwarts, where she inflicts herself in full measure on select students and faculty members whom she, with undeniable malevolence, wishes to attack.

Umbridge: To take umbrage is to have "a feeling of pique or resentment at some often fancied slight or insult." This is certainly how Dolores Umbridge responds at the slightest criticism. A synonym, offense, is even more telling: "something that outrages the moral or physical senses," "the act of attacking," "the act of displeasing or affronting," and "a breach of a moral or social code." All of these perfectly describe the true nature of Dolores Umbridge, a career bureaucrat with fascist tendencies who will stop at nothing to achieve her despicable goals.

Cassandra Vablatsky

The author of *Unfogging the Future*, she is a celebrated seer. Professor Trelawney is her great-great-granddaughter.

Vablatsky is probably a wordplay of Helena Petrovna Blavatsky, an occultist who wrote *Isis Unveiled* and *The Secret Doctrine*.

See "Professor Sibyll Trelawney."

Professor Vindictus Viridian

He is the author of *Curses and Counter-Curses (Bewitch Your Friends and Befuddle Your Enemies with the Latest Revenges: Hair Loss, Jelly-Legs, Tongue-Tying, and Much, Much More)*.

Vindictus: "Vindictive," the root word of Vindictus, is from the Latin *vindicta*, which means "revenge"; vindictive means "disposed to seek revenge" and "intended to cause anguish or hurt."

Professor Viridian's first name fits him perfectly, given the title of his book.

Viridian: a "durable bluish-green pigment."

This is very telling as well, since durable means it is long-lasting, and green is a color associated with envy and jealousy. In *Anthony and Cleopatra*, Shakespeare wrote that envy was "the green sickness."

Lord Voldemort (Tom Marvolo Riddle)

Justifiably the most feared in all the wizarding community, Voldemort is a dark wizard whose powers are so strong that it is thought only Professor Dumbledore could match or exceed them. Known to his followers, the Death Eaters, as Lord Voldemort, he is generally referred to in the wizarding world obliquely: You-Know-Who or He-Who-Must-Not-Be-Named. Few dare to speak his name outright, though Professor Dumbledore does not hesitate to do so.

After Tom Riddle Sr. learned that his wife was a witch, he abandoned her; she subsequently died giving birth to her son, after naming him Tom Marvolo Riddle. (The middle name is that of his grandfather on his mother's side.)

Raised in a Muggle orphanage, Tom Riddle Jr. attended Hogwarts (Slytherin House), but returned to the hated orphanage during holidays and the summers. A brilliant student, according to Professor Dumbledore, Tom Riddle showed exceptional promise, first as a prefect, then as a head boy.

Hating his Muggle father, young Tom began using the name Voldemort among his closest friends—the first sign of disassociation with his father. Tom Marvolo Riddle, when rearranged, spells "I am Lord Voldemort."

After leaving school, he went back to the "Riddle House" in Little Hangleton and killed his Muggle father and his Muggle grandparents. Then he disappeared for decades, as he steeped himself in the dark arts, learning the lore of a dark wizard, and repudiating his Christian name to truly become Lord Voldemort. Embracing the dark side, traveling extensively, Voldemort sought power and immortality.

Voldemort drew others of like mind to him. With his disciples, the Death Eaters, they cut a bloody swath. Ignoring the Ministry of Magic decrees against using the three Unforgivable Curses—any one of which earns a lifetime sentence in the wizard prison Azkaban—Voldemort and his followers soon earned a well-deserved reputation as dark wizards of the worst kind, the kind hunted down by Aurors.

Each Death Eater proudly bore the Dark Mark, a skull-and-serpent design burned into the left inner forearm.

A reign of terror soon resulted when Voldemort and his followers enlisted the aid of giants to help them fight against the established order; many wizards and Muggles died as a result.

Responding to this crisis, Professor Dumbledore established the Order of the Phoenix. Those in the first gathering of the Order of the Phoenix, outnumbered by the Death Eaters, fought valiantly but were picked off one by one.

Hunting down the Potter family after learning of a prophecy that foretold his own death, Voldemort killed Harry Potter's father; Harry's mother died trying to defend her son from the Killing Curse. But Harry didn't die, which is why he is referred to in the wizarding community as "the boy who lived," a singular distinction, since no other person—Muggle or wizard—has ever survived such an attack.

The attack on Harry Potter, however, was not without price. The rebounding curse injured but did not mortally wound Voldemort. He lived, but he was disembodied, with his powers at a low ebb.

Hiding in a forest and biding his time, Voldemort regained his strength to formulate an attack against the wizarding world. The Death Eaters tested the prevailing winds and determined that, temporarily, it would be wiser to disavow their Dark Lord and pretend to have been cursed at his hand, but those were simply lies: The Death Eaters were just staying low, until their dark master regained enough strength to reappear and not only kill the child mentioned in the prophecy, but also mount an assault against the wizarding world at large.

Though Harry Potter would best him, as recounted in *Harry Potter and the Sorcerer's Stone,* Voldemort's defeat was merely temporary. Gaining strength and regaining his followers, Voldemort is poised once again to assault the wizarding world in his quest for power.

Though Minister of Magic Cornelius Fudge—a wizard in denial—repudiated the notion that Voldemort was back, the incontrovertible evidence proved otherwise, and it is clear that this time the stakes are at their highest: Either Voldemort will kill the boy cited in the prophecy, or the boy will kill him. Hanging in the balance: a world that will be overwhelmed with evil and covered in darkness, or a world finally made safe from this powerful dark wizard.

Voldemort: From the French, *vol* translates to "theft" or "flight," *de* translates to "of," and *mort* translates to "death." J. K. Rowling, who majored in French and the classics at the University of Edinburgh and who later taught French at Leigh Academy in Edinburgh, has stated in interviews that she made this name up. Nonetheless, the name is very suggestive, since Voldemort's principal goal is to cheat death and live forever. After a failed attempt to kill Harry Potter as a baby, Voldemort took flight, seeking refuge in an Albanian forest, and survived only by inhabiting the bodies of animals; in effect, stealing their bodies.

Not surprisingly, his followers are named Death Eaters, who cut a deadly swath through both Muggles and wizards alike.

Tom Marvolo Riddle: As noted, when rearranged, this spells out the anagram "I am Lord Voldemort." Long repudiating his given Christian name, he has become, in the eyes of his followers, the Dark Lord Voldemort.

Not only is his Christian name a riddle—deciphering it yields his preferred name—his middle name suggests the word "marvel," which means "strong surprise, astonishment." It is the reaction he produces when wizards find out—some only reluctantly admitting it—that he's indeed back, and on the attack, this time for keeps.

The dark lord is an archetype in literature and popular culture. A staple in fantasy fiction, the dark lord is usually offstage more often than not, powerful, geographically inaccessible (with strongholds in remote places), and has an insatiable lust for power. Indeed, the only hope is to destroy the dark lord before he destroys all in his path.

From the *Star Wars* saga (notably Darth Vader) to Tolkien's Middle-earth (the dark lord Sauron, formerly known as the Necromancer), the dark lord is either destined to turn toward darkness or predisposed to do so. In either instance, the end result is the same: Might versus Right, black versus white, dark lord/wizard against the white lord/wizard—the eternal struggle between darkness and the light.

Adalbert Waffling

The author of *Magical Theory*, he is a famous magical theoretician.

Waffling: from the root word "waffle," which means "evasive or vague speech or writing."

Given the subject matter, theorizing about magic, the definition of "theory" ranges from a less rigorous to a very rigorous meaning: less rigorous, "an assumption based on limited information or knowledge; a conjecture";

more rigorous, "a set of statements or principles devised to explain a group of facts or phenomena, especially one that has been repeatedly tested or is widely accepted and can be used to make predictions about natural phenomena."

Whether Waffling was in fact evasive or vague when writing about magical theory is a matter of conjecture; what we do know is that he's famous, which suggests accomplishment.

"Honest Willy" Wagstaff

This fraudulent wizard sells defective goods and passes them off as quality goods. In one instance, the defective wands he sells cause inadvertent burns; in another, he sells loose-bottomed cauldrons—a dangerous situation—which is why he draws the attention of the Ministry of Magic.

Willy: This name is similar in sound to *wily*, which means "deceitfully clever." This is certainly an apt name for someone who pawns off defective goods as substantial.

Wag: This name is also suggestive, since it means "talk rapidly." A con artist is usually a fast talker, overwhelming the listener with a barrage of words.

Staff: This is similar in sound to *stiff*, which is a slang word meaning to cheat someone.

This man is an out-and-out fraud, which explains his nickname: He is anything *but* honest, a fact that is so well known that people mock him for it.

Celestina Warbeck

Known as the Singing Sorceress on the WWN (Wizarding Wireless Network), the wizards' equivalent of radio broadcasting, she is a very popular singer.

Celestina: A celesta is "a musical instrument consisting of graduated steel plates that are struck by hammers activated by a keyboard."

Warbeck: suggests the words "warble" and "beckon." To warble is "to sing (a note or song, for example) with trills, runs, or other melodic embellishments." And to beckon means to summon.

For a singer, both names suggest her musical talent, though the name Melody, which is popular for girls, would also strike the right note.

Ron Bilius Weasley

The sixth son of Arthur and Molly Weasley, Ron follows in the family tradition by attending Hogwarts. (Their seventh child is a daughter, Ginny, who also attends Hogwarts.) As the last son to attend Hogwarts, the burden of expectation is high: Bill, Charlie, and Percy distinguished themselves, respectively, as head boy, Quidditch captain, and prefect.

It doesn't help that Ron inherits his brothers' hand-me-downs: a robe, a wand, and the family pet, a rat. So, unlike some of the other students who attend Hogwarts for whom money is no object—including Harry Potter, who inherits a small fortune, and Draco Malfoy, whose parents are rich—money or, more accurately, the lack of it, is a constant concern.

Though not as academically gifted as Hermione and not as gifted as Harry Potter in athletic prowess, Ron nonetheless distinguishes himself in many ways, both major and minor, which earns him a coveted prefect slot, giving him bragging rights in his family: an important concern since two of his brothers, George and Fred, constantly double-team to treat him in a patronizing manner, though in a good-natured way.

A member of Dumbledore's Army (along with Hermione and Harry), and the Keeper on the Gryffindor Quidditch team, Ron Weasley is, slowly but surely, making a name for himself at Hogwarts.

The first person Harry meets on the train to Hogwarts, Ron proves to be a steadfast friend, and is proof that friendship and character trump connections and money—a fact that Harry underscores when he wisely rejects the offer of "friendship" from Draco Malfoy and sticks by Ron Weasley through thick and thin.

Bilius: Ron is named after his uncle Bilius; the root word "bile" is only somewhat suggestive as to Ron's character, since it means "an inclination to anger." Though Ron certainly is defensive about his family's lack of money and criticisms about his family from the likes of the Malfoys, his reactions are not out of line in terms of how others in his situation would respond. Therefore we can only assume that the name may be more associated with his uncle than with him.

The biles were two of the four vital fluids that defined one's health in medieval times. It was thought that the delicate balance of blood, phlegm, black bile, and yellow bile had to be regulated in order to maintain good health.

Weasley: On the face of it, this name seems more appropriate for Draco Malfoy or one of his lieutenants, since a weasel is a small brown mammal known for its destructive tendencies; moreover, the slang definition of the word *weasel* means to behave in a furtive manner, which fits Malfoy and his ilk.

On J. K. Rowling's website, in her FAQ section, she explains that she has "a great fondness" for the mammal, which is "not so much malignant as maligned," which explains why she chose the name.

Certainly, if anything defines the Weasley family, a familiar fondness, a warm affection, is omnipresent. This fondness extends beyond the family unit as well, especially from Molly Weasley, who is demonstrably fond of Harry Potter, treating him as if he were one of the family.

Weird Sisters

A popular band heard on the WWN (Wizarding Wireless Network). Visually distinctive, with "artfully ripped and torn" black robes (writes Rowling), its members include (in alphabetical order) Heathcote Barbary (rhythm guitar), Gideon Crumb (bagpipes), Kirley McCormack Duke (lead guitar), Merton Graves (cello), Orsino Thruston (drums), Donaghan Tremlett (bass), Myron Wagtail (lead singer), and Herman Wintringham (lute).

The all-male band is also known for being hirsute. (Professor Lupin would fit in.)

Weird: "Of or pertaining to witchcraft; caused by, or suggesting, magical influence; supernatural; unearthly; wild; as, a weird appearance, look, sound, etc."

Shakespeare drew on Norse mythology for the Weird Sisters

Three Weird Sisters: A Muggle Band

There is a musical group called Three Weird Sisters who have issued two compilations of music, released on compact disc: "Rite the First Time" and "Hair of the Frog." Though not biologically linked, these sisters in spirit, once three but now four, include: Teresa Powell, Brenda Sutton, Gwen Knighton, and Mary Crowell.

From their website (www.three-weirdsisters.com): "They *are* weird (or at least their repertoire and presentation of songs is weird), everything from renaissance ballads to 'country on a harp' to science fiction with a twist. . . . They play the folk clubs, music fests, gatherings, and conventions near their homeland of Atlanta, Georgia. . . . Together, these women make a unique blend of instruments and voices described as 'what the Carter family would have sounded like if they'd done filk/folk/Celtic/blues/[insert music type].'"

who foretold destiny in *Macbeth.* Norse myth held that the three Fates wove the tapestries of fate, the web of life for all people: Urth (or Wyrd) represented the past, Verthandi represented the present, and Skuld represented the future. These three crones controlled an individual's destiny.

Kennilworthy Whisp

He is a fanatic of Quidditch who has written extensively on the subject. His only book published for Muggles is *Quidditch Through the Ages,* which was published by Whizz Hard Books in Diagon Alley. Mr. Whisp makes his home in Nottinghamshire.

His first name may come from the town of Kenilworth, southeast of Birmingham in central England. Its most famous landmark is the Kenilworth Castle.

The word "whisp" has several meanings, but the most apt one in reference to his name may be that he's a small person.

Willy Widdershins

A shady character, he was responsible for the regurgitating toilets that plagued Muggles, which came to Arthur Weasley's attention, since his department deals with the misuse of Muggle artifacts. But Widdershins was a victim of his own prank after one of the toilets exploded, injuring him, which led to his capture. (He likely went to St. Mungo's Hospital for treatment.)

To avoid prosecution, he reported to Dolores Umbridge, who then reported to Cornelius Fudge, that he had overheard members of Dumbledore's Army talking at their first meeting at Hog's Head in Hogsmeade—fortuitous news that earned him a reward: immunity from prosecution.

Willy: similar to the word "wily," which means "full of wiles; cunning."

Widdershins: "in a left-handed, wrong, or contrary direction." This name is telling, since this wizard runs contrary to the law as a way of life.

He is indeed a wily wizard who will sell others down the river, so to speak, to save himself, as he did with the Hogwarts students who thought they were gathering in anonymity, only to discover they were not.

Lord Stoddard Withers

He is a Magical Creatures specialist who breeds flying horses. His attempts to interest the public in a new sport incorporating polo (flying horses) and Quidditch never took flight.

Withers: His last name has a dual meaning in this instance. Regarding horse anatomy, the "withers" is the region of a horse's back that is at the base of the horse's neck. It would be an area slightly forward from where a saddle would be positioned, which would obviously be needed for a game involving a flying horse.

The name also suggests lack of interest in the proposed sport, since wither means "to lose vitality, force, or freshness." Interest in his proposed sport simply shriveled up.

Bowman Wright

A metal charmer who invented the Golden Snitch used in Quidditch. Use of the Golden Snitch replaced the use of the Snidget, the bird that was nearly hunted to extinction due to its early use in the popular wizarding sport. Wright's idea of the Golden Snitch took flight and became an integral part of the sport.

In its most general definition, a wright is a person who "constructs or repairs something."

Homonym: One can also say that he had done the right thing by inventing a magical, mechanical substitute for the Snidget, an endangered species.

The name fits an inventor, an inveterate tinkerer who is always looking to improve things to make them right.

Section 3

All Things in the Magical World

Arthur Weasley, a wizard who works at the Ministry of Magic in the Office of Misuse of Muggle Artifacts, remarks that he wonders how Muggles manage to get by without magic. The answer is that Muggles manage to get by with magical things invented by technology.

Wizards are able to buy Omnioculars with which to record and play back fast-moving events like sports tournaments, but Muggles can buy their equivalent, which are now available from several manufacturers—a high-powered pair of binoculars with a built-in video camera.

The wizarding world and the Muggle world, as the entries in this section show, are closer than you think.

Amulet

When Hogwarts students are afflicted, seemingly at random, with the curse of petrification, Neville Longbottom, who has problems in all his classes except Herbology, uses a green onion as an amulet to protect himself.

At first glance, using an onion would seem to be a preposterous notion, but in folklore, the lowly onion does have protective powers, which is why ancient Egyptians used it in charms to keep ghosts away from children. To protect one's house, stick a small white onion with black-headed pins and put it in a window; this is supposed to protect against evil intruders. What Neville had in mind, most likely, was carrying it to protect himself from venomous beasts.

Perhaps Neville thought a basilisk was on the loose and would petrify him with a single stare. Whatever his concerns, Neville knows full well the effects of petrification, as a reluctant and remorseful Hermione Granger had to cast the *Petrificus Totalus* (full body bind) curse on him to stop him in his tracks, in *Harry Potter and the Sorcerer's Stone*.

Given that the wizarding world is filled with all sorts of dark denizens and creatures that go bump in the night, it seems logical that there would be a host of amulets appropriate for virtually every situation, but there is not. If a Hogwarts student were to rely on the old standbys—amulets of proven worth—these would include not only natural but man-made objects.

On the website the Lucky W Amulet Archive (www.luckymojo.com), Cat Yronwode provides links to numerous amulets and talismans, all designed to protect the wearer, or holder, from harm.

Would any of them have helped Neville Longbottom against the curse of petrification? It's hard to say, but one thing is for sure: As an excellent student of herbology, he knew that the Mandrake root is the restorative that Madam Pomfrey would administer if he were to be petrified, so relying on folk wisdom by carrying an onion may not have been such a bad idea, after all.

Apparating

For witches and wizards who have a great deal of self-confidence and have passed the Apparation test, which is given by the Department of Magical Transportation at the Ministry of Magic, this form of instantaneous travel certainly beats using Floo powder, riding a flying carpet, having to hail (and wait for) the Knight Bus, flying a broom in possibly bad weather, or having to find a Portkey.

The procedure is not, however, risk-free; if it is done incorrectly, a witch or wizard could literally find him or herself in pieces—two of them, in fact; half of the person would be left behind at the original location and the other half would be at the intended destination. The half-arsed result is called "splinching," which is the opposite of "splicing" (to bring together).

Apparating at long distances, such as across an ocean, is also very problematic. The longer the distance, the more unreliable the result.

All of which explains why the traditional broomstick remains the most popular means of transportation in the wizarding world.

Arithmancy

> Oh, it's wonderful! It's my favorite subject!
>
> —*Hermione Granger*

To Professor Severus Snape, Hermione Granger is, as he puts it, an insufferable know-it-all; to Professor Lupin, she's an exceedingly clever witch; to Draco Malfoy, she's a source of constant frustration because her grades are consistently higher than his own; but to everyone else, she's a sterling example of how hard work pays off—a model student at the top of her class, she's earned everyone's respect.

It figures that Hermione Granger, a methodical planner, would find solace in Arithmancy because it's not, as she derisively terms reading tea leaves, "wooly."

Taught by Professor Vector—an altogether appropriate name—the class uses *Numerology and Grammatica* as its principal text, which defines the principles behind Arithmancy, which is numerical prophecy.

"Number is All," said Pythagoras, a sixth-century Greek who is best known for being the founder of geometry. Pythagoras believed that everything in life was interrelated and could be expressed numerically, using numbers one through nine. It was not so much a tool for divination, predicting the future, as it was to understand things the way they are in the present.

The numbers in your birthdate, added up and reduced to either a master number (11 or 22) or a single digit, provide a look into your present, into who you are. Similarly, using a conversion table to assign a single-digit number to each letter of your name provides a look into your future.

Here's the conversion table:

I	2	3	4	5	6	7	8	9
A	B	C	D	E	F	G	H	I
J	K	L	M	N	O	P	Q	R
S	T	U	V	W	X	Y	Z	

Now, it's time for a quiz: If your name is Harry James Potter and you were born on July 31, 1980, what is your birth number and what is your name number?

Birth number: 7 + 3 + 1 + 1 + 9 + 8 + 0 = 29 = 11

Name number:

Harry: 8 + 1 + 9 + 9 + 7 = 34 = 7

James: 1 + 1 + 4 + 5 + 1 = 12 = 3

Potter: 7 + 6 + 2 + 2 + 5 + 9 = 31 = 4

Name total: 7 + 3 + 4 = 14 = 5

Thus Harry Potter's birth number is 11 (a master number) and his name number is 5.

According to Ann Fiery, author of *The Book of Divination,* the following is what the numbers 11 and 5 mean for Harry Potter. Birth number 11 is a master number and, as such, is significant. "Their recipients are especially perceptive and talented, but they are also especially fraught. Their lives are full of vigorous battles, ending sometimes in triumph, sometimes in defeat. They are the embodiment of the saying 'From him to whom much has been given, much will be exacted.'"

In Harry Potter's case, great things are expected from him, and, based on what he's done in the tales chronicled in books one through five, he is a child of destiny and is fulfilling his great potential.

The name number, the number of destiny, seems rather accurate, as well. "As a number of destiny, Five ensures an adventurous life. The roller coaster of ups and downs is too alarming for most people, but destiny Five, with his love of variety, likes the wild ride."

Certainly Harry Potter has had a wild ride thus far, but it's not been one of his making. In any event, perhaps it's time to consult another source, just to make sure. Personally, I'd bypass Professor Trelawney, who, according to Professor Dumbledore, has made only two accurate predictions in her life, and go straight to the centaurs, whose visions look skyward to find the answers in the stars.

Astrology

> The fault . . . is not in our stars but in ourselves.
>
> —*William Shakespeare*

Firenze the centaur, who lives in the Forbidden Forest, would disagree with Shakespeare. To Firenze, the stars in the heavens *do* reveal the destinies of all. "Observe the heavens. Here is written, for those who can see, the fortune of our races," he tells Harry's Divination class.

Seeing is believing, but the gift of seeing is not easy to acquire; in fact, according to Professor Trelawney, the gift is beyond the abilities of some—notably Hermione Granger—but, like Firenze, those who have it can decipher its secrets and unlock the mysteries of life and those within them as well.

In our fast-paced Muggle world where people don't have the luxury of time to get to know one another, the interrogatories at first meetings are predictable: What do you do for a living? And, for perhaps a personal insight as to character, the astrological query, "What's your sign?"

Imagine what it's like at the Three Broomsticks when Hogwarts graduates get together to celebrate, drinking butterbeer and mingling, getting to know one another. You might overhear any number of intriguing things:

"I'm studying to be an Auror." (High marks. Cool.)

"I'm going to work at Gringotts." (Boring.)

"I'm going to Romania to study dragons." (Awesome.)

"I'm going to be lost in the bowels of the Ministry of Magic as a bureaucrat at a desk job." (Awful.)

A conversational shortcut: "What's your sign?"

"Astrology is the queen of the divinatory arts," writes Ann Fiery, in *The Book of Divination,* in which a detailed explanation of astrology is provided. The short answer is that it's a pseudoscience (something that has the appearance of having a scientific basis but does not), in which the movements of celestial bodies are said to influence human lives and events, a notion to which Firenze subscribes.

In fact, for many years, astrology was held in high esteem, since it encompassed "natural astrology" (astronomy) and "judicial astrology" (astrology as we know it today). But in the sixteenth century, as Copernicus, Galileo, and Kepler began the scientific exploration of the heavens, it was clear that the tides of fortune for astrologers were changing. It didn't help astrologers that in 1585, Pope Sixtus V officially

condemned astrology, followed by further condemnation in 1631 by Pope Urban VIII.

To put things in a historical perspective: Alchemy is to chemistry as astrology is to astronomy. In other words, astrology is regarded by scientists as being in the same league as other forms of divination, like reading tea leaves. Astrological horoscopes found in daily newspapers are considered by the masses to be a form of entertainment—fun but not something to take seriously. (For this reason, they are most often found on the comic pages.) Astrologers who take this subject seriously would snort in disgust at the daily dispensation of horoscopes in newspapers, since these snippets simply refer to the Sun sign, which is an important component of a horoscope, but by no means the only component.

According to Ann Fiery's *The Book of Divination:*

> The full horoscope shows the placement of all the planets in the signs and in the house. . . . The astrologer's task is to interpret the forces represented by these planets according to both their position and their relationship to one another. It sounds simple, but it's an outrageously complicated task, for the position of each element bears on every other element, creating a vast number of permutations that have to be interpreted. A full horoscope contains between thirty and one hundred indicators to analyze and then synthesize.

Fiery says that even with a computer program like the Io Edition of Time Cycles Research's Graphic Astrology program, the computational task is made easier, but the arduous task of interpretation still remains.

A discussion of the planets, signs of the zodiac, houses, and aspects is far beyond the scope of this entry. For those who want an informative discussion, consult *The Book of Divination*. And for those of you who want to try your hand at astrology, a good place to begin is the "TCR Astrology: The Io Series" website (www.timecycles.com), which will, at least, make the computation aspects—the science of astrology—easier; afterward, as Fiery suggests, you'll then have to explore the art of astrology.

Astronomical Model: Galaxy

A trip to Diagon Alley for Harry Potter is inevitably a frustrating experience, since he must be careful to preserve his inheritance for the purchase of necessities, not the luxuries for which he can only window-shop.

One of the luxuries is a model of a galaxy in constant movement. If he owned this precious item, he wouldn't have to take Astronomy class, for he would hold in his hands a functioning, magical model. An astronomical model of (presumably) our galaxy, suitable for desktop display, would be a stellar object to own, and would likely cost many Galleons.

Not to be confused with the solar system (the sun and the surrounding nine planets), a galaxy contains an estimated 100 billion stars. Our own solar system is part of the Milky Way galaxy.

Astronomical Model: Solar System

For use in her Divination class, Professor Trelawney has a glass dome containing a miniaturized model of the solar system, hanging in empty space; the model displays the sun and the nine surrounding planets—our solar system.

The solar system is comprised of the sun and the planets Earth, Jupiter, Mars, Mercury, Neptune, Pluto, Saturn, Uranus, and Venus, as well as the miscellaneous objects orbiting these planets, such as moons, comets (bodies of ice), and asteroids (bodies of minerals). The solar system is what the centaurs see when they look heavenward to practice divination.

For a Muggle interested in astronomy, the best way to view the heavens is to visit a planetarium, which houses a domed ceiling on which is projected a representation of the night sky. Capable of compression so that planetary and stellar movements that would otherwise take years to view can be seen in minutes, the first planetarium was built in Germany in 1924 by the Carl Zeiss Optical Works.

Planetariums usually offer a live, guided tour of the night sky. My local planetarium (the Virginia Living Museum in Newport News, Virginia) offers such a presentation. From its website (www.valivingmuseum.org):

> Join us in the planetarium theater for this live, guided tour of the current night sky. One of our staff astronomers will take you on a journey through the evening sky, pointing out constellations, planets, galaxies, star clusters and other objects of interest visible in the sky for that night. Special events, such as meteor showers and comets, will be discussed as appropriate.

If there is no local planetarium, an affordable alternative is to buy a kit. The Discovery Channel (www.discovery.com) offers in its store, for $29.95, a Star Theater Home Planetarium, which is a globe that projects in 360 degrees a representation of the heavens. The accompanying audio recording supplements the light show. A portable Stellarscope shows the heavens in a handheld tube (from www.mcdonaldobservatory.org, $39.95). Obviously, neither item will offer the sense of space that can be experienced at a planetarium, but they are cost-effective alternatives, and light-years cheaper than the magical model that Professor Trelawney uses in her classroom in the North Tower of Hogwarts.

Bezoar

In Professor Snape's Potions class, the interrogative teacher sees Harry Potter among his pupils and decides to put the famous boy wizard to the test, asking question after question, none of which Harry can answer. Hermione attempts in vain to catch Snape's attention. Practically levitating off her seat, Hermione is anxious to answer the question, where can one find a bezoar? Harry doesn't know, since, unlike Hermione, he hasn't read the textbooks before first term.

Derived from the Persian word *pâdzahr,* meaning "protection from poison," the bezoar is a hard stone found in the intestines of ruminant animals, including cattle, sheep, goats, deer, and giraffes (according to www.dictionary.com). This stone was once believed to be a universal antidote to poison.

Broomstick

A wizard or witch in the market for a new broomstick—the flying kind, not the sweeping kind—will almost surely make his or her way to Quality Quidditch Supplies, a retail store in Diagon Alley, where the latest models are on display in the picture window.

When Harry Potter gazes longingly at a state-of-the-art Firebolt, a flying broom capable of going from zero to 150 miles per hour in seconds, displayed there, he wistfully thinks about owning it because he feels the need for speed. Unfortunately, its prohibitive cost discourages him, and so he regretfully passes it up; he instead has to be content with window-shopping until fortune smiles on him. (A good thing, too, since a Firebolt is so expensive that it would have required a sizable withdrawal from his Gringotts bank account, making a serious dent in it.)

In the wizarding world, the means of transportation include Apparating, Floo powder (named after a chimney's neck, the flue, and perhaps a pun on the word "flew"), a Portkey (the magical equivalent of the *Star Trek* transporter beam), and the old standby, the broomstick.

Constructed in the traditional fashion with twigs, the flying broomstick is a favorite means of locomotion because it's fast, portable, convenient, and reliable. In short, it's the ideal means of travel. The only question is which model to buy. As with cars in the Muggles world, broomsticks come in a wide configuration of makes and models. Because sitting on a broom is clearly uncomfortable, especially for long flights, the Cushioning Charm, invented in 1920 by Elliot Smethwyk, allows the witch or wizard to ride comfortably on a cushion of air a few inches off the broom. (I can't imagine that Jocunda Sykes riding the Oakshaft, one of the earliest sporting brooms, could have endured her successful trans-Atlantic flight without the comfort of a Cushioning Charm.)

From the Oakshaft (1879) and Moontrimmer (1901) to the newest model, the Firebolt, flying broomsticks are constantly engineered to fly faster, higher, and with more stability. (In fact, the Firebolt's individual birch twigs are aerodynamically designed to enhance flight stability and speed.) For those who prefer to do their research before buying, a handy guide, *Which Broomstick* (the wizarding equivalent of *Consumer Reports*), lists all the currently available models.

Obviously, Quidditch players are principally interested in the latest model, which gives them a competitive edge as they whiz through the air, rocketing past the spectators below and, it is hoped, the competition.

Priced for every budget, flying broomsticks are likely to be found in every wizarding family, just as the Broomstick Servicing Kit will likely be found as well, since keeping one's broom in tip-top shape simply makes good sense.

Historically, the early brooms were constructed of bundled twigs wrapped around one end of a long stick. The image of a witch on a broomstick—characterized perfectly when the Wicked Witch of the West, astride her broom, flies across the skies above Emerald City and spells out in smoke, "Surrender Dorothy"—is firmly entrenched in folklore and popular culture. The witch is usually a hag, and the broom is usually nondescript.

The origins of brooms for witches can be found in the pagan fertility rites when men and women mounted not only brooms but also poles and pitchforks, jumping up and down, and dancing wildly. It must have been quite a sight, but from that evolved, in the sixteenth and seventeenth centuries in Europe, the popular notion of the witch astride the broom.

What made the broom fly was "flying ointment," which was rubbed on it. Often, the witch's familiar would ride on the broom as well. The flying ointment, however, usually contained hallucinogenic ingredients, so it's more likely that a woman whose skin came in contact with the broomstick, as she held it or used it to sweep the floor, truly believed she was flying, when in fact it was a flight only in imagination.

In *The Encyclopedia of Witches and Witchcraft,* by Rosemary Ellen Guiley, the author explains:

> According to lore, witches flew to the sabbats, sometimes carrying along demons or their familiars in the shapes of animals. They also rode their brooms to fly out to sea in order to raise up storms. Legend has it that novices sometimes fell off. On witch festival nights such as Walpurgisnacht, townspeople laid out hooks and scythes to kill any witches who fell off their brooms. They also rang church bells, which has the power to ground broomsticks and knock witches off them.

Though "flying" witches are a thing of a past, the broom is still used today by Wiccans, mostly for symbolic reasons. Called a "besom," the broom is used to purify areas by symbolically sweeping them clean.

Cauldron

Hogwarts School of Witchcraft and Wizardry provides a shopping list of things that first-year students must bring to school, including one "cauldron (pewter, standard size 2)," as noted in *Harry Potter and the Sorcerer's Stone.* The preferred place to buy a cauldron is at a retail store in Diagon Alley, where traditional and magical cauldrons are for sale.

At Hogwarts, cauldrons are omnipresent in Professor Snape's potions class; they are traditionally used to brew potions, as do three witches in Shakespeare's play *Macbeth*. The second witch intones (IV:1):

> Fillet of a fenny snake,
> In the cauldron boil and bake.
> Eye of newt and toe of frog,
> Wool of bat and tongue of dog,
> Adder's fork and blindworm's sting,
> Lizard's leg and howlet's wing,
> For a charm of pow'rful trouble,
> Like a Hell broth boil and bubble.

Made of cast iron, pewter, copper, or bronze, the cauldron was used for normal household duties, from cooking to cleaning, as well as for magical purposes.

In Irish legend, the cauldron has a special significance: A magical cauldron, a gift from the hero Bran to the King of Ireland, brought life to dead soldiers; the king would reanimate fallen soldiers to fight for him. The army was invincible with this never-ending supply, until the cauldron was destroyed when Bran's half-brother leapt into it, since it could not hold the living but only the dead.

Chocolate

In *Harry Potter and the Prisoner of Azkaban,* Harry first encounters the dreaded apparitions, the dementors, on a train ride to Hogwarts. Boarding the train to look for the escaped convict Sirius Black, the dementors' presence profoundly affects Harry, as his friend Ron Weasley observes: "You went sort of rigid and fell out of your seat and started twitching—"

Drowning in cold and in despair, Harry is saved by Professor Lupin, who, when Harry is revived, gives him a piece of chocolate and urges him to eat it. Harry tentatively takes the proffered gift and wonders why the professor gave it to him, but discovers that eating it instantly restores warmth.

J. K. Rowling's inspiration for the restorative powers of chocolate may be found in popular literature—notably, Roald Dahl's famous children's classic, *Charlie and the Chocolate Factory,* which she considers his masterpiece—and the popular notion that chocolate is medically good for you, as "medicine" for melancholy. And at least one study suggests that dark chocolate *is* in fact good for you. In the study, conducted by Dr. Mary Engler, 21 adults were divided into two groups, half of whom got Dove bars with high cocoa content, and half of whom got Dove bars with the flavonoids taken out.

The study, the results of which appeared in the June 2004 issue of the *Journal of the American College of Nutrition,* revealed that those who got the high-cocoa-content Dove bars showed better blood vessel dilation. As the study report explains: "Like other dark chocolate bars with high-cocoa content, this one [the Dove Dark Chocolate bar] is loaded with something called epicatechin. Epicatechin is a particularly active member of a group of compounds called plant flavonoids.

Chocolate Frogs

In the Muggle world, Nestlé makes "the very best" chocolate, though perhaps Godiva, Hershey, and Ghirardelli would dispute it; but in the wizarding world, at least among children, the Chocolate Frog remains a favorite.

In *Harry Potter and the Sorcerer's Stone,* Harry is on the Hogwarts Express, a train that is taking him and his classmates directly to Hogwarts. Sharing a train compartment with Ronald Weasley, Harry is understandably concerned that Chocolate Frogs are indeed enchanted frogs made of chocolate, but Ron reassures him that they are simply ordinary chocolate, though the real treat is in the cards featuring famous witches and wizards in moving pictures. When Harry explains that in the Muggle world pictures don't move, Ron is stunned and says, "Weird!"

Flavonoids keep cholesterol from gathering in the blood vessels, reduce the risk of blood clots, and slow down the immune responses that lead to clogged arteries." (Note: The study was funded, in part, by the American Cocoa Research Institute, a nonprofit group funded by the chocolate industry, which provided the chocolate used in the study.)

No less an authority than the Yale-New Haven Nutrition Advisor (http://www.ynhh.org/online/nutrition/advisor/chocolate.html) cites a study conducted by Andrew Waterhouse that "chocolate was found to have potent antioxidants called phenols. These antioxidants are the same types found in red wine." Cocoa phenols were found to prevent the bad choles-terol from causing plaque buildup in the arteries. In another study, cocoa inhibited LDL oxidation two hours after consumption. Waterhouse also found "that the darker the chocolate, the more phenols it contains."

Despite the medical assertions that dark chocolate is good for you, all nutritionists agree that eating a little may not be such a bad thing, but like everything else, it should be in the context of a balanced diet.

Crystal Ball

In *Harry Potter and the Prisoner of Azkaban,* when Professor Trelawney peers into her crystal ball to look into the future, she doesn't really see any-thing, but she pretends that she does in order to be more convincing to her students. (The only times she has made accurate predictions, she has gone into a trance and then doesn't remember what she has said.)

Professor Trelawney's use of the crystal ball is consistent with its usage in history. Also called scrying (divination of future events), crystal ball gazing has a long tradition. When a seer peers into the crystal ball, the ball will cloud up, become misty, and a vision will appear.

Rowling, of course, is not the first to use crystal balls in popular fiction. In J. R. R. Tolkien's *The Lord of the Rings,* crystal balls (called palantíri) are used both to communicate and to foresee the future. (The wizard Gandalf, when confronting Saruman at his tower at Orthanc, narrowly misses getting clobbered by one when Grima Wormtongue heaves it out of the window. It didn't take a crystal ball to see Saruman's white-hot fury at Grima's foolish-ness, for the palantir was Saruman's sole means of communicating with the Dark Lord Sauron.)

Before the invention of the crystal ball, people looked in anything reflec-tive, like water or shiny metals, in an attempt to scry. Not surprisingly, the medieval church condemned its practice, crediting it as devil's work, but years later, in Victorian England, scrying enjoyed a resurgence in popularity, along with other methods of divination, like palmistry.

Note: The crystal ball should not be confused with a witch ball, which is a colored, hollow glass globe originally used by fishermen to provide buoy-ancy for their nets, which came to be associated with superstitions at sea—thus its name.

For those who wish to try their hand at divination, crystal balls are avail-able at the Gift Emporium (www.phoenixorion.com), in sizes ranging from two inches ($10.95) to eight inches ($347.95).

Curse

The opposite of a blessing, a curse is given to bring evil upon someone. In the wizarding world, curses are a way of life, which is one reason why Hogwarts students attend classes in Defense Against the Dark Arts, since dark wizards do not hesitate to use curses in combat, including the Unforgivable Curses. So named because their use means the users can expect no mercy when the Ministry of Magic puts them on trial, the Unforgivable Curses include the Cruciatus Curse, the Imperius Curse, and the most feared of all, the Killing Curse. Using any of these means a lifetime sentence in Azkaban prison, with no possibility of parole. (Not that it matters: Chances are good that madness will result after even a short incarceration.)

Not surprisingly, Lord Voldemort and his Death Eaters are well practiced in the employment of the Unforgivable Curses, as all Aurors, the bad wizard hunters, know.

There are numerous curses that can be inflicted on someone, but these three are unquestionably the worst.

The Cruciatus Curse causes excruciating pain. Sometimes, the pain is so great that it drives the victim mad.

The Imperius Curse makes the victim a slave of the spell-caster—a living zombie, in one sense. The distinction is that a zombie is a reanimation, brought back from the dead, whereas the victim of this curse is alive. In both instances, however, the victim has no free will.

The worst is the Killing Curse, which produces a jet of green light, accompanied by a rushing sound. Against this curse, invoked by saying *Avada Kedavra* (similar in sound to the magical word *abracadabra*) and pointing one's wand at the victim, there is no defense and instant death results.

No one has successfully withstood an attack from this deadly curse, except Harry Potter, which is why he's celebrated in the wizarding world as "the boy who lived." That he survived the curse at the hands of one of the most practiced and deadly wizards in the world—Lord Voldemort, the Dark Lord—is unprecedented.

Note: The curriculum at Hogwarts does teach curses, but only to upper-class students, in their sixth year (out of seven).

Curses have been around for thousands of years, but to put real power behind the curse, invoke a demon and have him do your bidding.

Curses can also be placed on places, to preserve them from trespassers, as suggested by what happened to people who unwisely raided the Egyptian tomb of King Tutankhamen, better known as King Tut. The history of people who have gotten killed or injured makes for fascinating, if morbid, reading and is certainly compelling.

The King Tut Curse began claiming its victims in 1922, when an Englishman, Howard Carter, discovered King Tut's burial grounds. A great archeological discovery, King Tut's tomb was then explored by teams of archeologists, who mysteriously fell ill and subsequently died, in the 1920s. Predictably, the word spread that the tomb was haunted, that it had been cursed, but the fact remains that we can't know for sure. One theory states that the preserved vegetables had grown toxic mold, but this strikes the scientific community at large as speculative.

Cursed Opal Necklace

If you find yourself in Knockturn Alley at Borgin and Burkes, a retail store known for its curious collection of Dark Arts items, you may find yourself entranced by the bewitching opal necklace. If so, you wouldn't be alone: Nineteen Muggles died because of that cursed necklace. This being the case, you might be able to wrangle a good price for it, though the cost of ownership may be more than you want to pay.

In ancient Rome, opals were highly prized, second only in value to emeralds. Later, in the Middle Ages, it was considered to be a lucky stone. Today, however, it has taken a bad turn and some people consider it unlucky.

This cursed opal necklace recalls the Hope Diamond, considered to be the most cursed gem in history. Weighing 44.52 carats, the gem was reputedly pried out of the eye of a statue of Sita, a Hindu goddess. That is legend, but the fact remains that some of those who have come in contact with this precious gem have paid for it . . . with their lives. A French jeweler, Jean Baptiste Tavernier, was killed in India by a pack of wild dogs; the crown jewels (including this one) were stolen from Louis XVI and Marie Antoinette, both of whom were beheaded; a grieving Dutch diamond cutter named Wilhelm Fals died after his son Hendrick stole this precious gem from him; the son later committed suicide.

The list of dead continued for some years afterward; currently, the diamond is housed in the Smithsonian Institution in the United States, where it is hoped there will be no more names added to its necrology.

Dark Arts: Defense

Considering that Lord Voldemort is gathering his power and his followers, the Death Eaters, to his banner, it seems ironic that Hogwarts has had a

bad run of professors who have taught Defense Against the Dark Arts, or attempted to do so. In Harry Potter's first year at Hogwarts, the stuttering Professor Quirrell proved to be two-faced. In Harry's second year, the self-inflated Professor Gilderoy Lockhart was exposed as a poseur. In Harry's third year, Professor Remus Lupin, an effective teacher, turned out to be a real howler. In Harry's fourth year, Professor "Mad-Eye" Moody deserved the Evil Eye. In Harry's fifth year, Professor Dolores Umbridge, a bureaucrat from the Ministry of Magic, had a positive knack for not teaching anything useful, prompting Harry by default to teach the class on his own, in defiance of school policies and invoking her umbrage.

Will Hogwarts *ever* see a Defense Against the Dark Arts teacher who will stick around for more than one year?

Though Potions Master Severus Snape wants the job, he's been unable to secure it. Clearly, Professor Dumbledore has other plans for Professor Snape, or feels that putting Snape in that job would create an equally difficult vacancy to fill for Potions Master.

Nonetheless, defense against the dark arts is a very real concern, since some witches and wizards go bad. You may see them lurking about in Knockturn Alley, or you may not see them at all, until they gather at the command of Lord Voldemort, who has recruited a handpicked cadre of dark witches and wizards who feel the balance of power will shift to them, if they succeed in their aims.

Dark Detectors: Foe-Glass, Sneakoscope, Secrecy Sensor

Foe-Glass: a mirror-like device that, as your enemy approaches, becomes clearer and more distinct.

Sneakoscope: a gyroscopic-looking device that whistles when someone untrustworthy is nearby.

Secrecy Sensor: an item that detects evil (in any form) approaching.

Considering the kinds of evil creatures that roam, haunt, and otherwise inhabit the Harry Potter universe, up to and including the Dark Lord himself, it makes perfect sense for the wizard to have this trio of detection equipment, and thus be prepared for all eventualities.

In the Muggle world, there are similar items, including some that are classified top secret and cannot be discussed, except on a "need to know" basis.

Muggle Foe-Glass: Surveillance cameras, from ground-based to satellite-mounted, have become increasingly sophisticated and are capable of recording your image, comparing it to a database of known suspects, and giving a probability as to a positive match. These cameras are used in airports world-wide as a countermeasure against terrorism. The idea is to photograph and positively identify the foe before he boards the plane. Naturally, the closer the foe comes to the cameras, the more distinct the likeness, and the better the picture, with a correspondingly greater likelihood of a positive match.

Muggle Sneakoscope: The equivalent Muggle tool is the old-fashioned but still reliable polygraph (nicknamed "Polly"), more commonly known as the lie detector. It can't actually detect a lie, but measures the body's physi-ological changes that occur as a result of questions being answered; there-fore, the results obtained by "Polly" are questionable and, depending on your location, may not be admissible in court. Invented in 1895, but per-fected in the 1900s, the use of the polygraph remains controversial.

Muggle Secrecy Sensor: There is no Muggle equivalent to this useful device, since it detects an unquantifiable element. But wouldn't it be handy to have? Imagine all the people you could eliminate from your life from the outset by knowing in advance if evil lurks in their hearts!

Divination

> I think Divination seems very wooly. A lot of guesswork, if you ask me.
> —*Hermione Granger*

Hermione Granger feels that Divination is not a rigorous academic sub-ject, but others, notably Professor Trelawney, would vehemently disagree. Though many forms of divination seem ludicrous, from Aeromancy (divina-tion by atmospheric conditions) to Xylomancy (divination by burning wood) and everything in between, the fact remains that in the Department of Mysteries at the Ministry of Magic, thousands of prophecies are carefully stored in glass spheres, each marked as to the sender, recipient, and subject matter.

Divination, more art than science, attempts to foresee the future by var-ious means, which puts a great deal of reliance on interpretation. For this reason, Hermione Granger feels it's guesswork, but as seers will tell you, it's not guesswork: Those who have the Inner Eye can pierce the veil, so to speak, and look beyond to see and intuit what most people cannot.

Professor Sibyll Trelawney, who teaches this subject at Hogwarts, is more often wrong than right in her predictions. Even so, the subject is part of the

Methods of Divination

These are too numerous to mention, but some of the more "wooly" ones include:

· Axiomancy (divination by axes)

· Cephalomancy (divination by skulls)

· Geloscopy (divination by laughter)

· Moleosophy (divination by blemishes)

· Myomancy (divination by rodent behavior)

· Tiromancy (divination by cheese)

curriculum at Hogwarts, and thus is taught to all students, beginning in their third year.

Significantly, the two correct predictions by Trelawney involved Lord Voldemort. Going into a trance, speaking in a toneless voice, and coming out of it with no knowledge of what she said, Trelawney seems to possess the Inner Eye, though apparently it's not a skill that she can tap into at will.

Just as significantly, she is the great-great-granddaughter of Cassandra Vablatsky, who was very highly regarded in her time as an authentic seer. In Muggle legend, Cassandra was celebrated for her prophetic utterances until she lost her power when the god Apollo, who had given her the gift, took it back after she spurned his advances, with the result that her celebrated gift proved ironic: though she was accurate in her divinations, no one took them seriously.

Professor Trelawney's first name is "Sibyll." *Sibylla,* from the Greek, means "prophetess", and there were up to ten sibyls who were considered oracles, and thus held in high regard in ancient Greece. Of them, the three most famous ones were the Cumaean (located near Naples, Greece), Delphic (in Delphi), and Erythraean (on the Ionian coast, near the island of Chios).

Today, the general public considers all forms of divination to be of entertainment value only, but those who practice the arts believe it, though none of it holds up to scientific scrutiny.

In *The Book of Divination,* author Ann Fiery provides a no-nonsense look at the subject. Covering astrology, metoposcopy, oracles, numerology, orneiromancy, phrenology, alchemy, tasseomancy, runes, haruspicy, talismans, chiromancy, geomancy, rhabdomancy, and tarot, Fiery takes the subject seriously and treats it with respect.

"This book is no more than a dabble in the deep waters of Western divination," states Fiery in her introduction. While that may be true, for Muggles who want to get their feet wet, it is a good place to start.

Dreams . . . and Nightmares

In their fifth year, Hogwarts students study dream interpretation in Professor Trelawney's class on Divination. Inigo Imago's *The Dream Oracle* is the standard text, which reportedly holds the key to unlocking the secrets of dreams and their hidden meanings.

It's a subject that is on everyone's minds, so to speak, since everyone dreams nightly, but the most vivid and memorable dreams occur during deep sleep called REM (rapid eye movement) sleep.

When Harry Potter is in REM sleep, what, exactly, is he dreaming, and what do they—his dreams and nightmares—mean?

In ancient Egypt, a troubled person would sleep in a temple and, the next morning, a priest known as the Master of Secret Things would patiently listen as the person recounted a dream and interpret it for him or her, in the hope that the information would in some way help or solve the problem at hand.

In later years, however, dream books supposedly held the key. The earliest such dream book—*Oneirocritica: The Interpretation of Dreams* by a Greek named Artemidorus—listed different dreams and their symbology, but later books delved more deeply, offering more scenarios and symbology.

Beyond dream books, the field of psychology beckons. Sigmund Freud, who wrote *The Interpretations of Dreams,* believed that a dream was the pathway to the unconscious and held that dreams were wish fulfillment. Carl Jung felt differently, believing that the *remembered* dream is not wrapped in mystery or symbology, but clearly contains its actual meaning.

Some people hold that dreams are prophetic in nature, whereas others feel dreams are an extension of one's real life, or that nightmares identify inadequacies. In Harry Potter's case, all three apply: he dreams someone will be coming to take him away (true); he dreams (on several occasions) of locked doors (highly suggestive of his imprisonment in the Muggle world); and he has nightmares that speak to his inadequacies as a wizard and his fractured life. His prophetic dreams may be the most interesting because they foreshadow the final, fatal (for whom?) confrontation with Voldemort, the Dark Lord.

E

Evil-Looking Masks

It's not surprising that you'd find masks at Borgin and Burkes, a disreputable place in Knockturn Alley where dark witches and wizards do their shopping. And although we have no specific idea of what *kinds* of masks Mr. Borgin carries in his store, we can presume they are of evil origin.

The word "mask" is suggestive of evil origins in itself, for to mask something is to hide or disguise it. Or it can actually be a false front, worn to conceal one's identity. In either case, honest people need no reason to hide themselves behind a false name or a facade.

Could it be that Mr. Borgin is carrying a selection of death masks? If so, these were likely made with wax (as the Romans did) or thin gold plate (as the Egyptians did), reproducing the face of a dead person. Alternately, Mr. Borgin could be stocking a more traditional mask, often used to represent harmful spirits, and worn during religious ceremonies.

Sometimes, the masks are not only monstrous, but also monster-sized. According to the online *Encyclopædia Britannica:*

> In New Britain, members of a secret terroristic society called the Dukduk appear in monstrous five-foot masks to police, to judge, and to execute offenders. Aggressive supernatural spirits of an almost demonic nature are represented by these masks, which are constructed from a variety of materials, usually including tapa, or bark cloth and the pith of certain reeds. These materials are painted in brilliant colours, with brick red and acid green predominating.

Extendable Ears

Used to manage mischief, the flesh-colored Extendable Ears is a listening device invented by Fred and George Weasley to eavesdrop. They find it particularly useful when listening in to conversations at Sirius Black's house, the headquarters of the Order of the Phoenix.

There are several Muggle equivalents of Extendable Ears, including a handheld sound amplifier (sensitive enough to pick up bird calls 100 feet away), a pinhole microphone (sensitive enough to pick up a whisper in a 30-by-30-foot room), and wireless microphone systems.

Naturally, though it's relatively easy to "bug" a room, it's also just as easy to "debug" the room by using electronic sensing equipment that will identify their presence, so would-be eavesdroppers won't necessarily be able to manage their mischief.

For those who want to find out what top-secret, highly classified products are currently available, that information is on a need-to-know basis, so if you don't already know, fuggedaboutit.

Floo Powder

In the wizarding world, there are several means of locomotion, from the mundane (the Hogwarts Express) to the magically marvelous, including using Floo powder.

A pun on the words "flue" (the long, vertical neck of a chimney) and "flew," the Floo powder, invented by Ignatia Wildsmith in the 1200s, is easy to use: Grab a handful of the silvery powder, throw it into the flames of an open fireplace, step into fireplace, and *clearly* announce your destination. Then, poof, you're off!

Regulated by the Department of Magical Transportation at the Ministry of Magic, the Floo Network is an interconnection of all fireplaces. Keep in mind that if you don't enunciate properly, you may not wind up where you wish to go, as Harry Potter finds out when, instead of winding up in Diagon Alley, he finds himself in Knockturn Alley. (Fortunately, Rubeus Hagrid just happens to be in the neighborhood and rescues him.)

In Muggle history, witches were traditionally thought to mount their broomsticks and fly up the chimney to ride the night sky. Those flights, however, were mostly flights of imagination.

There is, alas, no Muggle equivalent of Floo powder, but in the wizarding world, one hazard presents itself: If a fireplace is sealed, which is something you wouldn't necessarily know before undergoing the trip, imagine how uncomfortable it would be to be stuck in the narrow flue! Ask Fred, George, Ron, and Arthur Weasley, who found themselves in just such a predicament, as recounted in *Harry Potter and the Goblet of Fire*.

Flying Carpet

Though in use around the world, with the largest concentration in the Middle East, a flying carpet, a charming way to fly, is listed in the Registry of Proscribed Charmable Objects. In other words, it's illegal to use a charm to enchant a Muggle rug.

Unlike Floo powder or a Portkey, a flying carpet has more in common with a broom, since time in flight is a consideration. In other words, if you are in a hurry, forgo a flying carpet: not that you have much of a choice in the British wizarding world.

If you live outside Britain (therefore beyond the Ministry's jurisdiction), you do have a choice, and a flying carpet will offer more leg room than a broom. For instance, King Solomon's flying carpet was reported to be room-sized, with his throne positioned in its center and his entourage surrounding him. And when flying above clouds or on cloudless days, a canopy of birds conveniently provided cover against the sun.

Goblet of Fire

As recounted in *Harry Potter and the Goblet of Fire*, the Goblet of Fire is a magical cup that selects the names of the school champions to compete in the Triwizard Tournament. It is contained in a bejeweled wooden chest. Only those who seek to become a champion should put their names in the cup, for it's a binding contract.

In *Indiana Jones and the Last Crusade*, Professor Indiana Jones is faced with the decision of his life: He must choose the true Holy Grail among dozens of cups and chalices, ranging from a simply hewn wooden cup to a massive bejeweled chalice; only one is the legendary Holy Grail from which one can drink and enjoy eternal life; choosing any of the false Grail cups will bring instant death. Fortunately, Professor Jones chooses wisely.

Said to be the cup used by Jesus Christ at the Last Supper, as well as the cup used by Joseph of Arimathea to catch the blood flowing from Christ's wounds as he hung dying on the cross, the Holy Grail was the highly sought-after object among King Arthur's Knights of the Round Table, which included the pure Sir Galahad. In the Middle Ages, the cup (or chalice) was thought to be imbued with a magical aura.

Many are called, but few are chosen: While not an object of desire, the Goblet of Fire will consider all who wish to compete in the Triwizard Tournament. In the end only four champions from the three European wizarding schools are selected. (Normally, only one champion from each school would be chosen, but in this case the goblet is tricked into thinking there is a fourth school.) Like the Arthurian Knights who sought the Holy Grail, the schools' champions seek their grail, defined as "any greatly desired and sought-after objective; ultimate ideal or reward."

Gobstones

A popular wizarding game, Gobstones is one at which you definitely play to win, for losers will be spat at by the Gobstones with a disgusting fluid.

Wizards with more Galleons than sense can buy the solid gold set, available at Diagon Alley, but most prefer the less expensive edition.

Gob: Depending on whether the word is used formally or informally (i.e., slang), it can mean several things, most of them unpleasant. A gob is "a small mass or lump," which is what you'd expect from a spitting Gobstone. The word "gobshite" means "wad of expectorated chewing tobacco," which is rather disgusting. In the British slang expression "Don't you gob at me!" gob means "to spit." It is also slang for "mouth," as in "Shut your gob!" So a stone with a mouth could certainly spit at you.

H

Hand of Glory

Like other magical artifacts found at Borgin and Burkes, there's nothing glorious about the Hand of Glory; indeed, it's a disgusting item that even Lucius Malfoy rejects, when his son Draco expresses an interest in owning it. In *Harry Potter and the Chamber of Secrets*, the unctuous proprietor, Mr. Borgin, upon spying Draco Malfoy coveting the Hand of Glory, tells Lucius, "Your son has fine taste, sir." Lucius, who knows the history of the unsavory item, replies, "I hope my son will amount to more than a thief or a plunderer, Borgin." A disappointed Draco Malfoy leaves the store empty-handed.

According to *Secrets Merveilleux de la Magic Naturelle et Cabilistique du Petit Albert* (*Marvelous Secrets of Natural and Cabalistic Magic*), a grimoire by Albertus Magnus published in 1772 in Cologne, Germany, this is how to make a Hand of Glory:

> Take the right or left hand of a felon who is hanging from a gibbet beside a highway; wrap it in part of a funeral pall and so wrapped squeeze it well [to extract the blood]. Then put it into an earthware vessel with zimat, nitre, salt, and long peppers, the whole well powdered. Leave it in this vessel for a fortnight, then take it out and expose it to full sunlight during the dog-days until it becomes quite dry. If the sun is not strong enough, put it in an oven heated with fern and vervain. Next, make it a kind of candle with the fat of a biggeted felon, virgin wax, sesame, and ponie, and use the Hand of Glory as a candlestick to hold this candle when lighted.
>
> After breaking into a house, the thief should recite: "Hand of Glory shining bright, lead us to our spoils tonight!" And the Hand of Glory will shine on.

A note to curious Muggles: An actual Hand of Glory can be seen at the Whitby Museum in North Yorkshire, England.

Hangman's Rope

An artifact found at Borgin and Burkes in Knockturn Alley, a hangman's rope is indeed a grisly item. Who, one wonders, would want to buy one for its intended use, except a Death Eater? And who would want such an item for souvenir purposes?

With its traditional eight coils around the neck of the rope, the hangman's noose has seen more than its share of victims, both just and unjust. In the Muggle world in England until 1808, for example, hanging was considered just punishment for all sorts of "crimes," including attempting suicide (if you didn't succeed, the judicial system certainly would) and, if you were aged 7 to 14, for showing "strong evidence of malice."

Early methods of hanging were primitive. Simply slip the noose around the victim's neck and let the victim hang until dead. Unfortunately, it sometimes took a long time, since death by strangulation wasn't instantaneous. Subsequent improvements in the art included using a machine to hoist the victim, or having the victim trigger his own death by stepping on a metal plate that initiated the hoisting mechanism.

The hangman's noose found itself around the necks of many innocent victims, including so-called witches who, as an alternative to being burned at the stake (inefficient and time-consuming), would find themselves hung from on high. An accused witch usually didn't have far to travel to the gallows, since nearly every English town had its own.

Herbology

Taught by the aptly named Professor Sprout, herbology is the study of magical plants. Students should expect to get their hands dirty in this class, which is taught in the Hogwarts greenhouses. Herbology's reference books include *Encyclopedia of Toadstools* and *One Thousand Magical Herbs and Fungi*.

Unlike a Muggle greenhouse, Professor Sprout's greenhouse is hazardous, and so requires special tools: Dragon-hide gloves and ear muffs are standard issue. Even the manure is apparently special, for dragon and mooncalf dung are used for fertilizer.

Principally used for potion-making, herbs require the proverbial "green thumb," an affinity for things that grow in gardens. In Gryffindor, just as Harry Potter excels in Defense Against the Dark Arts classes and Hermione is a whiz with figures in Arithmancy, Neville Longbottom, a hapless student who seems all thumbs in all his other classes, has a talent for herbology that flowers under the tutelage of the gentle Professor Sprout, who is also the head of Hufflepuff House.

Muggles practice herbology, but mostly for medicinal purposes, especially in Asia. The Chinese, for instance, have long advocated mixing herbal "cocktails" as remedies. (In the United States, such herbal remedies are employed in alternative medicine, which has taken root among people who feel conventional medicine is needlessly invasive.)

In medieval times, herb gardens were commonplace. In addition to their use in flavoring food, herbs were used as medicines.

Hogwarts Express

Ah, finally, a form of locomotion that Muggles are comfortable with—if only they could board it!

When Harry Potter is taken to King's Cross Station in London to board the train to Hogwarts, he realizes that Rubeus Hagrid has forgotten to explain *how* to get to the Hogwarts Express, a shiny red train whose northern terminus is Hogsmeade station, where everyone disembarks. Temporarily derailed, Harry is understandably concerned because the train leaves promptly on September 1 at 11 A.M. If he misses it, well, he doesn't even want to think about it.

Fortunately, Harry overhears Molly Weasley as she escorts her children through King's Cross Station, where Harry watches in amazement as they make their way to a train platform that Muggles can't see—platform nine and three-quarters.

The train platform is between platforms nine and ten, and accessible to those in the wizarding world. But to get through, one must run at full speed at the brick barrier between platforms nine and ten. On the other side, a gleaming red steam train awaits to carry the students and faculty to the school.

With the exception of prefects, who have two compartments reserved up front, seating is random, so you don't know who will be in your compartment. Fortunately for Harry Potter, his compartment is shared by Ron Weasley and not Draco Malfoy, which would have made for a very long and unpleasant ride to Hogwarts. Malfoy, who caught wind that Harry Potter was on the train, had to come by his compartment to take a look and see for himself that *the* Harry Potter was on the train, which was the beginning of a beautiful un-friendship. In fact, Malfoy is ready to pick a fight, until he's discouraged by Scabbers, Ron Weasley's pet rat.

Because of the length of the trip, refreshments are available. A witch pushing a trolley cart offers all the finest food and candy a hungry wizard would want, including "Bertie Bott's Every Flavor Beans, Drooble's Best Blowing Gum, Chocolate Frogs . . ." All, of course, more palatable than what Ron Weasley's mother prepared for him to take on the train, corned beef, which Ron readily admits isn't his favorite.

The Hogwarts Express makes six runs a year: once when the school session starts, once when the school session ends, and four in between for vacation (to and from home at Christmas and Easter).

Muggles can, of course, get on a train at King's Cross Station, but they will look in vain for platform nine and three-quarters.

The infrastructure of the U.K. train system is maintained by Network Rail, which employs more than 20,000 people that staff its 2,500 stations and maintain its 21,000 miles of tracks. The system is comprised of numerous railway companies, with colorful names like Anglia Railways, Arriva Trains, and the famous London Underground, to name a few. For general information about the train system and schedules, go to www.rail.co.uk.

Howler

> "What's the matter?" said Harry.
> "She's—she's sent me a Howler," said Ron faintly.
> . . . .
> "What's a Howler?" he said.
> But Ron's whole attention was fixed on the letter, which had begun to smoke at the corners.
>
> —*from* Harry Potter and the Chamber of Secrets,
> chapter 6, "Gilderoy Lockhart"

Having lived most of his life in the Muggle world, Harry Potter has no idea what a Howler is, but he's about to find out. It likely has something to do with Ron Weasley hijacking the enchanted Ford Anglia to take Harry and him to Hogwarts after they fail to get through to platform nine and three-quarters.

Seated at the Great Hall for breakfast, the students who spy the infamous red envelope know what to expect, and poke fingers in their ears. With great trepidation, Ron opens the red envelope, which explodes, and he hears the voice of his mother a hundredfold in volume, as she excoriates him, to his great embarrassment, with all eyes and ears on him. After the message is delivered, the red envelope conveniently explodes, like a firecracker, and then burns to ashes.

A "howler" is slang for "a laughably stupid blunder," which is why Ron got his Howler.

In the Muggle world, there's fortunately no equivalent item, but there *is* such a thing as a red howler, a species of monkey found in Central and South America. Due to a large bone in its throat, the howler monkey can be heard up to three miles away. The sound it makes is very distinctive, a loud whooping sound punctuating the air. The red howler, however, is not prized for its loud voice; it's prized for its flesh in some countries and so, like other species, it's being hunted to extinction.

Human Bones

No doubt a fine selection of these can be found at Borgin and Burkes, where all sorts of evil oddities and curiosities can be obtained for the required Galleons, Sickels, or Knuts.

Dark wizards use human bones for purposes of divination and necromancy (communication with the dead to predict the future), so it would make sense that Borgin and Burkes would have a good inventory on hand.

Muggles, however, used them for another purpose, equally bizarre. In Europe, during the Renaissance (supposedly the period of enlightenment), human bones were used for decoration in churches and monasteries. This proved to be so popular that the practice continued for several centuries afterward. The prevailing thought back then was that the bones symbolized the impermanence of life—a grisly reminder to the meditating monks who were living on a physical plane but meditating on an ethereal one.

The tourist with a taste for the macabre might want to visit the Church of Saint Francis in the Portuguese city of Evora, which bears the legend: "We bones in here wait for yours to join us." Inside, the walls and vaulted ceiling are constructed of skulls, and leg and arm bones. In the Carmo Church, at the seaside town of Faro in Portugal, another macabre monument to the once-living can be seen: 1,250 skeletons line every inch of this small chapel.

It's hard to imagine who would find either place a suitable house of worship, though Baba-Yaga, the Slavonic Goddess of Death, would feel right at home. According to www.godchecker.com, which lists gods from various cultures and religions, this bizarre goddess probably didn't have many houseguests:

She lives in a house built of human bones, complete with bone fence with inset skulls whose eye sockets light up in the dark. And it is a mobile home—it runs around supported on gigantic chicken legs. If this doesn't make you chicken out, her own eyes turn humans to stone, and her mighty mouth has knives for teeth. She can also pole herself around in a giant pestle and mortar, which she uses to grind up and unpetrify her victims.

Invisibility Cloak

Q: If you were Harry and had an invisibility cloak what would you use it for?
J. K. Rowling: I'd sneak into a few places. I can think of loads; 10 Downing Street [the Prime Minister's residence] would be a good start.
—*J. K. Rowling, in an online interview* (Comic Relief, *March 2001*)

In *Harry Potter and the Sorcerer's Stone,* Harry receives the usual sort of Christmas gifts (his first gifts ever)—a sweater from Ron Weasley's mother, and candy—but he also receives an unusual gift from an unnamed source: an invisibility cloak, which he is told in an accompanying note was previously owned by his father, James Potter. The cloak will prove useful to Harry, concealing him from view from everyone, though "Mad-Eye" Moody can still see him.

Greek legend recounts two instances in which the wearer dons an article of clothing to become invisible, not a cloak but a cap that belonged to the Greek god of the underworld, Hades—a kingly gift given to him by the Cyclops, the one-eyed sons of Uranus and Gaia.

The cap proves useful to Perseus, who dons it before confronting the Graeae, three deities who share a single eye and tooth, passed among one another as needed. Though the Graeae can sense his presence outside their cave, they can't see him, and so the sole eye is passed to the Graeae who is in a position to see him, as is the sole tooth. As they are passed from hand to hand, Perseus snatches them and the Graeae, now blind and toothless,

The Real-World Invisibility Cloak

The U.S. military has been pursuing technologies termed "adaptive camouflage" that would help vehicles blend in with their surroundings, but a civilian—Kazutoshi Obana, the founding head of the Virtual Reality Society of Japan—devised a coat that renders the wearer invisible, or at least it seems so. It appears that you can look through the coat and see what's behind the person, but it's an illusion created by a video camera linked to a projector shining on a coat made of microscopic reflectors. In fact, this basic idea is the basis for Richard Schowengerdt's Project Chameleo, which he hopes will shield top-secret facilities in the United States from radar and sonar detection.

have to strike a bargain for their return. Perseus offers them back in trade for directions to Medusa, one of three Gorgon sisters.

Perseus finds her on a remote island. She has the face of a beautiful woman but an unusual crown of hair made of serpents. To look directly upon Medusa means instant death, since seeing her turns the viewer to stone. Perseus uses a highly polished shield, provided by the goddess Athena, to view Medusa indirectly and thus escapes the stony fate of others who had confronted her.

The "cap of darkness" (as Hades called it) was also used by the messenger of the Gods, Hermes, who donned it in a battle against the giants, who fought against the Gods. In battle, Hermes killed the giant Hippolytus.

Later, Athena, in battle against the war-god Ares, wears it and becomes invisible, assisting Diomedes, who wounds Ares. The wound forces Ares to return to Olympus, where he is healed.

Knight Bus

Welcome aboard the Knight Bus! Capable of taking you anywhere in Britain, this triple-decker, purple-colored bus is driven by Ernie Prang and its conductor is Stan Shunpike. It provides "emergency transport" for the stranded witch or wizard.

Arriving with a loud flash and a bang, the Knight Bus providentially appears out of nowhere to pick up a stranded Harry Potter, who is happy to board it and zoom off to the Leaky Cauldron, where the Minister of Magic, Cornelius Fudge, is waiting for him.

The Magic Bus

For younger readers who want to "board" a Magic School Bus, go to Scholastic's website (http://place.scholastic.com/magicschoolbus/home.htm) and enjoy an interactive site that will transport you.

A double wordplay on "Knight"—meaning, appearing at night, and a medieval knight that rescues those in distress—the Knight Bus charges off at breakneck speed as it makes its appointed rounds.

The double-decker bus unique to Britain has largely disappeared from her roads. According to the online guide to the United Kingdom (http://gouk.about.com), the double-decker bus is vanishing:

London's landmark jump-on, jump-off red double-decker buses are disappearing from the capital's streets. First introduced fifty years ago, the cost of maintaining the buses, called Roadmasters, has become too expensive. The buses are slowly being replaced with new "bendy buses" which not only carry more passengers, but are also more accessible for the infirm and disabled. The official Routemaster Association calculates that at the current replacement rate, all buses will have disappeared by the end of 2005. Decommissioned buses are available for sale; prices vary depending upon the condition of the bus.

Latin

> *Q. There is a lot of Latin in the spells in your books. Do you speak Latin?*
>
> Rowling: Yes. At home, we converse in Latin. [Laughter]. Mainly. For light relief, we do a little Greek. My Latin is patchy, to say the least, but that doesn't really matter because old spells are often in cod Latin—a funny mixture of weird languages creeps into spells. That is how I use it. Occasionally you will stumble across something in my Latin that is, almost accidentally, grammatically correct, but that is a rarity. In my defence, the Latin is deliberately odd. Perfect Latin is not a very magical medium, is it? . . . I take a lot of liberties with things like that. I twist them round and make them mine.
>
> —*J. K. Rowling, answering questions from the audience at the Royal Albert Hall (London, June 28, 2003)*

Far from being a dead language, as some students today think, Latin is alive and well. In fact, it's still spoken daily, in Vatican City, where it is not only the official tongue but the official language of the Roman Catholic Church as well.

In the Muggle world, Latin words and phrases have become a part of everyday life: a priori, ad hoc, ad hominem, ad infinitum, ad nauseam, et cetera. But thanks to the popularity of the Harry Potter books, there's been a worldwide resurgence of interest in Latin, since it is the language used to cast charms and spells. To know Latin is to speak the spell-language of witches and wizards in Harry Potter's universe.

When you think of it, it makes perfect sense for Rowling to employ Latin as the wizards' language because, in the Middle Ages, it was the principal language among writers and scholars. Second, the language is "fixed"; unlike a modern language, the vocabulary is set in stone, so to speak, so words won't change their meanings.

Also, why go to the trouble of inventing a language when an existing language will do the job? After all, inventing a language—its vocabulary, grammar, and various dialects—is no easy matter: J. R. R. Tolkien, who wrote *The Lord of the Rings*, developed several, but then he had a big advantage over most authors, for he was a professional philologist. (He also helped edit the *Oxford English Dictionary*.)

Besides, using a language that is well known internationally lends authenticity to the fictional universe.

The list of charms and spells, all spoken in Latin, is beyond the scope of this book, but here are a few of the ones that begin with the letter "A."

- *Accio:* a charm used to summon an object

- *Alohomora:* a charm used to open a locked door

- *Aparecium:* used to make invisible ink turn visible

- *Avada Kedavra:* the Killing Curse (the single most deadly curse that can be uttered)

As to what they translate to in Latin: A little homework won't hurt you, will it? Go look it up, as J. K. Rowling would say. "And saying the magic words properly is very important too," according to Professor Flitwick.

Lunascope

A device used to view the phases of the moon. Professor Dumbledore has one in his office. (Presumably, Professor Lupin keeps one handy, as well, wouldn't you think?)

The alternative is to use a moon chart to look up the various phases of the moon. Whether a lunascope or moon chart is used, it serves a dual purpose: astronomical studies and astrological predictions. Or, if you fear a full moon, these devices serve a *very* useful purpose!

Luna: from the Latin meaning "moon."

Scope: from the Greek meaning "to watch, to look at."

Muggles with access to the Internet can, in effect, have their own lunascope. The University of Texas's McDonald Observatory provides at its website (www.stardate.org/nightsky/moon) a real-time "lunascope" that shows the moon phases. Simply use the drop-down menus to select a month and year, and the correct phases of the moon for that time period will be shown. A useful set of links provides FAQs about astronomy in general as well.

Magic Camera

When Harry Potter, Hermione Granger, and the Weasley family go to the bookstore Flourish and Blotts in Diagon Alley to stock up on textbooks, a photographer from the wizarding newspaper the *Daily Prophet* shows up with his magical camera in hand. Capable of taking magical pictures in which the person photographed moves about the photo frame, or leaves the frame entirely, the camera produces a cloud of purple smoke with each blinding flash.

In Muggle history, photography began in the 1500s with the Camera Obscura, which used a portable "camera" (lightbox) to project traceable images for artists. The next major development came in 1826 when two Frenchmen, working independently, invented the daguerreotype process. Modern photography wasn't in the picture until 1900, when Kodak mass-produced the camera, leading to an explosion of interest. In 1935, color film was invented; in 1947, the "instant" camera was invented by Polaroid; in 1990, the APS film format, adopted by a consortium of camera and film manufacturers, allowed for flexible formatting and ease-of-loading film, but the real revolution came later with the invention of digital cameras that finally freed photographers from film and the requirement to develop it and print "wet" pictures.

Similarly, flash photography developed slowly, starting with a slow-burning magnesium ribbon that took up to 20 seconds to combust, which made it useful only for static subjects. Adding oxygen to magnesium, flash powder ignited with a blinding flash of white light and generated a cloud of white smoke—a dangerous proposition. As films developed—orthochromatic and panchromatic—flash powder was modified to produce different kinds of light sensitive to those specific emulsions. One of the formulas included strontium and barium salts, which were used to produce green and red light, according to "Photography in the Dark" (http://photography.about.com). Not surprisingly, injuries and fires were a very real risk.

The portable flash cube, used in Kodak cameras, and flash bulbs (1930)—

capable of generating considerable light, though the bulbs ignited with a blinding flash, and the bulbs themselves were hot enough to burn flesh if touched immediately afterward—were eventually replaced by the electronic flash gun, which is still the standard.

Even though photographers in the wizarding world rely on old-fashioned purple-colored flash powder, magical photos have the virtue of being able to take moving pictures (like the Muggle invention, the camcorder) and their subjects can actually vacate the picture frame. As Arthur Weasley observes, Muggle technology is a poor substitute for magic.

Magic Mirror

When asked by Stephen Fry in an interview at a public talk at the Royal Albert Hall in London (June 26, 2003) what she would see if she looked into the Mirror of Erised, J. K. Rowling replied:

> I would at the moment probably see myself very much as I am because one of the most wonderful things that could possibly have happened to me has just happened: I've just had another child. So I see myself and my family, but there would be room in the background for a few other things.
>
> I've always said that I would see what Harry sees which is my mother alive again and there would probably be room to see over my shoulder something like a scientist inventing a cigarette that would be healthy—that would be lovely—and I can think of a particular journalist I'd like to see being boiled in oil over my other shoulder.

In *Harry Potter and the Sorcerer's Stone*, Harry, under cover of darkness and his invisibility cloak, is searching the Restricted Section of the Hogwarts school library, where he hopes to find information about Nicholas Flamel.

The search does not go well and, after one of the books he picks up begins shrieking at top volume, he drops it in surprise and runs for it. Fortunately, the invisibility cloak shields him from the view of Argus Filch, whose watchful eyes search in vain for the trespasser.

Filch seeks out Professor Snape and dutifully reports that someone is footloose in the Restricted Section, but neither Filch nor Snape can see Harry, who takes refuge in an unused classroom that harbors a tall, gold-framed mirror. It is the Mirror of Erised and, as Harry looks longingly at it, he sees not only himself, but also many others, including a woman who resembles him, especially her eyes. It is his mother, and the man next to her is his father.

Harry is almost nose-to-mirror as he experiences mixed emotions: joy and wonder and sadness. He has looked into the Mirror of Erised (read: Mirror of Desire) and seen his innermost desire—to see his parents, whom he never knew, since they were killed by Lord Voldemort when he was an infant. To Harry, it is a wonderful, but bittersweet, moment, especially when he realizes the truth of what he sees.

The word "mirror" is derived from the Latin word *mirus,* which means "wonderful." It is a perfect symbol for what Harry sees and experiences: a sight to wonder at, but, alas, an illusion. No wonder a mirror is also called a *looking glass.*

Before the invention of glass mirrors in the Middle Ages, standing bodies of water served as simple mirrors. In fact, in Greek myth, an extraordinarily handsome young man named Narcissus sees his reflection in a pool of water and falls in love with himself.

The first mirrors were used in the classical era by Greeks and Romans, and consisted of a highly polished metal disk. Later, mirrors were backed by a mixture of tin and mercury to provide their reflective surface; subsequently, mirrors had silver backs; today's mirrors have aluminum backs.

In appearance, the Mirror of Erised resembles the cheval glass, which is full-length (perfect for dressing purposes), framed, and freestanding on its own feet.

Mirrors in fantasy fiction and popular culture reflect our fascination with them. In fantasy fiction, mirrors are often portals to other worlds, most notably in Lewis Carroll's *Through the Looking Glass,* a land where everything, and everyone, is reversed. In popular culture, in Disney's *Snow White* and Dreamworks' *Shrek,* mirrors show and tell their owners what they want to see and hear.

In the wizarding world, however, mirrors have their own distinct personalities. In *Harry Potter and the Chamber of Secrets,* when three of the Weasley boys help Harry escape from the Dursley residence and take him to their enchanted home, a talking mirror over the kitchen mantelpiece barks at Harry, "Tuck your shirt in, scruffy!"

In *Harry Potter and the Prisoner of Azkaban,* when Harry is rooming in the Leaky Cauldron before the school session starts, the mirror in his room gently admonishes him when it sees him trying to tame his characteristically wild hair, "You're fighting a losing battle there, dear."

Magic Wand

When Harry Potter goes with Rubeus Hagrid to shop for school supplies in Diagon Alley, the single most important item to buy is the wand. It's the item, we are told, Harry is most eagerly anticipating purchasing, though he will soon learn that it's not so much that he chooses the wand. The wand, we learn, chooses the wizard. It is, perhaps, destiny.

At Ollivander's: Makers of Fine Wands since 382 B.C., the store owner, an old man named Mr. Ollivander, assists Harry, as he has assisted scores of others, including Harry's parents, James and Lily Potter.

The wand that "chooses" Harry is an unusual one, for Fawkes, the phoenix that gave his wand its core feather, only gave one other feather, for the wand wielded by Harry's nemesis, Lord Voldemort.

The key feature of a wand is its ability to focus its hocus pocus to enhance a spell's effects. It is made from various woods—willow, mahogany, rosewood, hornbeam, ash, oak, vine wood, and beech, to name a few—and its length varies. But the key element of the wand is its core, which is magical: a phoenix feather, unicorn hair, veela hair, or dragon's heartstring.

It is not enough, of course, to own a wand. A witch or wizard must be

instructed in its proper use, which means knowing the art of spell-casting and the various incantations necessary to get the desired results consistently.

Unlike, say, a broken pair of glasses, which can be fixed with a simple command of *oculus reparo,* wands cannot be repaired; in fact, a broken wand is best retired. Unable to focus its magical energies when broken, the wand and its waning powers cannot even be fixed with Spellotape: The results can backfire on the wand's owner, as Ron Weasley discovered.

Important safety tip: Don't be cheeky and carry a wand in the back pocket, because, as "Mad-Eye" Moody pointed out, your buttocks are at risk!

Perhaps some enterprising Hogwarts student should design a leather arm or side holster in which to secure the wand, since the question arises: When riding a broom, where, exactly, does a wizard put his wand to keep from losing it?

Muggles associate wands with frivolous purposes—notably joke or trick wands that recall the kind Fred and George Weasley might sell—but wands actually have a long and distinguished history. Though street performers in the Middle Ages used them principally to misdirect the audience's attention—magic as sleight of hand, or wand, in this case—magicians used them to focus their spells, as do Harry Potter and his classmates.

The earliest known use of wands dates back to Europe, where druids fashioned them out of wood from sacred trees. Today, Wiccans use wands fashioned from wood, but also from metal.

Magic Words

Just as Professor Flitwick explains that wands must be properly used with the correct techniques of swishing and flicking, the utterance of the magic words is also important. Hermione Granger emphasizes and then demonstrates this when, after Ron Weasley repeatedly mispronounces a spell, she rolls her eyes in mock chagrin and correctly pronounces the levitating spell *"Wingardium Leviosa!"* (It comes in handy later when Harry Potter, Ron, and Hermione are under attack by a mountain troll in a girls' bathroom at Hogwarts, and a resourceful Ron uses it to levitate the troll's club; Ron then drops it on the troll's head.)

Remember, as Hermione Granger points out, it's pronounced "lev-e-*oh*-sa," not "lev-e-oh-*sa*." In spell-casting, the difference between using the right word with the right pronunciation and the right word with the wrong pronunciation is, to paraphrase Mark Twain, the difference between lightning and the lightning bug.

In choosing a language to form the basis of spell-casting, J. K. Rowling had three options: Use an invented language with nonsense words with no philological underpinnings, use an invented language with a complete vocabulary and grammar (as philologist J. R. R. Tolkien did for several languages spoken and written in Middle-earth), or use an established language. In Rowling's case she used Latin and modified it to suit her needs.

Magical Megaphone

Used outdoors, this magically enhanced megaphone allows speakers to be heard over large crowds, as is the case during Quidditch matches at Hogwarts, with play-by-play narration provided by an ebullient Lee Jordan, who also has a tendency to get distracted and talk about the latest flying broom's performance, and not the match itself. (The alternative to a magical megaphone is to point a wand at your throat and say *"Sonorus"*—the Latin word for "sound.")

The Muggle equivalent is a megaphone, but obviously not magical. Primitive man used hollow bones and such naturally produced items as conch shells to produce a booming sound that could be heard for long distances.

Today's handheld, cone-shaped megaphones are available in various wattages, typically from 8 to 25 watts, with a range of 300 to 1,000 yards. Electronically amplifying a person's voice, these megaphones simply improve on nature's design. Using one of these modern marvels, the owner never needs to ask, "Can you hear me *now?*"

Mandrake

When Hogwarts students are afflicted with Petrification caused by the indirect stare of the basilisk (a direct gaze causes death), as recounted in *Harry Potter and the Chamber of Secrets,* there's only one course of action: Take the victims to the hospital wing, where they are under the tender care of Madam Poppy Pomfrey, who watches over the students, her brood, like a mother hen clucking over her baby chicks.

It takes a keen eye to discern whether or not the petrified victim is alive or dead, but Madam Pomfrey has a lot of hands-on experience and can quickly detect the condition, and apply the necessary antidote. (A ghost, too, can be petrified, in which case they turn in color from semitransparent to dark gray.)

When afflicted with Petrification, there is only one cure: applying a potion made of Mandrake. Fortunately, Professor Sprout keeps a ready stock of this plant in the greenhouse, not only for her Herbology class but for use in potion-making.

Professor Sprout is well aware of the auditory dangers in extracting the Mandrake from the soil and thus instructs her students to don earmuffs, which provide protection against the Mandrake's unusual, piercing cry.

Taking its name from the genus *Mandragora* of the nightshade family, the mandrake is a plant found in southern Europe, identifiable by its short stem and distinctive greenish-yellow flowers. According to myth, its thick, fleshy root somewhat resembles the human form and, when uprooted, it will emit a piercing sound that can kill, unless one's ears are protected. Because people cannot directly touch the mandrake, the traditional method of safely extracting it is to use a black dog to pull it from a safe distance via a cord wrapped around the top of the plant.

The mandrake root actually has medicinal purposes. It contains a poison, hyoscyamine, which was used in the Middle Ages as a narcotic.

Marauder's Map

Argus Filch is a squib, a person with no magical abilities, with pureblood parents. He appears to be all-seeing, aided by his cat, Mrs. Norris, so in order to evade him, and other prying eyes, the ideal magical device to own is the Marauder's Map. A one-of-a-kind item invented by James Potter, Sirius Black, Remus Lupin, and Peter Pettigrew when they were students at Hogwarts, the map was secured some time ago by Filch, who stored it in a file of confiscated students' goods. He did not keep it under lock and key and since he could not put a locking charm on the file cabinet, it was easy pickings, and was subsequently filched by the inveterate pranksters George and Fred Weasley.

The map, though, changed hands when the Weasleys decided that Harry Potter needed it more than they did, since he would otherwise be confined to quarters, so to speak, having to stay behind at Hogwarts when other students were allowed to go on weekends to Hogsmeade, the nearby wizarding community.

Harry uses the map to make his way surreptitiously to Hogsmeade and back without detection. When he is finished using the map, he simply says, "Mischief Managed!" and the map's features are cleared.

What the map does is provide real-time location and tracking of any person, creature, or ghost. Even something as small as a rat can't escape detection, as the map will show its location and, with a dotted line, reveal its trail.

In short, this magical tracking device has all sorts of applications beyond making one's way to Hogsmeade when you don't have a guardian's pass—the dilemma Harry Potter faced. (Any Auror, a witch or wizard who hunts dark witches and wizards, would find this an especially useful tool.)

When you're the richest man in the world—when, in other words, your name is Bill Gates—you can afford all the high-tech toys you want, one of them being a tracking system for your personal residence, which doubles as place to conduct business. Of course, with its 20,000 square feet, the house is easy to get lost in, but don't worry: An integral part of the house is its 100+ computers that control every aspect of it, from heating to lighting, and much more.

Unlike the average house, the Bill Gates high-tech modern mansion keeps track of guests and their preferences from the time they enter the house until the time they leave. Guests are given a small, inconspicuous pin that attaches to their shirt; this pin acts as a tracking device that, as they go from room to room, is their silent servant, turning lights on and off, and selecting music and artwork individualized to their personal tastes, once it's been programmed. (Of course, once they leave, the pin is electronically wiped clean for reuse.)

Though most homes will never be outfitted with such high-tech gadgetry, the fact remains that individualized tracking is now a way of life. Invented by the U.S. military to provide real-time tracking and location-finding for any point on the globe, the global positioning system (GPS) employs 24 satellites that will provide a "fix" with any GPS receiver, which are now so popular that small, handheld units retail for as little as $150. As with any technology, it has its good and bad points. Though civil libertarians cry "Big Brother!" when a discussion of this kind of technology is brought up in the context of individuals, the fact remains that it's a near-foolproof way to keep track of people, especially children, mentally impaired people who might wander off the premises, or unimpaired people who are directionally challenged.

The latest wrinkle is to use RFID (radio frequency identification) tags to track young schoolchildren. These small tags can be placed on clothing, book bags, nametags, or other possessions, and they let the school system know exactly where their students are at all times, since children can, and do, wander off. In that instance, mischief is certainly managed!

Mrs. Skower's All-Purpose Magical Mess Remover

For house-witches or house-wizards who find a mess on their hands, a magical mess remover would certainly come in handy! No doubt doing magic can be, at times, a messy endeavor, especially in a Potions class at Hogwarts, so it's likely that the school's janitorial staff keeps an ample supply of this on hand for everything from Mrs. Norris's regurgitated hairballs to the noxious green slime from a mountain troll's nose.

Muggles rely on more conventional means, a chemical all-purpose cleaner. It's just the thing to have on hand to keep a house clean.

Chances are you won't have to deal with some of the magical messes those in the wizarding world have to contend with, but it's nice to know that with modern-day, concentrated mixtures, you won't have to mess with mess and can spirit away those pesky stains and odors, so you can tidy up your affairs.

Omnioculars

Quidditch is a fast-moving game—so fast, in fact, that it's impossible to keep up with all the action, unless you own a pair of Omnioculars.

The wizard who thought of this ingenious device likely had sports events in mind, because this invention not only records the action, but also provides instant replay; in case you miss it, purple-colored written commentary overlies the recording.

Likely available in Diagon Alley at Quality Quidditch Supplies, Omnioculars aren't cheap. They'll set you back ten Galleons.

Omni: from the Latin *omnis,* which means "all."

Ocular: from the Latin *oculus,* meaning "eye." Hence "done or perceived by the eye."

Imagine being at the Superbowl and stuck up in the "nosebleed" section. Wish you had a pair of Omnioculars? I bet you do. Fortunately, the technowizards at Bushnell (www.bushnell.com) have invented just such a gadget for your inspection. From its website:

> Bushnell's Instant Replay™ binocular is a serious, high-performance binocular with a dual personality. The Instant Replay

can record a 30-second continuous video loop, allowing you to capture and review sports action on the LCD screen right after it happens. Or, you can choose to take high-quality digital photos. This is essential gear for team coaches and scouts, birders and wildlife observers, big-game hunters and anyone who enjoys recording photographs or movies. Now you can easily view, download, edit and keep your favorite movie clips or stills. Powerful, easy-to-use and loaded with advanced features, the Bushnell® Instant Replay binocular sets the standard for excellence in image-capturing binoculars.

This amazing invention, which is studded with all sorts of buttons and knobs, can be yours for only . . . $400.

Palmistry

> Many witches and wizards, talented though they are in the area of loud bangs and smells and sudden disappearings, are yet unable to penetrate the veiled mysteries of the future.
> —*Professor Trelawney, in* Harry Potter and the Prisoner of Azkaban,
> *chapter 6, "Talons and Tea Leaves"*

First-year Hogwarts students begin their divination studies by reading tea leaves in the first term and the hands of palms (palmistry) in the second.

A method of divination also called chiromancy, palmistry first began in India, then migrated to China and later westward to Greece and beyond.

A palm reader "reads" both hands and examines their various lines; when read separately and considered together, the palms give a picture of the person, but also suggest the road ahead and the paths to take.

Though most people who engage the services of a palm reader are principally interested in piercing the veil, so to speak, to know a little about their own future, some in the palm-reading community are quick to point out that palm reading is firmly rooted in the present. At the Palmistry Center (www.palmistry.com), Dr. Ghanshyam Singh Birla states: "The original intent of palmistry was for personality assessment and counselling. One's emotional tendencies, social attitudes, conscious awareness and subconscious fears, blockages and strengths can be understood in great detail through this in-depth system. . . . You cannot make predictions with palmistry."

Be that as it may, whether merely a parlor game or a serious field of interest, palmistry is a handy introduction to the ancient art of divination.

Pensieve

The Pensieve is a shallow bowl with markings around its rim. When one looks into it, one sees nebulous white, liquid light. The Pensieve doesn't collect things but thoughts. By emptying one's mind into this device, it allows one to think more clearly. It's also used to store temporarily thoughts one wants to keep from other people.

Professor Dumbledore keeps one in his office for ready use. He lends it to Professor Snape, who reluctantly teaches Harry Potter the art of Occlumency, which will allow Harry to protect himself from Lord Voldemort's invasive mental powers.

Pensive: from the Latin *pensar,* "to ponder," and defined as "musingly or dreamily thoughtful."

Muggles don't have the advantage of being able to own a Pensieve, but the technique of clearing one's mind by emptying one's thoughts is an age-old technique, practiced in many religions, notably Buddhism. The technique works, according to Redford Williams's article "The Trusting Heart" (*Psychology Today,* Jan.–Feb. 1989): "As described by Harvard Medical School cardiologist Herbert Benson in his pioneering book, *The Relaxation Response,* meditation is perhaps the most effective means of emptying one's mind of all thoughts."

Philosopher's Stone

Deep in the bowels of the earth, beneath London, the subterranean vaults of Gringotts bank—the bank for the wizarding world—contain many treasures, including those that can be counted (like gold Galleons) and those that cannot, like the mysterious parcel wrapped up and stored behind the magically protected door of vault #713.

Killing two birds with one stone, Rubeus Hagrid goes to Gringotts for two reasons: to allow Harry Potter to withdraw money from his parents' vault, and to retrieve the mysterious, innocuous-looking parcel from vault #713, a package which obviously has great value. It, in fact, contains the fabled Philosopher's Stone, the only one known to exist, now sought by the Dark Lord Voldemort for its gift of immortality.

The "holy grail" of Western alchemists, the Philosopher's Stone was thought to be a substance that could not only transmute base metals into gold but confer immortality as well.

The Philosopher's Stone dates back to the eighth century, when the prevailing thought was that all metals were comprised of four qualities—cold, moist, hot, and dry. By rearranging these four, alchemists felt that transmutation was possible: lead, for instance, could be changed to gold.

This idea took root as alchemists pursued this fruitless endeavor. Not surprisingly, despite the considerable and costly efforts put forth to achieve the Philosopher's Stone, results proved elusive: indeed, contemporary metallurgy has put forever to rest the notion that transmutation as envisioned by the alchemists was achievable. Nonetheless, the lure of gold—not to mention the lure of immortality—proved irresistible, with the result that instead of fortunes being made, fortunes were in fact lost. Alchemists, after all, could not achieve the impossible.

Note: There is some confusion attendant to the title of Rowling's first book, published in the U.K. as *Harry Potter and the Philosopher's Stone*, and in the U.S. as *Harry Potter and the Sorcerer's Stone*. While most publishers outside the U.S. have stuck to Rowling's original title (or a close translation of it), the U.S. title has simply lent confusion to the issue, since there's no historical basis for a "sorcerer's stone," as there obviously is for the "Philosopher's Stone."

Portkey

The logistics of getting the worldwide wizarding community in one place at nearly the same time is daunting, but where there's a will, there's a way. In fact, there are several ways, but the most efficient, especially for a group of witches and wizards who like to travel in packs, is to teleport by using a Portkey. Through this ingenious magical device, cleverly disguised as a useless Muggle artifact like an old boot, it's easy to teleport to the site of the Quidditch World Cup, as recounted in *Harry Potter and the Goblet of Fire*. Many of the 100,000 witches and wizards who showed up from all over the world used a Portkey to get to the stadium.

Teleportation is nothing new in the Muggle community, at least since September 8, 1966, when the crew of the Starship Enterprise began transporting themselves—down to a planet's surface or back up to the starship—by means of a teleportation beam.

It's a handy way to travel, but the physics of it is daunting. Imagine "faxing" a person, disassembling a trillion trillion atoms that comprise the average human being and then reassembling them perfectly, with every atom in place, just where it should be, and doing so in a near instantaneous fashion. In such matters, being close is not nearly good enough; in fact, even being a few molecules off could have a catastrophic effect.

The question remains: *Is* teleportation possible?

In a word, yes.

In a story reported by Paul Rincon for *BBC News World Edition* online (June 16, 2004), two teams managed to "teleport qubits (the quantum form of the digital bits 1 and 0) from one atom to another with the help of a third auxiliary atom."

Rincon explains:

> First, a pair of highly entangled, charged atoms (or ions) are created: B and C. Next, the state to be teleported is created in a third ion, A. Then, one ion from the pair—let's say B—is entangled with A. The internal state of both these is then measured and the result sent to ion C. This transforms the quantum state of ion C into that created for A, destroying the original quantum state of A.
>
> The teleportation took place in milliseconds and at the push of a button, the first time such a deterministic mechanism has been developed for the process.

He adds that this "strange behavior" was noted by physicist Albert Einstein, who called it a "spooky action."

Spooky, indeed!

So, does this mean that people will one day be able to get their atoms scrambled from one place and perfectly reassembled at the other end?

These days, science is looking more and more like magic; that is to say, the results achieved look miraculous. In this case, it's theoretically possible.

Kevin Bonsor ("How Teleportation Will Work" on www.howstuff works.com) says that the process would involve what's called "biodigital cloning." In other words, because of the laws of physics, you'd have to die at the disassembly site, and then be "reborn" at the assembly site. Explains Bonsor, "Their original mind and body would no longer exist. Instead, their atomic structure would be recreated in another location, and digitization would recreate the travelers' memories, emotions, hopes and dreams. So the travelers would still exist, but they would do so in a new body of the same atomic structure as the original body, programmed with the same information."

Sounds like a great way to save a lot of time traveling—or does it? Given that people make mistakes and computers occasionally fail, would *you* want to take the chance that every atom in your body will be accurately disassembled to be reassembled elsewhere?

Thanks, but I think I'll take the bus. . . .

Quill Pen

Potter47: Did you come up with "Sugar Quills" from Charlie and the Chocolate Factory? *I believe there were "Sugar Pencils" in that book.*

Rowling: Oh dear, I don't know whether I did or not. Not consciously, anyway. But it's not a very difficult idea to come up with; we all suck the ends of pens and pencils (or I do), so it seemed logical to make them taste nice, and at Hogwarts, obviously, they use quills!

—*J. K. Rowling, in an online interview at www.worldbookdayfestival.com*
(March 4, 2004)

The Muggle world hasn't relied on quill pens (made from a sharpened bird feather) for writing implements since the 1800s, but in the wizarding world they are not only commonplace but standard issue at Hogwarts. Though not on a list of required items to get before attending school, quill pens are in daily use at Hogwarts, where students dip them into bottles of ink to write notes on parchment.

Sometimes, however, even the commonplace becomes extraordinary: In *Harry Potter and the Order of the Phoenix,* Harry is bedeviled by Professor Dolores Umbridge, who wants to make a point—and a sharp one, at that—with Harry, who finds himself in detention, under her watchful eye.

In Pen and Ink

Curious readers can try their hand at writing with a quill pen, if they want to get a feel for what it is like to be a student at Hogwarts, writing with such implements on parchment. The Esoteric Emporium (http://esotericaofleesburg.com) offers genuine pheasant quill pens with metal nibs for $12.50 each, along with ink in a rainbow of colors, made in Italy and packaged in the traditional small bottles with rubber stoppers and sealing wax.

Seeking to punish him for his candor in her class, Umbridge has devised a particularly painful punishment, since she wants her "message to sink in," as she puts it. (What a real bi—, er, witch.)

The message does indeed sink in, for as Harry writes without ink with the bedeviled quill pen, the words magically appear on the back of his right hand. The cursed pen cuts into his flesh, its message repeating again and again, appearing and disappearing, until detention is over.

Harry Potter literally gets the message.

Fortunately, most scribes don't find themselves in such painful circumstances, but even constructing a quill pen was no easy task. After selecting a bird feather from a goose, crow, turkey, or swan, the feather had to be trimmed to expose the point. Then inserting it in hot sand both strengthened it and enhanced its flexibility. After trimming the point with a knife to create a nib, the pen was finally ready for use. Dipped and redipped into ink, the nib would become worn from writing and need to be resharpened periodically.

Used carefully and deliberately, the nib was capable of producing lines of varying thicknesses and handwriting of unsurpassed beauty; indeed, during the medieval era when monks copied manuscripts, many were works of art (known as illuminated manuscripts) with elaborate designs, flowing script, and various colored inks.

In later years, the metal-nibbed pen replaced the traditional feather quill pen, which became obsolete. Today the fountain pen (with a reservoir of ink in its barrel), ballpoint pen, mechanical pencil, and plastic-tipped pen have entirely replaced their early cousin, but not without a price: The slow, deliberate process of writing with a quill pen forced contemplation on the writer and ensured legibility.

R

Remembrall

A marble-sized object that, when touched, glows red if the person who's holding it has forgotten something. When not in use, the marble has the color of white smoke.

Remember: from the Latin *memorari,* meaning "to be mindful of." Synonyms: remember, recollect, recall, remind, reminisce.

Old technology: string around the finger. Advantage: inexpensive. Disadvantage: The string reminds you to remember *something,* but do you remember just what?

New technology: from www.NeverForget.com, computer software that acts as an electronic string-around-the-finger. Running on the PC platform only, NeverForget Personal Reminder Software acts as your personal information servant.

Rusty, Spiked Instruments

Rusted from disuse, these spiked instruments on sale at Borgin and Burkes were likely used for nefarious purposes such as torture.

In Muggle history, spiked instruments were freely used by the church and state to extract "confessions" from the victims, who would admit to virtually anything if the torture would stop.

The human mind, capable of inventing fiendishly clever and diabolical devices, created numerous torture tools that were especially useful during periods of religious persecution, when few were spared. Such persecution is rightly called a witch hunt, and the "ordeal" (using torture instruments) to inflict pain and suffering, often on innocent victims, was the order of the day. After all, when hunting for a witch, the authorities are almost certain to find one.

The less said of these monstrous devices, the better, but the modern-day fascination with them remains undiminished: A group of men promoting themselves as "independent Italian scholars" have assembled a grisly collection of torture devices that have toured around the world. According to www.torturamuseum.com, the exhibit has been "shown in many historical and prestigious venues all over Europe, in Tokyo, in Argentina and Mexico, . . . [it] has always raised the interest of millions of visitors and the press, not only for its great visual impact, but also for its clear message against the violation of human rights."

Screaming Yo-Yos

As you can imagine, Argus Filch has a long list of forbidden items, which he has doubtless confiscated over many years as the caretaker at Hogwarts. One such forbidden item is the screaming yo-yo. Imagine what a disruptive noisemaker this would be in a classroom. Just take the yo-yo for a "walk" and hear it scream loudly!

Muggles have enjoyed yo-yos since their invention in China more than 4,500 years ago, according to *The Yo-Yo Book,* by John E. Ten Eyck. Yo-yos, constructed of terra cotta, can even be found in Greek museums.

The modern yo-yo—a name coined by a Filipino man named Pedro Flores—translates as "come-come." When in his native Philippines, he carved wooden yo-yos and, as a bellhop in southern California, he played with his yo-yos, attracting a crowd. The response he got from the public was so positive that he started the Flores Yo-Yo Company.

In 1929, Donald Duncan bought the company from Flores, and added a new twist—the looped slip-string, which allowed the yo-yo to perform more elaborate tricks. The yo-yo then acquired the name Duncan Yo-Yo.

Ever "Walk" the Dog? "Do" the Three-Leaf Clover? "Light" the Skyrocket? "Show" the Lunar Eclipse? These tricks, and more, are part of the repertoire of advanced yo-yo players who can make their yo-yos do a lot more than simply go up and down.

Some fun facts about yo-yos:

• Although the doll is considered the oldest toy in the world, the second oldest is the yo-yo.

- In 1932, the first yo-yo competition, held in London, was won by a 13-year-old boy.
- The most expensive yo-yo ever was sold at auction for $16,000. Given by country music star Roy Acuff to President Richard Nixon, the yo-yo was signed by Nixon and given back, and was sold after Acuff's death.
- Market experts in the 1920s predicted the yo-yo's early demise. It was, they said, merely a fad. But the predictions proved to be wrong: Half a billion Duncan yo-yos have sold since then.

Seven-Lock Trunk

This useful trunk holds a wealth of objects. It is secured with seven locks, and the contents of the chest vary depending on which lock is unlocked. For instance, if you want spell books, unlock the *first* lock; if you want a miscellany of items, including an invisibility cloak, quills, and broken Sneakoscopes, unlock the *second* lock.

In the wizarding world, it's quite likely that a locked container of any kind has, in addition to key entry, magical protection. As unsuccessful thieves have discovered, breaking into a Gringotts bank vault is hazardous to your health. After opening vault #713, Griphook the bank goblin volunteered the information that if anyone but a bank goblin had attempted entry, he'd be sucked through the doors and held prisoner, which would prove to be a terminal experience: If Griphook the goblin told the truth, they check the vaults about once a decade.

Likewise, in the Muggle world, breaking into secured areas has become an increasingly difficult proposition because of the high-tech countermeasures. On the assumption that locks can be picked or broken, passwords can be filched, and keys or cards can be duplicated, the security technowizards have latched onto biometrics as the answer.

According to Simo Liu and Mark Silverman ("A Practical Guide to Biometric Security Technology" at www.computer.org), a biometric lock is the most secure because "it can't be borrowed, stolen, or forgotten, and forging one is practically impossible."

The key to biometric security is a seven-step process that records, stores, and then compares the person undergoing the biometric procedure; fingerprints, hand geometry, retina scan, iris scan, face recognition, signature verification, and voice authentication (or a combination thereof) comprise the current state-of-the-art methods used for biometric ID.

"Biometrics," say the authors, "measure individuals' unique physical or behavioral characteristics to recognize or authenticate their identity." The key word is "unique." Obviously, a combination of biometric tests would enhance security, since it'd be increasingly difficult, if not impossible, to get past a battery of well-designed biometric challenges.

Modern-day wizardry, high-tech solutions like biometrics will become increasingly prevalent in the workplace, where security is an issue. Clearly, getting past the modern-day electronic three-headed dog Cerberus would be, if not mission impossible, then mission difficult indeed.

Sorting Hat

> I'll eat myself if you can find
> A smarter hat than me.
> —*The Sorting Hat, singing in* Harry Potter and the Sorcerer's Stone

Just as it's wise not to judge a book by its cover—especially in the wizarding world, where looks can be not only deceiving but downright hazardous, as Harry Potter has found out on several occasions—it's also wise not to underestimate the battered, frayed, and dirty Sorting Hat. The hat serves two useful functions: to decide which house a new student should be in at Hogwarts, and to provide an early warning system when the school is faced with great danger.

First-year students encounter the hat in the Great Hall, where it is placed on a stool, awaiting each student as his or her name is called. The student then walks up to the stool, puts on the hat and then, after some cogitation, the hat decides where to place the student.

When not in use, the hat resides in Professor Dumbledore's office, where it occasionally makes comments to those who gain access to that inner sanctum.

Though its singsong verses delight the students, the Sorting Hat has a more serious side. Originally, the hat was simply a plain old wizard's that belonged to one of Hogwarts' founders, Godric Gryffindor; however, after being bewitched by all four founders, the Sorting Hat came to life, with its own intellect and personality.

So what sort of hat *is* the Sorting Hat? Well, according to J. K. Rowling, there's more to the Sorting Hat than meets the eye, as will become apparent in books six and seven, when Hogwarts is likely threatened from danger without, and possibly from danger within.

Spellotape

This sticky tape is used for repairing broken items.

Some things are the same everywhere. In both the wizarding world and the Muggle world, things break and need a temporary fix, which is why tape can be found in both.

The wizarding world's version is called Spellotape, which is the same product in the Muggle world as 3M's product Magic Mending Tape, with which you can "mend it, seal it and secure it with this permanent transparent tape. Non-yellowing tape disappears when applied, and stays invisible over time. Can be written on."

Sounds pretty magical to me.

Note: As discerning readers know, the U.K. and U.S. editions of the *Harry Potter* series are not identical in text; the U.K. versions use British words, whereas the U.S. versions "helpfully" translate British usage to American. Therefore a "jumper" in the U.K. is published as "sweater" in the U.S.

Similarly, Cellotape in the U.K. is the commonly known see-through, adhesive tape (Scotch Tape in the U.S.); hence its name in the wizarding world, since it essentially fulfills the same function, though with a magical twist: Repaired with Spellotape, Ron's wand malfunctions.

Staring Glass Eye

Among other curiosities that can be found in Borgin and Burkes is a staring glass eye. Its mere presence in the Dark Arts retail store is indicative of its malevolent nature, probably connected in some fashion to the Evil Eye, which is a baleful stare from someone wishing you ill will or deliberate harm.

Once you are the recipient of the Evil Eye, anything can happen. From minor inconveniences to death, the power of the Evil Eye cannot be overstated. The fear of the Evil Eye is so great in Turkey, for instance, that parents deliberately cover their newborns for 40 days to ward off jealous glances, and adults use a brooch in the form of a blue-glass eye to protect themselves.

Tasseography: The Art of Reading Tea Leaves

At Hogwarts, students typically rely on hard work and brainpower to carry the day, but sometimes that's not enough, as Hermione Granger discovers. In *Harry Potter and the Prisoner of Azkaban*, she—along with her friends Harry Potter and Ron Weasley—is stymied by the mystical mutterings of Professor Sibyll Trelawney, who teaches Divination.

Unlike the other classes Hermione is taking, Divination presents a unique challenge. As Professor Trelawney explains, it is "the most difficult of all magical arts," because it can't simply be taught out of a book. A student who lacks "the Sight"—a gift, according to Trelawney—will find Divination maddeningly difficult.

Professor Trelawney lives in her own world. Her classroom is anything but traditional—it is described by Rowling as a cross between an attic and a tea shop—and her subject matter is clearly nontraditional. Divination, the art of telling the future, is no easy subject to master, as the third-year students discover.

The first term's studies concentrate on telling the future by reading tea leaves—tasseography. Using *Unfogging the Future* as a guide to recognizing patterns left in the teacup, Professor Trelawney finds herself teaching a roomful of skeptics, including Harry, who admits he can't see anything except the obvious: the dregs of the tea leaves.

Reading tea leaves for their cosmic meanings is as ancient as the Chinese culture, which is where the practice likely began, dating back to the sixth century. Soon thereafter, as Dutch traders brought tea to Europe, it became the beverage of choice, especially in England, which to this day is a nation of tea, not coffee, drinkers, despite Starbucks's best efforts.

Professor Trelawney's method of preparing tea leaves for reading is fairly straightforward: Drink the tea until only the dregs remain, then use your left hand (considered sinister) to swirl the dregs three times, turn the cup upside down, emptying its contents, and wait for the cup to drain. Then read the tea leaves: The leaves closer to the rim suggest an imminent occurrence; the leaves toward the center suggest an eventual occurrence.

Today's divination students will obviously not be able to consult the book of choice—*Unfogging the Future*—but there are plenty of websites that provide this information. Also, if you want a book, consult Sasha Fenton's *Tea Cup Reading: A Quick and Easy Guide to Tasseography.*

What's Brewing?

If you have a taste for tea, go to the Ability website (www.ability.org.uk/tea.html) and drink your fill of information about the world of tea, from its history and traditions, to museums, tea parties, glossaries of tea terms, and much more. If your thirst for tea cannot be quenched by knowledge alone, check out www.alltea.com, where you can order tea of every variety, by brand or type, or join the Tea of the Month Club.

Tents

In the wizarding world, you can't judge a book by its cover, nor can you judge a tent from its shell. Case in point: When the Weasley family shows up en masse to attend the Quidditch World Cup, their borrowed tent appears to be a two-person pup tent, but inside, it is the size of a three-room apartment, complete with furnishings. Ranging from modest to magnificent, the tents at the World Cup collectively housed 100,000 witches and wizards who showed up from around the world to see their favorite Quidditch players compete.

Tent: from Latin *tendere,* "to stretch out."

Intended as portable shelters for nomadic people, tents run the gamut from small to large, simple to fancy, round and square, and civilian to military. Mentioned in the Old Testament of the Bible and in Greek literature, tents have traditionally been utilitarian, though Persian tents were known for their opulence. The simplest tents had a single pole with an opening at the top for the smoke hole, but more elaborate tents had multiple poles and were correspondingly larger in size.

Tents today come in every conceivable configuration, from small, one-person tents designed for camping and backpacking, with lightweight aluminum poles and lightweight fabrics, to military tents that can be interconnected to produce multi-room dwellings, large enough for a field hospital, garages for vehicles, operations centers, shower facilities, and troops.

Timepiece

In the wizarding world, clocks and watches are magically functional. For instance, at the Weasley residence, the kitchen clock and the living room clock don't tell the time, at least in the conventional sense. The kitchen clock tells the chores that need to be done, as well as whether or not you're late. And the clock in the living room indicates where someone is by his physical location or if he's in danger (mortal peril).

There's even a mechanism for turning back the hands of time, so to speak: The Time-Turner does just that, which is why it's a controlled device under the jurisdiction of the Ministry of Magic.

As for wristwatches, they, too, differ in design. Professor Dumbledore's watch has planets on its face instead of the traditional numbers.

As times have changed, so have timepieces. Early timepieces included the sundial, the hourglass, and water clocks, but none of them proved to be accurate enough for daily use. It was time for a change.

There's some dispute as to who invented the first mechanical clock, but most experts believe that Pope Sylvester II invented it around 996.

As time went by, technological improvements rendered the purely mechanical clock obsolete. A quartz analogue watch used a piezoelectric quartz element at its heart to drive its mechanism. Later, digital watches with light-emitting diodes (LEDs) were all the rage. Then the invention of the LCD (light crystal diode) made LEDs obsolete.

Watches today not only tell the time, but also provide a wealth of information at one's fingertips: built-in calculators, barometers, altimeters, thermometers, GPS technology, computerized linkups—you name it. If it has not been invented, it probably will be soon.

Time-Turner

Short on time? Wish you had more?

That's the problem Hermione Granger faced, but in her case she had one of the most controlled items in the inventory of the Ministry of Magic: a Time-Turner, which can turn back or move forward the passage of time. Loaned to her by Professor McGonagall, the Time-Turner allowed Hermione to "double up" on her classes—an arrangement that, in the end, proved too taxing.

Obviously, such a device could have severe repercussions, as countless writers have imagined in stories involving time travel. The latter can get, as some characters have discovered, confusing; worse, it can alter the future, as the characters in Ray Bradbury's "A Sound of Thunder" discover, when one hunter strays off a timepath and accidentally steps on a butterfly, which forever alters the course of history, but not for the better.

H. G. Wells's *The Time Machine* (published 1895) is perhaps the best-known story about time travel, in which the Time Traveler goes forward to 802,701 A.D., and discovers two races (the Eloi and the Morlocks), one of which steals his time machine, placing him in jeopardy, possibly for an eternity.

Which raises the tantalizing question: Is there such a thing, or theoretically, could there be such a thing, as a Time-Turner?

Until recently, the answer, unequivocally, was "no." Too many paradoxes involved, said the conventional scientists. Even experts such as Dr. Stephen Hawking, who holds the post of Lucasian Professor of Mathematics at Cambridge, would have said "no way."

Today, Hawking concedes the possibility, since the field of quantum physics may have solved the time conundrum. Dr. Michio Kaku, a professor of theoretical physics at the City University of New York, wrote an essay titled "Is Time Travel Possible?" in which he says that Dr. Hawking has changed his mind, believing that time travel is possible but not necessarily practical.

Theoretical physicists, who think on a completely different plane from mere mortals, are the kinds of people who believe a dozen impossible things before breakfast . . . like time travel.

For those who want to know more about the tantalizing, mind-stretching field of quantum mechanics, take the time to view Stephen Hawking's official website (www.hawking.org.uk). And be prepared to have your mind expanded by a brief history in time.

Vanishing Cabinet

Someone ought to talk to Peeves the Poltergeist, since he thinks the best use of a vanishing cabinet is as a bomb. Anyone know where the Bloody Baron is?

As recounted in *Harry Potter and the Chamber of Secrets*, Peeves dropped a vanishing cabinet on the floor, in the classroom above Filch's office, which caused Filch to exit, stage left.

A crowd pleaser and one of the favorite illusions of Muggle magicians, the vanishing cabinet, usually constructed of black with gold trim, is large enough to house a Muggle. Typically, the magician will have a beautiful assistant climb into the cabinet and, after a few theatrical taps of the wand and the requisite magic words, he opens the door to the cabinet to reveal . . . nothing.

This illusion is so convincing that a Muggle magician named Don Juan Cardoza, who made members of the audience vanish, offered a $1,000 reward if anyone could explain how he did it. No one could, of course, but don't expect a magician to tell you either, since they are bound by a code of secrecy.

Fortunately, for the magically inclined Muggle, there are plenty of resources available on the fine art of illusion—er, magic. A good place to start is www.misdirections.com and Alexander's Magic Shop (www.conjuror.com).

Wizard Chess

In the first *Star Wars* movie (1977), confusingly retitled by George Lucas as *Episode IV: A New Hope*, there's a scene aboard Han Solo's spaceship, the Millennium Falcon, in which a pint-sized robot, R2-D2, is playing a chesslike game with Han's copilot, a large hairy mammal (named Chewbacca) from the Wookie race.

The 3-D chesslike game being played features animated characters that physically interact. At one point, R2-D2 makes a move that will clearly favor him, but C3PO, a protocol android, urges R2-D2 to "Let the Wookie win" because, as Han Solo had pointed out, Wookies are sore losers and pull people's arms out of their sockets when they lose.

The equivalent game in the wizarding world is chess, with a twist. Players are not likely to get bored with the board pieces, since they are animated, move about the board, and have violent tendencies, smashing each other to bits. How cool is *that?*

When wizard chess is played on a regulation-sized board, 12 inches square, it's fun to watch it, but quite another matter when the board is life-sized and the destruction on the playing field can be hazardous to your health, as Ron Weasley found out when he had to sacrifice his piece in order to let Harry Potter and Hermione Granger advance (recounted in *Harry Potter and the Sorcerer's Stone*).

Well done, Ron. Simply smashing!

With the notable exception that in wizard chess the pieces are animated, the wizarding version

The Harry Potter Chessboard

For Harry Potter fans who want a classy reproduction of the actual gameboard and pieces seen in the movie version, Noble Collection has manufactured the ultimate chess board. Measuring 20 inches square, the Plexiglas playing board is the field of battle for the 32 die-cast zinc chess pieces that range in height from 2.5 to 5.5 inches. And it's yours for only $295, from http://noblecollection.com.

and the Muggle version are identical. Invented in Persia in the sixth century A.D., the game of chess quickly spread eastward, and from there, around the world.

Sometimes called "the royals' game" because of its popularity among royalty since medieval times, chess is the thinking person's board game, as victory is dependent not on chance but on brainpower and strategic thinking.

The goal of the game may sound simple—put your opponent's King in checkmate, in a position where he cannot escape, at which point the game is over—but it's not: The interrelationship among the pieces as they move is what makes the game interesting and endlessly challenging.

Wizard's Wireless

A wizard's radio that uses magic for reception.

Only those in the wizarding world can tune in to the WWN, the Wizarding Wireless Network, on which there's presumably the usual mixture of news, entertainment programs, and advertising. One popular program is the "Witching Hour," which features Celestina Warbeck, a singing sorceress, along with Weird Sisters, a popular group.

Molly Weasley has a wizard's radio in her kitchen, as is noted in *Harry Potter and the Chamber of Secrets.*

The Muggle equivalent is not the World Wide Web or the shortband wireless radio, but the ordinary, garden-variety radio, which had its origin in 1895 when Guglielmo Marconi gave a demonstration using the wireless telegraph. In 1897, he founded the Wireless Telegraph and Signal Company, and in 1898 he set up his "wireless" factory in Chelmsford, England. After using Morse code to make the first transmission overseas, Marconi sold the British military his radio communication systems for ship-to-ship and ship-to-shore transmissions.

The first commercial radio station went on the air in the United States in 1920, and the popularity of radio exploded. Soon there was a radio in virtually every home. For an audio taste of what it was like during the Golden Years of radio, go to www.old-time.com.

Operating on the electromagnetic spectrum from 3kHz to 300GHz, the radio spectrum now encompasses a wide range of signals, including AM, FM, television, citizen's sideband, cellular phones, taxis, police, and wireless LANs.

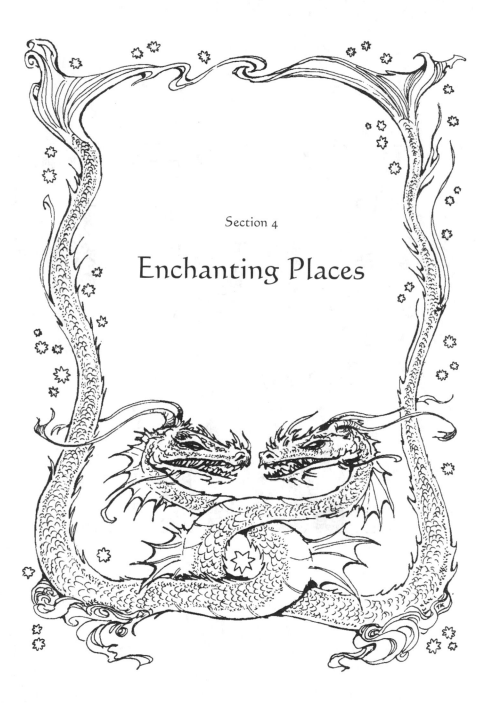

Section 4

Enchanting Places

Whether in Hogwarts, Hogsmeade, or Diagon Alley, the (literally) enchanting places that form the landscape of the wizarding world sound similar to those of the Muggle world, but with a twist. The wizarding world's post office, for example, delivers mail, but uses owls; the apothecary (or "drugstore" to Muggles) carries the usual supply of ointments, balms, and medical remedies, but they include things you'd never find at the local pharmacy, like root of asphodel or a bezoar.

This section looks at some of the most prominent places in the wizarding world, and their historical counterparts in the Muggle world.

Apothecary: Slug and Jiggers

A retail store in Diagon Alley, this is where witches and wizards go to get the ingredients needed for potion-making. Doubtless Professor Snape goes to Hogsmeade for his supplies, but if the local store is out, all he needs to do is get to this apothecary.

Considering what the store carries—herbs, powders, animal parts, and feathers—the apothecary is likely to have a fowl, and foul, smell.

Slug: a terrestrial gastropod, related to the land snail.

Jigger: a unit of measure used almost exclusively for measuring liquids. A "double jigger" of alcohol was instituted by King Charles I in 1625 to increase tax revenues.

Apothecary: from the Latin *apotheca*, meaning "storehouse."

In Greek legend, Hygeia was tasked by Asclepius, the god of the healing art, to act as his apothecary. In the Middle Ages, the apothecary was essentially a medical practitioner who provided herbs to physicians. Later, medical practitioners became pharmacists and physicians became doctors. The prescribed herbs were thought to have magical powers to cure; some herbs were obviously curative, but others were not; trial and error determined which was which, leading to the science of pharmacology. As the role of doctors and surgeons evolved, the role of the apothecary was eventually restricted to that of a pharmacist.

Azkaban

This wizard's prison, established by the Ministry of Magic's Department of Magical Law Enforcement, is located in the North Sea, on a tiny island far from civilization. Its remote location and forbidding surroundings make it an ideal place to house hardened criminals; unfortunately, some who should be there are not, and some of those who shouldn't be are.

A fortress of solitude in many ways—geographically, and mentally—Azkaban is a place justifiably feared by all witches and wizards because incarceration means a slow death. Imprisoned in their own minds, inmates go slowly mad; forced to relive their most horrible memories, again and again, they lose their will to live and often stop eating. Azkaban is guarded by the feared dementors, spirits whose soul-sucking "kiss" is their most deadly weapon.

The facts about Azkaban:

1. It is located on an island.
2. It was built for the most hardened criminals.
3. It is considered escape-proof.

Given those three factors, one inspiration for Azkaban may be the similar-sounding Alcatraz prison, on Alcatraz Island in the middle of San Francisco Bay in northern California. A maximum security prison from which there was never a successful escape—meaning, an inmate who escaped and lived to tell about it—in its 29 years of operation, Alcatraz was permanently closed in 1963.

Nicknamed "The Rock" because of how it juts up from the bay, Alcatraz was home to hardened criminals like Al Capone, who cut a bloody swath across Chicago.

Another possible inspiration for Azkaban is the Château d'If, located in the Mediterranean Sea in the bay of Marseille, France. Best known for its fictionalized portrayal as the prison where Edmond Dantès was wrongfully imprisoned, from which he subsequently escaped (in *The Count of Monte Cristo,* by Alexandre Dumas), this prison principally housed religious detainees, mostly French Protestants. As with Alcatraz, there are no documented instances of a successful escape.

211

Cauldron Shop

Cauldrons are an essential part of every witch's or wizard's tools of the trade. In fact, first-year Hogwarts students will find a standard-sized pewter cauldron on their school shopping list. Cauldrons are indispensable for mixing potions, especially for students who use them in potions class taught by Professor Snape.

In Diagon Alley, cauldrons—both magical and nonmagical—can be bought at the cauldron shop, which is located just as you pass through the portal from the Muggle world to the magical world at the Leaky Cauldron. In fact, it'll probably be your first stop, since every wizarding household needs a functioning (i.e., nonleaking) cauldron.

Cauldron: from the Latin *calidus,* meaning "warm."

The most famous cauldron in literature is surely the one used by three witches in Shakespeare's *Macbeth,* in which the cauldron is used to mix a nasty potion.

Once a part of every household in medieval days, the cauldron today can mostly be found in the hands of modern-day witches, Wiccans, who use it for many purposes, including potion-making.

Because cauldrons are not stock items at your local K-Mart, they must be mail-ordered from specialty houses. One such place is the Magick Cauldron (www.magickcauldron.com), where the smallest cauldron, made of cast iron, is available for $9.95, and they go up in price to $49.95 for the large potbelly model, which measures 5.5 inches in diameter and 7.5 inches high.

The Daily Prophet

The newspaper of the magical community, the *Daily Prophet* covers the entire wizarding world. Hardly a bastion of traditional journalism, the *Daily Prophet* is the mouthpiece of the Ministry of Magic and employs the likes of Rita Skeeter, a reporter with a nose for gossip and a talent for tabloid journalism.

Rowling has little, if any, love for journalists, who have shown up at her doorstep to demand interviews. As she has discovered, the press is persistent. (In fact, her disdain for some journalists, the ones who step across the line, is so great that during an interview with Stephen Fry at the Royal Albert Hall in June 26, 2003, she admitted that there's one particular journalist she'd enjoy seeing boiled in oil!)

Rowling concedes, though, that most journalists are simply trying to do their jobs, but it didn't stop her from creating a fictional character that she feels typifies the bloodthirsty types who want to suck information out of her—the Rita Skeeters of the world.

Muggle newspapers have been around for a long time. In fact, in ancient Rome, the *Acta Diurna* ("daily acts") kept its citizenry informed about local events of interest. But it wasn't until the invention of movable type (metal slugs set in "beds") that modern newspapers came into being.

In England, in 1702, the *Daily Courant* began publishing, followed by the *Times* in 1785, and the *Observer* in 1791.

Later, with the invention of high-speed presses and mechanical typesetting, papers began being printed in significantly higher print runs, which not only increased their circulations but allowed the publisher to reduce the cost of the paper so that anyone could afford one. (In New York City in 1933, the *Sun* cost only one penny.)

Paper circulation grew throughout the 1900s, but current circulations are down—a trend that began in 1990. According to "The State of the News Media 2004," an annual report on American journalism (www.stateofthe newsmedia.org), "just more than half of Americans (54%) read a newspaper

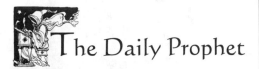

The Daily Prophet

Available only to Brits, the newspaper the *Daily Prophet*—in fact, a three-page newsletter—was mailed to those who joined the Official Harry Potter Fan Club, with content by Rowling.

Its first issue came out on July 31, 1998, with a cover price of 7 Knuts. Unfortunately, only four issues were published, and it then folded permanently.

If you want news of the wizarding world, the best source of information is Rowling's own website, at www.jkrowling.com.

during the week, somewhat more (62%) on Sundays, and the number is continuing to drop."

The drop is attributable to a number of factors: the popularity of news and cable TV, the rise of alternative and specialty publications, and the World Wide Web, where readers can get real-time news online from their favorite publications.

Actually, when you think about it, the fanciful idea that wizarding newspapers can show moving pictures isn't all that unusual in the Muggle world; after all, online papers do feature video clips with animation, and sound as well.

E

Eeylops Owl Emporium

Because an owl is on the approved shopping list of pets (along with toads and cats) for Hogwarts students, Eeylops Owl Emporium in Diagon Alley does a brisk business year-round in owls of all species. In fact, as recounted in *Harry Potter and the Sorcerer's Stone,* Rubeus Hagrid buys a snowy white owl for Harry as a birthday gift, noting that it's really the pet of choice for a student.

> Tell yeh what, I'll get yer animal. . . . I'll get yer an owl. All the kids want owls, they're dead useful, carry yer mail an' everythin'.

Harry names his owl Hedwig, who shares the same name as Saint Hedwig,

Queen of Poland, and Saint Hedwig of Andechs, Duchess of Silesia. (On her website, Rowling says that she found the name in a book about "medieval saints.")

There appears to be no direct linkage between "Eeylops" and anything in history, so we may assume this is simply the name of the store's current owner or founder.

"Emporium" comes from the Greek word *emporion*, from *emporos*, meaning "traveler, trade." Defined, it means "a place of trade," "a commercial center," "a retail outlet," and "a store carrying a diversity of merchandise."

On a purely speculative note, *Eey* is pronounced "eye" and when combined with "lops," suggests Cyclops, the one-eyed giant of Greek mythology. *Eeylops* could be a simple wordplay on those elements, since an owl is far-sighted and cannot see anything a few inches from its face.

In the wizarding world, owls are the principal means of communication, used to carry messages on little scrolls tied to their legs. In fact, at Hogwarts, there's even an Owlery, housing hundreds of owls, located at the top of the West Tower.

In the Muggle world, owls are neither messengers nor pets, since they are birds of prey that need open spaces for flight and are wholly unsuited for pets, a message Rowling reinforced on her website: "If anybody has been influenced by my books to think an owl would be happiest shut in a small cage and kept in a house, I would like to take this opportunity to say as forcefully as I can: YOU ARE WRONG. The owls in the 'Harry Potter' books were never intended to portray the true behaviour of real owls."

Florean Fortescue's Ice Cream Parlor

In *Harry Potter and the Prisoner of Azkaban,* Harry finds himself with a little time on his hands before school starts, and spends some of it at Florean Fortescue's Ice Cream Parlor. No doubt the free sundaes that Fortescue gave Harry were inducements, but the store owner also happened to be quite knowledgeable about medieval witchcraft, about which Harry was writing a school paper.

The history of ice cream, or iced cream, as it was originally called, goes back to Roman days, when the Emperor Nero had runners retrieve ice, obtained from nearby mountains, which would be combined with fruit toppings to create the world's first "ice cream."

It wasn't until the eighteenth century when traveler Marco Polo came back from the east with recipes for flavored ice food that the next evolution in ice cream occurred. In Italy, Italian cooks refined the recipe and came up with flavored ice and sherbet, which are mainstays today in Italy: *Gelato* ("Italian Ice Cream") is found virtually everywhere in Italy, on every street corner, it seems. But it's not the ice cream Westerners are accustomed to eating.

Here's the real scoop on what is considered Western-style ice cream: A frozen desert with ten percent or more milk fat, combined with sweeteners and flavorings, ice cream was actually brought to the attention of Americans by Ben Franklin, who had traveled to Italy and brought the recipe back.

What most people don't know is that with cheaper ice creams, half of it is comprised of air whipped into the mixture. (More expensive ice cream, like Cold Creamery, has little or no air mixed in, giving it a creamier, richer texture.)

So, how popular is ice cream? According to www.makeicecream.com, 98 percent of all U.S. households buy ice cream, and each American consumes 23 quarts of it annually, though Americans aren't the world record holders in terms of consumption—that honor goes to New Zealand.

Some cool facts about ice cream: vanilla is the most popular flavor, and chocolate syrup is the favorite topping.

Of course, ice cream can be made at home, if you have the right equipment—from the hand-cranked wooden bucket with the metal "collar" in its center to the sleek, modernized, all-electric ice cream maker—and if you absolutely want the freshest ice cream imaginable. *Very* cool!

Flourish and Blotts Bookstore

For the most recent books of interest to the wizarding world, there's only one place to go in Diagon Alley: Flourish and Blotts bookstore.

Before each new school term, young witches and wizards, accompanied by their parents, come to Flourish and Blotts to buy the required textbooks. (Note: Muggle parents have been known to show up, as well; one year, Hermione Granger is present with her Muggle parents, who are dentists.)

Since the wizarding world doesn't have (as of yet) the equivalent of online bookselling, and since some of the books are not only heavy but downright dangerous, making them very unsuitable for owl delivery, getting the required textbooks usually means a trip to the store itself.

As expected, some of its inventory is unconventional, to say the least. At Flourish and Blotts, you can't judge a book by its cover—if, indeed, you can even see it: *The Invisible Book of Invisibility* became a problem for its bookseller, for obvious reasons; then there's *The Monster Book of Monsters,* which lives up to its name, with a cover that bites viciously.

It is at Flourish and Blotts that Harry Potter, Hermione Granger, and the Weasleys first encounter the flamboyant Professor Gilderoy Lockhart, whose books are required reading the year he comes to Hogwarts to teach Defense Against the Dark Arts.

At Hogwarts, students write with a quill pen on scrolls of parchment, which was how books were "published" in the Middle Ages—a monk would hand-copy each book, often decorating it with elaborate flourishes and designs, called illuminations, hence "illuminated manuscripts." This was a slow and tedious process, which meant that hand-copied books were individual treasures, affordable by few; consequently, books were often chained to prevent theft. In the fifteenth century, however, the printing of books took a giant leap forward when books were mass-produced: Johannes Gutenberg combined two technologies—movable type and the printing press—to create multiple copies of books.

Today, books are manufactured by a variety of methods: short-run "instant" printing, traditional printing with photo-offset plates, digital (i.e., electronic) books, and texts of books online. Despite the new technologies, however, the traditional printed and bound book has stood the test of time and, judging from its popularity, doesn't look like it will go the way of parchment anytime soon.

Forbidden Forest

First years should note that the forest on the grounds is forbidden to all pupils. And a few of our older students would do well to remember that as well.

—*Professor Albus Dumbledore, addressing Harry Potter and his classmates in the Great Hall after the Sorting Hat has assigned them to their respective houses, in* Harry Potter and the Sorcerer's Stone

In *Harry Potter and the Sorcerer's Stone*, as punishment for breaking cur-
few, four students—Harry Potter, Hermione Granger, Neville Longbottom,
and Draco Malfoy—report to Argus Filch for detention; he takes them to
meet Rubeus Hagrid, who decides on the appropriate punishment. Predictably, Filch paints a dark picture of what awaits them in the aptly named
Forbidden Forest, where Hagrid will lead a search mission to rescue, or put
out of its misery, a dying unicorn.

The Forbidden Forest, or Dark Forest, is a staple in fantasy fiction. In
The Wizard of Oz, as they search for the Wicked Witch of the West, Dorothy
and her companions venture with trepidation to the edge of a spooky forest
where a red-eyed owl blinks ominously and a sign warns them: "I'd turn back
if I were you." It's all the warning the Cowardly Lion needs, and he turns to
run, as the Tin Woodman and Scarecrow pick him up and the Lion is ped-
aling air. In Oz's Dark Forest, Dorothy and her friends discover that the forest's animals are terrorized by a giant spider, until the Cowardly Lion kills it
and, in gratitude, the animals make him their king.

In Tolkien's Fangorn Forest, after the Orcs run for cover after the Battle
of Helm's Deep, they seek refuge in the nearby forest. From a distance,
Gandalf and company see the forest come alive after the Orcs enter, and
none of the Orcs survive the encounter.

It is a dark forest where Hansel and Gretel are lured by a wicked witch
living in a remote cottage.

In Harry Potter's case, given the admonition from Professor Dumbledore, it seems odd that for breaking one rule, the students would deliberately have to break another rule: to go into the appropriately named forbidden forest.

G

Gambol and Japes Wizarding Joke Shop

A favorite destination in Diagon Alley—especially for Hogwarts students, notably George and Fred Weasley—Gambol and Japes offers the finest in novelty items, guaranteed to wind up in Argus Filch's file cabinet if confiscated. (I'm sure that Filch has a pretty good collection of products sold by Gambol and Japes.)

George and Fred are indeed the merry pranksters at Hogwarts. You never know what new deviltry they are cooking up, though the tricks they pull on Professor Dolores Umbridge are well deserved.

If George and Fred were Muggles, they wouldn't have the advantage of being able to shop for magical novelty items, but there's more than enough Muggle mischief to be had—*if* you know where to shop.

In the United Kingdom, at The Joke Shop

(www.the-joke-shop.com), you can buy the kinds of products George and Fred would find rather useful at Hogwarts, including stink bombs (Dungbombs in the Potter universe), a sprayable bottle of authentic-smelling fart gas (perfect for spraying in Argus Filch's or Professor Umbridge's office), devil bangers (loud noisemakers), a pea shooter with ammo, a pen that shocks, and foaming sugar (works wonders with hot drinks).

Because the Weasley boys, who have invented their fair share of magical novelties, eventually set up their own shop in Diagon Alley, as recounted in *Harry Potter and the Order of the Phoenix,* with Weasleys' Wizarding Wheezes, it's not likely that they frequent Gambol and Japes as much as they used to, except to keep on top of the competition.

The store, by the way, is aptly named. Consider its word origins.

Gambol: "to skip about in play: frisk, frolic."

Jape: "to say or do something jokingly or mockingly."

Gringotts Wizarding Bank

When Harry Potter joined Rubeus Hagrid in Diagon Alley for a shopping trip, Harry rightly wondered how he could afford to pay for the various items on the students' list, since he didn't have any money. Fortunately, his parents had amassed a considerable sum and left it all to Harry, on deposit at the wizards' bank, Gringotts.

The only bank of its kind, Gringotts has two distinctions: First, it's run by goblins; second, it's guarded by magic spells and, reputedly, dragons. As with any bank, one's confidence in it is of paramount concern, which is why Gringotts houses not only the currency of wizards—Galleons, Sickles, and Knuts—but also one-of-a-kind valuables behind thick vaults, protected by

both magic and magical creatures. Consequently, there's never been a successful break-in at Gringotts, until it's discovered that vault #713, which Hagrid visited and removed a small package from, was subsequently broken into, though nothing was there to be taken. Clearly, it was the work of a dark wizard.

No one knows when banks

first began, but they weren't the sophisticated financial institutions we know today. In the beginning, banks principally handled currency only, mostly coins, but with the rise in mercantile trade, merchant bankers came on the scene to transact goods and offer bills of exchange, which had the advantage of not requiring shipping of actual coin or currency.

The modern bank as we know it had its origins in the seventeenth century in England, similar to Gringotts: The bank took deposits to be credited to an account, it dealt in foreign currencies, sorted money for profit, and acted as custodial agents, holding valuables within its vaults.

From what little we know of the banking system and Gringotts, the wizarding world relies on essentially the same mechanisms as Muggle banks. On its face, it seems to be a "cash and carry" system—no checks appear to be written and credit cards are nonexistent—and run by goblins, though the bank does employ witches and wizards, including Bill Weasley, who works as a curse-breaker.

Ingot: metal cast for refining.

Gringo: from the Greek *Graecus,* meaning "stranger." Used as an insult, a *Gringo* is a non-Hispanic person; more specifically, "a foreigner in Spain or Latin America especially when of English or American origin."

The root word for Gringotts Bank seems to explain the goblins' brusque manner in dealing with wizards. Matter-of-fact and by-the-numbers, the no-nonsense goblins are all business: no small talk, and not particularly friendly. At Gringotts, it's clear that the goblins have no love for thieves, and only a small tolerance for all others.

In European folklore, gnomes were said to be subterranean creatures, typically small in stature, who guarded precious treasures.

Fact: In 1956, the term "Gnomes of Zurich," referring to Swiss bankers, came into use when a British politician named Harold Wilson gave a speech in Parliament, part of which read:

> On September 5th, when the T.U.C. unanimously rejected wage restraint, it was the end of an era, and all the financiers, all the little gnomes in Zurich and other financial centres, had begun to make their dispensations in regard to sterling.

The Hog's Head

Located off the main street in Hogsmeade, with a sign that depicts a severed boar's head, bleeding on cloth. It's a telling sign that the place itself is somewhat disreputable. In 1612, it served as the headquarters for the goblin rebellion. It now serves as a meeting place for Hogwarts students holding their own class taught by Harry Potter, Defense Against the Dark Arts.

Patrons who frequent this tavern often go in and conceal themselves, suggesting their business is not entirely legitimate.

In any event, sanitation is a concern since the room reeks of goats, and it's best to bring your own glasses if you order a drink.

Harry Potter fact: The barman at Hog's Head is Albus Dumbledore's brother Aberforth, who, we are told, had a few misadventures with goats.

The earliest inns—if you can call them that—were merely empty huts designed to shelter travelers, with no amenities. Ancient Persia had a well-developed highway system of caravan routes and caravansaries, fortlike structures for travelers at regular intervals along the routes.

During the early Middle Ages in Europe, monks in monasteries provided lodging for the weary traveler, but, in time, inns (or lodging houses) were constructed by businessmen looking to make a profit—the first inns as we know them today. By the late sixteenth century, there were thousands of inns in Great Britain. Like the Roman inns, these inns were built around a central courtyard and were several stories high.

Today's inns—usually operated by large chain operations—are everywhere, providing affordable and safe lodging worldwide.

Honeydukes Sweetshop

Located in Hogsmeade, Honeydukes is a favorite stop for Hogwarts students who have a sweet tooth. Carrying a full line of magical and nonmagical candy, the store specializes in an extensive line of chocolate.

Though the proprietors live in an apartment above their store, they are unaware that, in the cellar, a trapdoor leads to a tunnel that connects to Hogwarts. This is how Harry Potter manages to sneak into Hogsmeade, since he doesn't have parental permission on his first outing. (Harry subsequently goes street legal and gets a guardian release from his godfather, Sirius Black.)

The list of stocked candy is too extensive to list here, but student favorites include Bertie Bott's Every Flavor Beans, Drooble's Best Blowing Gum, and Chocolate Frogs, all sold also on the Hogwarts Express.

Bertie Bott's Every Flavor Beans lives up to its name, from the temptingly delicious to flavors most would consider incdible.

Chocolate Frogs are among the students' favorites, since they include the collectable wizard cards.

Muggles who don't have access to the Hogwarts Express or Honeydukes can enjoy some of the treats, however. A bag of Droobles Best Blowing Gum ($1.95), Harry Potter Acid Pops (tart!), and Harry Potter Chocolate Frog and Collector's Card are but a few of the treats available. For Muggles who love jelly beans, Bertie Bott's Every Flavor Beans offers a complete selection: banana, black pepper, blueberry, booger, bubblegum, buttered popcorn, cherry, cinnamon, dirt, earwax, grape jelly, grass, green apple, lemon drop, sardine, spinach, toasted marshmallow, tutti-frutti, vomit, and watermelon.

Knockturn Alley

In *Harry Potter and the Chamber of Secrets,* Harry uses Floo powder for the first time and finds himself in Knockturn Alley, the wrong part of town that even by day is not a place to be. Catering to witches and wizards who favor the Dark Arts, it's a place that lives up to its name: a wordplay on the word "nocturnal." Knockturn Alley's retail stores include Borgin and Burkes, which is where Harry unwittingly arrives.

When Harry exits the store, he's accosted by an aged, mossy-toothed witch, a street vendor with a tray of what look like human fingernails, but he is rescued by Rubeus Hagrid, who happens to be in the area, shopping for Slug Repellent. Hagrid steers Harry clear of Knockturn Alley to where they are greeted with familiar sights: Diagon Alley and, in the distance, Gringotts Bank.

Even by day, the sinister characters, the seedy-looking witches and wizards, and the storefronts with questionable products (shrunken heads, giant black spiders, and poisonous candles) make Knockturn Alley a place to skirt, but imagine how dark and sinister it looks at night, for darkness (a dark alley) is always preferred for those who have dark business.

Nocturnal: "active at night."

Madam Malkin's Robes for All Occasions

After picking up the required textbooks from Flourish and Blotts, Hogwarts students go next door to get fitted for their school robes. First-year students need to get three sets of black work robes, along with a pointed hat, protective gloves, and a winter cloak, as noted on the students' list in *Harry Potter and the Sorcerer's Stone*.

Most Muggles don't wear robes and, in fact, would stand out if they did, since robes are usually worn only by people in specific professions. Typically worn by religious orders and judges, and for ceremonial occasions in academic circles (usually graduation), robes have traditionally been worn indoors.

Long, flowing robes are also associated with wizards. Merlin, a famous wizard from the Arthurian tales, is frequently depicted in a purple robe and sporting a tall conical hat, usually adorned with moon and star symbols.

For Potter fans who want to dress the part for a Potter celebration at a bookstore, a costume party, or a Potter party, go to www.AnniesCostumes.com, which carries a full line of hooded and nonhooded robes in sizes from small to large, from child to adult.

Madam Puddifoot's

Located off High Street in Hogsmeade, Madam Puddifoot's tea shop is, like others of its kind, small in size (cozy), and decorated with a feminine touch (small tables, frilly furnishings). It offers a light menu, with an emphasis on drinks and refreshments, notably tea. It is especially popular as a place for romantically inclined Hogwarts students to meet.

Tea has been around a long time, according to the Chinese, who date its existence back to 2700 B.C. But tea didn't take root in England until the 1600s, when the Dutch East India Company brought Chinese tea to London; drinking tea soon became a national pastime.

An offshoot: Tearooms—little cafes that serve tea in china cups, accompanied by the traditional favorite, jam on scones—are usually associated with

England, most notably the Lyons teashop, which opened its first retail establishment in 1894 and expanded to 250 teashops at its peak. Noted for its high-quality, proprietary tea blends combined with reasonable prices and good service, J. Lyons & Co. did brisk business for over a century, until it diversified and overextended itself, to the point where it had to sell out to Allied Breweries in 1978.

Muggles who want to know more about teas should stop by the Guide to Tea Shops in the United States and Canada, and Beyond, at www.cattea corner.com, which brews up reviews from customers who post online. In addition, there are lots of informative links, fun facts, and miscellany that are worth sipping.

Magical Menagerie

If you're a Hogwarts student and want to buy an owl, the place to go is Eeylops Owl Emporium, but if you want any other kind of pet, you'll have to go to the Magical Menagerie, also in Diagon Alley, where more exotic pets of all stripes can be found.

You may wish to pass on the purple toads, since they have fallen out of fashion as pets for students; cats are always popular. There's also a good selection of tortoises, rabbits, ravens, orange snails, rats, and furballs.

Menagerie: from Middle French *menagerie,* meaning "management of a household or farm." It is defined as "a place where animals are kept and trained especially for exhibition," and "a collection of wild or foreign animals kept especially for exhibition."

Muggles, for the most part, prefer dogs and cats over all other pets, but there are always those people who have a taste for the exotic, the unusual, the strange, or the different. In fact, a collection of such pets would be called a menagerie.

In the past, menageries were initially associated with traveling exhibits, notably Wombwell's Menagerie in England; and in the United States, Van Amburgh's Menagerie and the Zoological Institute of June, Titus, and Angevine.

Later, menageries became incorporated with circuses, where the wild animals—lions, tigers, elephants, and so on—were paraded for the enjoyment of the masses.

Obscurus Books

In association with Arthur A. Levine Books (an imprint of Scholastic Press), this obscure publishing house, located at 18a Diagon Alley in London, issued Newt Scamander's *Fantastic Beasts & Where to Find Them*, a definitive text with a foreword by Albus Dumbledore. A bestseller, this book is in its fifty-second edition.

About the author: Newton "Newt" Artemis Fido Scamander is renowned for his study of magic beasts, Magizoology.

Obscure: "To conceal in obscurity; hide" and "far from centers of human population."

Obscurus Books is something of an ironic title, since it has published (at least) one bestseller, which undoubtedly has made it well known among booksellers in the wizarding world. No doubt *Fantastic Beasts & Where to Find Them* is featured prominently at Flourish and Blotts, where it's a steady seller.

Notes Albus Dumbledore, from the back cover copy, "A copy of *Fantastic Beasts & Where to Find Them* resides in almost every wizarding household in the country. Now, for a limited period only, Muggles too have the chance to discover where the Quintaped lives, what the Puffskein eats, and why it is best not to leave milk out for a Knarl."

Muggles do indeed have an opportunity to buy this book, which is ghostwritten by J. K. Rowling, who published it to raise money for a charity, Comic Relief (www.comicrelief.com). Published in March 2001, this book, along with *Quidditch Through the Ages* by Kennilworthy Whisp (Whizz Hard Books, 129B Diagon Alley, London), has raised £15.7 million (USD $29 million) for charity.

Ollivander's: Makers of Fine Wands since 382 B.C.

When Rubeus Hagrid takes Harry Potter shopping for school supplies in Diagon Alley, one of the stops—the one Harry is most interested in—is Ollivander's, a retailer who has been in business since 382 B.C.

The store itself isn't much to look at. Its only furniture is a wooden chair for customers. The store's "shoebox" design, long and narrow, suggests its inventory: untold numbers of rectangular boxes that house magic wands.

The store owner has a very long memory, recalling not only every wand he has ever sold, but also its specifics; he clearly remembers selling wands to Harry's parents, and to Lord Voldemort as well.

After several abortive attempts at matching *the* wand to the wizard, the wand "selects" Harry. In retrospect, the wand is a perfect fit—he was destined to own it.

As recounted in *Harry Potter and the Prisoner of Azkaban,* Harry gets two letters—from Ron Weasley and Hermione Granger—in which Ron tells him that he and his family are in Egypt, which prompts Hermione to remark that "the ancient Egyptian wizards were fascinating." Hermione is right: the Egyptian wizards *were* fascinating.

According to Dr. Geraldine Pinch, in "Ancient Egyptian Magic" (www.bbc.co.uk):

> In Egyptian myth, magic (heka) was one of the forces used by the creator to make the world. Through heka, symbolic actions could have practical effects. All deities and people were thought to possess this force in some degree, but there were rules about why and how it could be used.
>
> Priests were the main practitioners of magic in pharaonic Egypt, where they were seen as guardians of a secret knowledge given by the gods to humanity to "ward off the blows of fate." The most respected users of magic were the lector priests, who could read the ancient books of magic kept in temple and palace libraries.

The Egyptian magicians, notes Dr. Pinch, harnessed the powers of metal wands and ivory wands as well. The metal wands were associated with the snake goddess; the ivory wands with powerful deities who could be called to serve the magician who held the wand, which is why the ivory bore decorations of the summoned deities.

Alivan's: Makers of Fine, Handcrafted Wands

Muggles, take note: Wands, wizard's brooms, Quidditch goggles, and selected apparel are all available at one of the most magical websites in the world, www.alivans.com, where Muggles can interact online.

The wands, each handcrafted and made of wood, range in price from $35 to $79 (black walnut or maple wand on the low end; and teak or rosewood with inlays on the high end); the brooms are priced from $49 to $79; and a wide selection of colorful scarves, ties, and other items is also available.

Take the virtual shop tour and select a wand, or, by answering a few questions, let a wand select you.

According to proprietor Finneas Alivan, a budding witch or wizard in search of a wand should keep a few things in mind:

Don't be fooled by a wand which is not what it seems to be.

Though it takes more time and costs a bit more to design wands from many different varieties of wood, the beauty and timelessness of the finished product is well worth it. This is exactly why every Alivan's wand is handmade from the actual wood specified on the wand description page (i.e., Ebony, Holly, Rosewood, Lignum Vitae, etc.) and specifically inspected one at a time before shipping to its new owner. A beautiful wand crafted of the finest wood is truly a piece of art to be enjoyed for generations to come.

From Our Master Wandmakers: What to Look For

Is the magic wand actually made of wood or does it just look like wood? This is a very common trend in "replica" wands. Be sure to read item descriptions carefully. You may see that there is no mention of these wands being made from wood at all; in fact, they are made from solid plastic or resin. If you are looking for a wand cast by the thousands from an injection molding system, then these would probably be a good choice. But I can think of no wizard who would be caught dead (or alive) with a wand made of plastic or resin—can you?

Are the wands made from different wood varieties, or are they made from one wood type and simply stained and finished in many colors and shades? This is done so the wands will look like many different wood varieties while all being made from the same type of wood. Remember, the properties of the wood are very important. It is very clear that one wood type does not work for all wizards and witches. Descriptions should state the wood that the wand is made from and include a synopsis of what makes that wood magical.

Post Office

In Hogsmeade, the local post office has several hundred owls, ranging in size from small Scop owls to the large Great Grays (up to 33 inches in length). The owl used to deliver a letter or package is chosen based on how quickly you want delivery.

Since the wizarding world doesn't use telephones, a reliable means of communication had to be established, and that turned out to be owl mail—airmail, as it were.

At Hogwarts, owls seem to be the most popular choice of pet, and for good reason. They're bloody useful, as Rubeus Hagrid might say. Most of the owls are seen during breakfast, when letters and packages are usually delivered. When the owls are not in transit, they are housed in the school's Owlery, located at the top of the West Tower.

In Britain, the mail system has been around since medieval times. Established in 1516 by King Henry VIII, the Royal Mail has a long and colorful history. With its distinctive red post boxes (each bearing the initials of the reigning monarch at the time of its installation), the Royal Mail delivered letters and packages twice daily, until 2004, when the second postal delivery was permanently canceled. For information about the Royal Mail system, go to www.royalmail.com.

Scribbulus Everchanging Inks

A retail store in Diagon Alley, this is where writing supplies—parchment, inks, and quill pens—can be purchased.

Scribbulus: The Latin word *scribere* means "to write."

Hogwarts students write the old-fashioned way, with implements more appropriate to the Middle Ages: bottles of ink, quill pens (traditionally sharpened feathers or sharpened metal nibs), and parchment (vellum).

Shrieking Shack

Though the blood-curdling screams that used to come from this house stopped years ago, the legend lives on. Boarded up and now silent, the shack shrieks no more, but its forbidding reputation is sufficient to keep the curious away. Even the ghosts at Hogwarts give it a wide berth.

Though contemporary houses have been known to be haunted—notably the Amityville Horror in New York—the haunted house as we traditionally know it is usually pre-1900, Victorian, and the older, the better.

Haunted castles, houses, and grounds are common around the world, and those in search of a spooky experience have no lack of places to see. Muggles who want to scare up a good time can check out www.haunted house.com for an updated list with weblinks to favorite haunts around the world. The armchair traveler, however, will find several books of interest, including the Discovery Channel's excellent *Discovery Travel Adventure Haunted Holidays,* which focuses on U.S. destinations, with a heavy emphasis on the south, especially Civil War ghosts.

Other recommended books include *Hans Holzer's Travel Guide to Haunted Houses, Historic Haunted America* by Michael Norman and Beth Scott, and *The National Directory of Haunted Places* by Dennis Hauck.

Three Broomsticks

Located in Hogsmeade, this is a tavern owned and operated by Madam Rosmerta. This retail establishment is a favorite watering hole for Hogwarts students and faculty, and popular with the wizarding community at large.

Pythagoreans considered the number three to represent harmony (composed of harmony and diversity), which is suggestive of the clientele who frequent this establishment. The rich diversity of people at the Three Broomsticks, a popular meeting place, is representative of the wizarding world—a contrast to the Hog's Head, which draws a rougher crowd.

Three is also suggestive of the witches in *Macbeth*, numbering three.

Broomsticks are iconic, not only for witches in Muggle history but for those in the wizarding world, who use them as a principal means of travel.

Whizz Hard Books

Whizz Hard Books, in association with Arthur A. Levine Books, published *Quidditch Through the Ages*, by Kennilworthy Whisp. Whizz Hard Books, like Obscurus Books, is located in Diagon Alley, though its address is different (129B Diagon Alley).

According to Albus Dumbledore, who wrote the foreword to the book, *Quidditch Through the Ages* is "one of the most popular titles in the Hogwarts school library." According to Dumbledore, it wasn't easy wrestling a copy from librarian Madam Pince's tenacious hands: He had to pry it from her fingers!

Perhaps a playful word pun on the word "wizard," this publishing company has likely enjoyed brisk sales of this book in Flourish and Blotts, and probably at Quality Quidditch Supplies as well.

Ghostwritten by J. K. Rowling, and co-published with *Fantastic Beasts & Where to Find Them*, this book was created as a fundraiser for a charity, Comic Relief (www.comicrelief.com).

Its author, Kennilworthy Whisp, is, as you'd expect, an ardent Quidditch fan who has written several other books on the subject, including *The Wonder of Wigtown Wanderers, He Flew Like a Madman*, and *Beating the Bludgers—A Study of Defense Strategies in Quidditch*.

Zonko's Joke Shop

Located in Hogsmeade, this novelty store is one of Fred and George Weasley's favorite hangouts. Carrying a wide assortment of joke items and gifts, including Dungbombs and Nose-Biting Teacups, Zonko's is a "must visit" store for Hogwarts students.

Zonked: British slang for "worn out, tired."

Muggles who enjoy perpetrating a joke at someone else's expense will find no lack of gag gifts and novelty items available to aggravate, harass, upset, and antagonize virtually anyone: shocking, exploding, and smelly instruments.

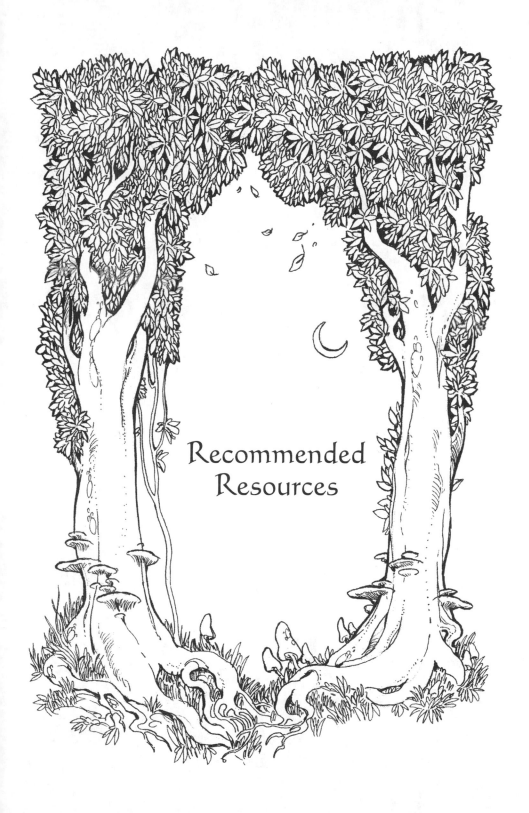

Recommended
Resources

Websites

There are countless websites devoted to Harry Potter and J. K. Rowling, but these are the indispensable ones:

1. www.jkrowling.com. The official website of J. K. Rowling, this is the first place to go for authoritative, up-to-the-minute information.

2. www.scholastic.com/harrypotter. The official website of Scholastic, publisher of the Harry Potter novels in the United States, this has a wealth of information.

3. www.harrypotter.com. The official website of Warner Bros., who licenses Harry Potter products and releases the Harry Potter films.

4. www.bloomsbury.com/harrypotter. The official website of Bloomsbury Publishing, Rowling's U.K. book publisher.

5. www.hp-lexicon.org. An unofficial fan website and recipient of a J. K. Rowling Fansite Award. The best reference source for information about the Harry Potter novels. Rowling herself sings its praises.

6. www.mugglenet.com. An unofficial fan website. The gathering hole for Potter fans worldwide. Run by fans for fans, it's the best general interest fansite.

7. www.fictionalley.org. An unofficial fan website. The best place for Harry Potter fan fiction.

8. www.scotsman.com. The electronic version of the *Scotsman,* which is

published in Edinburgh, where J. K. Rowling lives. It covers the local angle, which other media simply reprints. Go to the source.

9. www.hpana.com. An unofficial fan website that gathers news, reviews, interviews, and so forth from all over the world.

10. www.bbc.co.uk. The website of the British Broadcasting Corporation. It covers J. K. Rowling and Harry Potter news, reviews, interviews, and so on.

Books

Two books that Harry Potter fans will find indispensable are *Fantastic Beasts & Where to Find Them* (Newt Scamander, Obscurus Books, in association with Scholastic) and *Quidditch Through the Ages* (Kennilworthy Whisp, Whizz Hard Books, in association with Scholastic).

Both Newt Scamander and Kennilworthy Whisp are pen names of J. K. Rowling, who generously devoted her time in writing these books to benefit a British-based charity, Comic Relief (www.comicrelief.com), not to be confused with the American-based charity of the same name, which is also worthy of your support (www.comicrelief.org).

Rowling's support of Comic Relief (U.K.) has been instrumental in their success in raising money for all sorts of worthy causes. With these two books, the organization has raised £15.7 million, which has been used toward an international fund for children and young people. According to its website, the money goes

> to projects working in the poorest countries of the world. This means that as you're reading this, that money is hard at work making a real and lasting difference, helping improve the life chances of children and young people who were facing a terribly troubled future—many of them alone.
>
> This money is now helping children living and working on the streets of Guatemala City, young people working in horrific conditions in the carpet industry in Pakistan, and disabled children living in the slums of Bangalore.
>
> Some of the other countries this fund is reaching include Uganda, Bangladesh, Honduras, Russia, Croatia, and Kenya.

It's unfortunate and depressing that in stories about J. K. Rowling, much—too much, in fact—consists of speculation on her wealth or her financial ranking, when the free press could better serve the public at large by publicizing her support of Comic Relief and talking about these books that have done so much for so many people.

J. K. Rowling and Scholastic have donated 20 percent of the retail sales price of these books to Comic Relief.

As books, they stand on their own; as an insider's guide to the Harry Potter universe, they are valuable; and as fundraising vehicles, they are, simply, indispensable.

Please add these books to your collection or give them as gifts. And pass the word. As Albus Dumbledore wrote in *Fantastic Beasts*, "Proceeds from the sale of this book will go to improving and saving the lives of children around the world, which means that the dollars and Galleons you exchange for it will do magic beyond the powers of any wizard. If you feel that this is insufficient reason to part with your money, I can only hope most sincerely that passing wizards feel more charitable if they ever see you being attacked by a Manticore."

Well said, Professor Dumbledore!

Acknowledgments

Will the following people step forward to take a bow?

To the fine folks at Hampton Roads Publishing, especially Robert Friedman, Sarah Hilfer, Tania Seymour, and Jane Hagaman, who once again rolled up their sleeves and got to work to give this book their best efforts. Under a time constraint that would have forced most other publishers to use a Time-Turner, this book publishing company simply substituted with good old-fashioned hard work.

To Tim Kirk, artist extraordinaire, whose art lends just the right touch for this book. My thanks for putting me up and putting up with me as I went through his extensive art files.

To Britton McDaniel, who burned the midnight oil, and on short notice, to grace the pages of this book with her art.

To Colleen Doran, who provided the usual support behind the scenes, with advice, encouragement, and—when I needed a break—good fellowship.

To my wife, Mary. As the elves say in Middle-earth: Oio naa elealla alasse'.

Thank you, one and all.

FINIS

I think when I've finished the seven Harry Potter books, I will be finished with [his] world.

—*J. K. Rowling, in an online interview (October 2000)*
at Yahoo chat, sponsored by Barnes and Noble

Index

Note: Primary entries are in bold.

 A

Ability website, 201
Abominable Snowman, 3
Abracadabra, 5
Abraxan, 5, 112
Abraxas, 5
Acromantula, 6
Acta Diurna, 213
Acuff, Roy, 197
Aeromancy, 163
Aesalon, Falco, 79
Aethonan, 6
Agamemnon, 131
Agrippa, Cornelius, 80
Alas, I Have Transfigured My Feet, 109
Alcatraz prison, 210
Alchemy, 150
Alexander II, Tsar, 57
Alexander's Magic Shop, 204
Algie, Great Uncle, 68
Alivan, Finneas, 230
Alivan's, 230
American Cocoa Research Institute, 157
American Hopi Indians, 63
Amityville Horror, 232
Amulet, 145
Andersen, Hans Christian, 51
Anglia, East, 10
Animagus, 15, 79, 88, 113, 125
Anthony and Cleopatra, 133
Antipodean Opaleye, 24
Antivenin, 63
Antoinette, Marie, 160
Apollo, 131
Apollog, 164
Apothecary, 10, 70, **209**
Apparating, 146
Arachnida, 7
Aragog, 6, 8
Ares, 176
Aristo, Ludovico, 43
Arithmancy, 97, **147**
Armadillo, 7
Arnarson, Ingolfr, 102
Arrow-poison frog, 49
Artemidorus, 165
Artemis, 108
Ashwinder, 7
Astrology, 149

Astronomical Model: Galaxy, 151
Astronomical Model: Solar System, 152
Astronomy department, 125
Athena, 5, 113, 176
Atlante, 43
Auckley, 82
Auror, 38, 124, 114, 129
Austen, Jane, 16
Axiomancy, 164
Azkaban, 6, 100, 103, 123, **210**
Aztecs, 63

 B

Baba-Yaga, 173
Baggins, Bilbo, 28
Bagman, Ludovic, 81
Bane, 18
Banshee, 8
Banshee, Bandon, 8
Barghest, 10
Barkwith, Musidora, 81
Barnabus the Barmy, 81
Barnes and Noble, xiv
Barny the Fruitbat, 33
Bartimaeus Trilogy, The, 44
Bartsch, Jakob, 71
Basil, 123
Basilisk, 8, 19, 185
Bast, 16
Battle of Hastings, 98
Battle of Helm's Deep, 218
BBC, xvi
Beamish Hall, 82
Beamish, Oswald, 82
Beatles, xiv
Beaubatons, 5, 19, 89, 104, 112
Bede the Venerable, Saint, 101
Beetle, 9, 125
Beginner's Guide to Transfiguration, A, 128
Bellerophon, 5
Benson, Herbert, 190
Bermuda Triangle, 75
Besom, 155
Bezoar, 153
Bicorn, 10
Bigfoot, 4
Binns, Professor, 37, **82**
Biometrics, 197
Birla, Ghanshyam Singh, 190
Black, Andromeda, 105, 129

F

G

About the Author
and Illustrators

George Beahm wrote his first book, *The Vaughn Bode Index,* when in high school. He subsequently went on to publish many more nonfiction books, including *Muggles and Magic: An Unofficial Guide to J. K. Rowling and the Harry Potter Phenomenon.* Actively involved in the book industry since 1975, Beahm has also been a self-publisher, regional publisher, marketing director, publishing consultant, and packager.

Working with artists, Beahm established Flights of Imagination to publish and package their work. His websites are www.GeorgeBeahm.com and www.flightsofimagination.com.

Tim Kirk is a design director for Kirk Design, which draws on his vast experience in conceptualization, content creation, and art direction at Walt Disney Imagineering, where he worked for 22 years. Among his many credits at Disney, Kirk was the overall senior designer for Tokyo DisneySea, a $3 billion theme park, and he also played a key role in conceptualizing the popular Disney MGM Studio Tour Park in Walt Disney World. A five-time Hugo award winner for best art in the fantasy and science fiction field, Kirk has illustrated fanzines, calendars, limited edition books, and trade books for numerous publishers, including Ballantine Books, which issued his Tolkien illustrations, done for his master's degree in illustration, as the *1975 Tolkien Calendar.* A former artist for both Hallmark Cards and Current, Kirk designed greeting cards, jigsaw puzzles, wrapping paper, stationery, and books. In June 2004, one of Kirk Design's projects made its debut: The Science Fiction Museum and Hall of Fame in Seattle, Washington. Kirk Design's website is www.kirkdesigninc.com. Tim Kirk can also be reached through Flights of Imagination.

Britton McDaniel is a graduate of Virginia Commonwealth University, with a bachelor of arts in communication, arts, and design, with a concentration in illustration. She has also attended the Illustration Academy, working closely with top U.S. illustrators. A freelance artist, she runs the Britton McDaniel Studio. Her website, under construction, is www.BrittonMcDaniel.com. She can also be reached through Flights of Imagination.

MUGGLES AND MAGIC

An Unofficial Guide
to J. K. Rowling
and the Harry Potter Phenomenon

George Beahm

Illustrations by Tim Kirk

This book is not prepared, endorsed, or authorized by J. K. Rowling
or Warner Bros. and is not part of the Harry Potter series.

Gushing with enthusiasm and admiration, Beahm's compendium of Harry Potter trivia and essays should help tide over fans impatiently waiting for book six to come out. . . . Throughout, Beahm pitches the prose just right; it's both sophisticated enough to interest adults and lively enough to keep younger fans engaged.

—*Publishers Weekly*

Beahm offers a plethora of information, opinions, and facts that revolve around Harry Potter and the likes of J. K. Rowling. This general-interest guidebook includes sections on two movie adaptations, five books, merchandise and collectibles, and Harry Potter websites. . . . A 16-page centerfold of full-color photos as well as black-and-white photographs and illustrations throughout enliven the well-written, interesting text.

—*School Library Journal*

The Harry Potter fans declare the book enchanting!

I've been a Harry Potter fan for about six years, and a member of the online fandom for just about four, and this is the most useful printed resource I've seen for fans. Full disclosure here: I'm currently a [site] administrator with FictionAlley.org, a consultant for HPEducationFanon.org, and an editor at the-leaky-cauldron.org (and occasionally work with HP-Lexicon.org.) George Beahm has a fantastic overview of the best sites for Harry Potter information, and the format and organization make that information accessible to the newer fan, or the fan who's just realised that he or she is interested in discussing and theorizing about J. K. Rowling's books. . . . There are online resources, like the Lexicon, that have a lot of the information contained in this book, but you can't carry the Lexicon around. And I haven't seen another book with as much information about the different editions of the Harry Potter books, or as comprehensive a guide to the merchandise.

Also, as a fan of discussion forums and participating with other fans in working through JKR's clues and hints, I find it all to the good that Beahm doesn't push theories or speculation on the reader; he gives you the information you need, and may want to use to think about the books on your own and with other fans.

— *"Heiditandy" (Miami Beach, Florida)*

First off, this book is exactly what it claims to be: a general resource guide and reference book on J. K. Rowling and the phenomenon surrounding the Harry Potter books. It is not a book that focuses on spoilers, speculation, or inside knowledge of future Harry Potter novels or movies. Anyone looking for that sort of information will not find it here; however, someone interested in in-depth background information on Rowling, the writing of the first several Harry Potter books, and the reactions to her books and the movies should definitely pick up this companion.

The surprising depth and breadth of Potter-and-Rowling-related phenomena is one of the things that makes this book an excellent companion. . . . I would definitely recommend this book. It's worth the price just for having several of Rowling's more interesting quotes and the trivia quiz all in one place—not to mention everything else you get!—*Dabney Lyons (San Francisco, California)*

Muggles and Magic is the most comprehensive book I have found to date about the Harry Potter phenomenon. Written in a clear, honest, and delightful manner, it is sure to inform and charm its readers. The book delivers exactly what it promises.

I would recommend *Muggles and Magic* to all Harry Potter and J. K. Rowling fans. You won't be disappointed!—*a reader from Chicago, Illinois*

Hampton Roads Publishing Company

. . . for the evolving human spirit

HAMPTON ROADS PUBLISHING COMPANY publishes books on a variety of subjects, including metaphysics, spirituality, health, visionary fiction, and other related topics.

We also create on-line courses and sponsor an *Applied Learning Series* of author workshops. For a current list of what is available, go to www.hrpub.com, or request the ALS workshop catalog at our toll-free number.

For a copy of our latest trade catalog, call toll-free, 800-766-8009, or send your name and address to:

HAMPTON ROADS PUBLISHING COMPANY, INC.
1125 STONEY RIDGE ROAD • CHARLOTTESVILLE, VA 22902
e-mail: hrpc@hrpub.com • www.hrpub.com